ROUTLEDGE LIBRARY EDITIONS:
ECONOMICS AND SOCIETY

Volume 21

MARKETING IN A COMPETITIVE ECONOMY

MARKETING IN A COMPETITIVE ECONOMY

LESLIE W. RODGER

Routledge
Taylor & Francis Group
LONDON AND NEW YORK

First published in 1965 by Hutchinson & Co. (Publishers) Ltd.

This edition first published in 2026
by Routledge
4 Park Square, Milton Park, Abingdon, Oxon OX14 4RN

and by Routledge
605 Third Avenue, New York, NY 10158

Routledge is an imprint of the Taylor & Francis Group, an informa business

British Library Cataloguing in Publication Data
A catalogue record for this book is available from the British Library

ISBN: 978-1-032-97576-4 (Set)
ISBN: 978-1-041-15515-7 (Volume 21) (hbk)
ISBN: 978-1-041-15517-1 (Volume 21) (pbk)
ISBN: 978-1-003-67983-7 (Volume 21) (ebk)

DOI: 10.4324/9781003679837

Marketing in a Competitive Economy

LESLIE W. RODGER, B.Sc.(Econ.)

HUTCHINSON OF LONDON

HUTCHINSON & CO. (*Publishers*) LTD
178–202 Great Portland Street, London W1

London Melbourne Sydney
Auckland Bombay Toronto
Johannesburg New York

★

First published July 1965
Second impression July 1966

This book has been set in Times, printed in Great Britain
on Smooth Wove paper by Anchor Press and
bound by Wm. Brendon, both of Tiptree, Essex

Acknowledgements

THIS book is the product of many people's experience and of a wide exchange of ideas with business colleagues and associates.

The author wishes to express his gratitude to the following in particular:

Aubrey Wilson, Managing Director of Industrial Market Research Ltd., for his painstaking reading of the draft typescript, and for the many helpful observations and suggestions he made, especially on matters of industrial goods marketing; he has only himself to blame for this self-imposed chore, since the work might never have been written but for his persistent encouragement;

John Buck, Food Marketing Co-ordinator with the Unilever Organisation, for reading through the typescript and for his constructive comments and criticisms, with particular reference to consumer goods marketing;

Those working colleagues who allowed him to pick their brains and make use of certain ideas and material;

Mrs. Helen Capper and Miss Susan Brown, for their prodigious efforts in typing the final manuscript;

Last, but by no means least, his wife, for her understanding and patience during the many long evening silences.

Contents

Part Two

MANAGING THE MARKETING FUNCTIONS

Charts and Tables

Charts

Tables

Preface

THE need for the scientific study of marketing is dictated by the need to improve marketing technique, since it is now generally conceded that excellence of manufacturing technique alone is no longer a guarantee of commercial success. Much of marketing is concerned with the problem of disposing profitably of what is produced. This has been true of all stages and at all times of man's development from the most primitive tribal society to the complex technology-based society of present times, whether it be the mixed free-enterprise type economy of the United States of America or the rigidly planned state monopoly type of economy of the U.S.S.R.

The degree to which marketing has been studied or felt to have been a worthwhile subject for separate study has depended to a large extent on the relative strength of prevailing economic forces. So long as the basic economic problem was (and, for vast areas of the world, still is) one of 'how to produce enough', marketing was assumed to be an automatic process requiring little consideration beyond the fact that it had something to do with how products were finally distributed, used up, or consumed. As man's capabilities to produce in ever increasing quantities resulted in local surpluses in excess of basic requirements, the main economic problem became one of 'how to dispose of what is produced *at a profit*'. The rapid growth and dispersal of populations of users or consumers of goods and services focussed attention on the problems of physically moving production to where it could be used or consumed.

In recent times in the more mature economies of the United States, the United Kingdom, the countries of Europe and Scandinavia, marketing has come to be increasingly concerned not merely with the problem of how to dispose profitably of what is produced but also with the much more basic problem of 'what to produce that will be saleable and profitable', in other words, with nothing less than the profitable matching of a company's total resources, including manufacturing technique, to market opportunities. The marketing task is to identify, assess and realise the potentials of competitive markets.

The approach adopted in this book assumes conditions of competition, since these are the conditions that apply in our economy. These conditions of competition imply freedom of independent action on the part of business firms to increase profits by offering customers incentives to do business with them. These same customers are free to accept alternative incentives offered by rival firms. Such competition assumes freedom of business action and counteraction; freedom for the independent firm to offer whatever goods and services and special buying inducements it judges the customer will want and respond to; freedom of the customer to accept or reject what is offered; freedom for everyone to make their own mistakes and learn from them rather than having to do what other people think is best for them or happens to suit those in control.

Paternalism, no matter how benevolent, retards the development of mature judgement based on experience, and undermines the decision-making process in society, and ought, therefore, to be resisted. If, as Professor J. M. Clark has observed, 'competition is healthy in proportion to the quality of customers' judgements combined with the adequacy of environmental market conditions of customers' choice', then it cannot be made more healthy by removing the necessity to make decisions and the means of developing customers' power of judgement or by imposing on the market conditions which limit the freedom of customers' choice.

A competitive economy does not necessarily mean a free-for-all economy. Certain rules must be observed in order to preserve the best elements of competition and to protect society from harmful or noxious activities, cut-throat practices, fraud and misrepresentation. For such purposes, the State's role should be one of purposive intervention to prevent injustice and the abuse of excessive market power. It is the responsibility of the State to create the conditions most favourable to business growth and greater competitive efficiency, to create the economic climate within which business units are left to prepare their own plans in the light of their own best information, planning ability and competitive advantage.

During the past decade, few words in the business man's glossary can claim to have thrown so many traditional concepts, organisational methods and modes of conduct into the melting pot as the term 'marketing'. No other word can have provoked so much suspicion and even hostility among those business managers who may be fearful of losing the primacy and status they hold within their organisations and resentful of any attempt to change or encroach upon their established functions. One would be hard pressed to find another concept which has been the cause of so much heart-searching and reappraisal of business strategies among top management; or which, at one and the same time, has brought enlightenment to some but caused a good deal of misunderstanding and, possibly, disenchantment in others.

The great debate continues on the significance and place of marketing in our competitive economy. This book traces developments in marketing theory, explains the marketing concept in terms of both form (functions and organisation) and content (philosophy and purpose).

The author believes that, until quite recently, the marketing profession as a body has been singularly inarticulate in initiating outsiders into the scope and complexity of the subject and the vital role it plays in our competitive economy. This has been to the detriment not only of the business community as a whole but also of those who have been and are undecided upon following a business career, particularly university graduates from whose ranks must come an increasing proportion of the business and marketing managers of the future.

It is an easy way out of the problem to say that the only way of learning about marketing is to go out and do it. Marketing men, who are essentially practical men first and theorists second, have been perhaps a little too prone to adopt this approach with 'outsiders'. Although the author would agree that marketing is a highly practical business, he also believes that a particular piece of 'practice' becomes immeasurably more meaningful if it is allied to an understanding of why it is being done and how it fits into the whole. There is a great deal more that can be done to prepare a man for a business or marketing career—the growth in the number of marketing-oriented study courses, business schools and university chairs of marketing bears this out. This book is designed to help bridge that gap and to meet the needs of the aspiring young business executive.

It is directed towards three kinds of readers, each of whom it is hoped will find something of value in it. First, it is aimed at university undergraduates and students generally; second, at marketing practitioners who are at present engaged in a particular piece of 'practice' but who aspire to wider management responsibility; and third, at top business management. Among the latter, there will be those who have already developed or are in the process of developing the marketing perspective within their own organisations; there will be those who have not embraced the concept either because they are suspicious of it or do not feel able to implement it due to lack of knowledge or trained personnel; and there will be those who have tried it but, for one reason or another, have been disillusioned.

PART ONE

THE MARKETING PERSPECTIVE —A FUNCTIONAL APPROACH

1

The Development of Marketing Theory

(a) THE ECONOMIC DERIVATION OF MARKETING

MARKETING, taken in its broadest sense to mean *the organisation and performance of those business activities that facilitate the exchange of goods and services between maker and user*, is not new. There is sufficient evidence to suggest that the leading English-speaking economists of the eighteenth and nineteenth centuries, starting with Adam Smith and the so-called Classical economists (Torrens, McCulloch, Malthus, James Mill and Ricardo) and their successors in the Classical tradition (J. S. Mill, Marshall, Edgworth and Pigou), were quite well aware of the overall function of marketing, as defined above, in the national economy.

That they chose deliberately to leave out of account many of the real facts of business life in working out their economic theories should not be taken as evidence of their refusal to recognise their existence. The omissions were dictated by and entirely consistent with their conception of economic science, based as it was on assumptions which are now seen to be wholly untenable as a description of real-life economic processes. But, although marketing never came to be regarded by economists until the turn of this century as a subject worthy of separate and serious scientific study, an examination of their theories does provide some insight into the role of marketing in the economy as a whole.

The Classical economists' explanation of marketing—their terms 'exchange', 'commerce' and 'merchandising' may be broadly taken to cover what we have here designated as marketing—arose logically out of the principle of the division of labour, which was first expounded by Adam Smith in his treatise *Enquiry into the Nature and Causes of The Wealth of Nations*. He recognised the division of labour to be the single most important fact of economic life. From the division of labour and the specialisation of human activity to which it gave rise stemmed the ability to mass-produce, the need to exchange products and to develop the value and money mechanisms to facilitate this exchange.

Specialisation means different people concentrating on different tasks and without it there is no practical basis for exchange. Exchange presupposes at least two people, each of whom has something the other wants and who are accessible to each other directly or through some intermediary agency. The actual terms of exchange in any given instance, so the theory runs, will depend upon the relative values placed by each party on their own and the other's possessions, which, in turn, are functions of their comparative degrees of need and the availability of alternative sources of supply. The expected result of exchange is to leave both parties better off after the transaction than they were before it took place. Exchange involves not merely a transfer of values between the contracting parties but a positive gain in value arising from the fact that the possession and use of products after the exchange is greater than it was before the exchange.

For so long as each individual was completely self-sufficient, growing or killing his own food, making his own clothes, producing only what he needed to supply his basic wants, there was little possibility of exchange and no need for the market-place. Perhaps the most elementary form of social specialisation is the family unit where husband and wife, whether by natural endowment or inclination, specialise on the things they do best. Generally speaking, the man has been the bread-winner, the hunter, the farmer or the income-earner—whereas the woman has been the home organiser, the mother, family budgeter or the income-spender. The growing separation of the family household, viewed as a self-sufficient producing unit, from the household viewed as a consuming unit, brought about a major change of emphasis of vital significance for marketing. The household became increasingly concerned with the problems of earning and spending income and of choosing products through the exchange mechanism of the market-place and with ways of increasing the efficiency of these domestic operations.

The history of the growth of specialisation from the earliest tribal society which lived by hunting and fishing, through the pastoral, agricultural and handicraft stages to the complex industrial community of more recent times, is the history of the development of mass-production capability made possible by the application of the division of labour. This division of labour enabled individuals to cease being relatively inefficient Jacks-of-all-trades and to devote the greater part of their working time to carrying out a single form of activity and to concentrate on doing those things for which their inherited or acquired skills, aptitudes and experience best fitted them.

The extension of the same basic principle to firms, industries, even countries, whereby they tended to concentrate on performing those activities which gave them a comparative advantage over their competitors, by virtue of geographical location, accessibility of raw materials, capital, manpower resources, craftsmanship and technical know-how, opened up unlimited possibilities for creating an ever widening range of goods and services for the benefit of the whole trading community.

But if no basis exists for exchange without specialisation it is also true that without exchange specialisation is unworkable. When Adam Smith wrote that the division of labour was limited by the extent of the market, he was expressing the view that the extent of specialisation depended upon the ease with which exchange could take place, that is, upon the size, accessibility and degree of organisation of markets. Markets, in this sense, may be defined as any group of buyers and sellers who are in close enough contact with one another that the same price level will tend to operate in all sections for identical products. The extent of the market may refer either to its geographical coverage or to the size and degree of organisation of the group of individuals trading with each other. Markets are people, accessible to one another, and who have expectations of gaining from exchanges. The concentration of population, the development of easier and more efficient means of exchange (as exemplified by the progression from barter exchange to the use of money and later of credit) and quicker and more reliable communications between buyers and sellers have greatly facilitated the growth of specialisation and its concomitant, mass-production technique.

But the economies of large-scale production cannot be realised unless there is the possibility of large-scale selling which, in turn, rests on mass consumption. In other words, production technique capable of bringing about a greatly increased and more economical rate of output of a given product must be of largely academic interest in the absence of a comparable increase in the marketability of the output. The latter requirement depends upon the creation of a level of consumer demand sufficient to absorb the quantities and qualities of output at prices on which technical and commercial calculations can be based.

It is probably fair to say that in their explanation of the role of marketing in the economic system Adam Smith and his successors have been given less than their due. Adam Smith enunciated the principle of the division of labour from which stemmed the benefits of specialisation and the necessity for more efficient means of market exchange. Torrens, in one inspired passage, anticipated by more than a century one of the most widely used definitions of marketing—the process aimed at getting the right goods to the right people in the right place and at the right time. He wrote: 'Activities designed to make commodities available at either times or places where they are more in demand than at times and places at which they are available at the outset creates wealth or utility just as much as activities designed to change their physical composition.'[1] In other words, to the value (or cost) of manufacturing a given article must be added the value (or cost) of making it available when and where it is wanted by the potential user. From the marketing standpoint nothing has value unless it is available at the right time and place of use. The difference between the value of milk-on-the-farm and the value to the consumer of milk-on-the-doorstep or between a packet of ready-to-eat cereal lying in the manufacturer's warehouse and its value on the consumer's breakfast table represents the value added by marketing. Part of the final cost paid by the user is represented by the cost that would be incurred if the consumer had to go to the farm or factory himself and transport the product to his own home, and part by the cost of letting him know that a product is in fact

[1] R. Torrens. *The Economist Refuted.* Oddy 1808. p. 13.

available which is intended to meet his specific need. Torrens provided the economic justification for marketing middlemen, i.e. factors, wholesalers and retailers who collected in bulk and re-distributed in individual customer lots.

McCulloch, elaborating this argument, wrote: 'Merchants, or dealers, collect goods in different places in the least expensive manner; and by carrying them in large quantities at a time, they can afford to supply their respective customers at a cheaper rate than they can supply themselves. . . . They also promote the convenience of everyone, and reduce the cost of merchandising to the lowest limit.'[1] The marketing task, therefore, is seen to be to make goods and services available to consumers more efficiently and more economically than would otherwise be possible. Perhaps it is right and proper that Smith, who may be said to have started it all, should have a final word. 'Every man lives by exchanging, or becomes in some measure a merchant, and the society itself grows to be what is properly a commercial society.'[2] By substituting 'marketer' for 'merchant' and 'marketing' for 'commercial' the above quotation would stand as a fairly succinct account of our own life and times.

Production versus *Consumption*

The long drawn out theoretical argument as to which has primacy in the economic order—production or consumption—has always been a critical one for marketing. It is only in the last forty years or so that those who argued in favour of the pre-eminence of consumption in the economy or, at any rate, to the effect that consumption occupied a position co-ordinate with production, have come to the fore. Up to the turn of the century the great weight of economic argument held that production was the primary function and that distribution, if not unproductive, was, at any rate, less important than manufacturing. To understand why consumption was relegated to a secondary and passive role in the economic system it is necessary to return again to the theories developed by the Classical school of economists which dominated English economic thought for so many years.

Having acknowledged the existence of the marketing process, why did the Classical economists then proceed to concentrate almost their whole attention on production and distribution and give only the most summary treatment to consumption? For inasmuch as the study of the consumption function and, in particular, of consumer behaviour is fundamental to an understanding of the role and economic significance of marketing, the relegation of the consumer to the sidelines and the almost total disregard of the wants, expectations, motives and influences which go to determine his pattern of behaviour, had the effect of holding back for a

[1] J. R. McCulloch. *A Treatise on the Principles, Practice and History of Commerce* (Society for the Diffusion of Useful Knowledge, London). Baldwin & Cradock, 1833. p. 2.

[2] Adam Smith. *An Enquiry into the Nature and Causes of the Wealth of Nations.* 6th Edition. G. Bell and Sons, 1925. Vol. 1, p. 23.

hundred years or more the study of marketing as a separate discipline using scientific methods already well established in other fields of investigation.

The Traditional Approach to Economics

Robbins wrote in the mid-1930's: 'The traditional approach to Economics, at any rate among English-speaking economists, has been by way of an enquiry into the causes determining the production and distribution of wealth. Economics has been divided into two main divisions, the theory of production and the theory of distribution, and the task of these theories has been to explain the causes determining the size of the "total product" and the causes determining the proportions in which it is distributed among different factors of production and different persons.'[1] The fundamental reason for this approach is to be found in the conceptual framework within which the Classical economists arranged and interpreted the facts, or what purported to be the facts, about the economic environment with which they were familiar. It is no criticism of their prodigious analytical efforts that they constructed a framework which has since been largely discredited since they had to look at the problems of their generation, as we must look at the problems of our own, in ways which the existing state of knowledge, scientific methodology and analytical technique made possible at the time.

A brief outline of the main economic functions as they have been treated by most of the traditional economists will serve to show why marketing came to occupy a position of secondary importance. Broadly speaking, they broke down the field of economics into four parts—production, exchange, distribution and consumption. By production they meant the creation of 'utility' or the capacity of goods and services to satisfy human wants. Exchange involved the transfer of ownership of or title over goods and services and operated through the price mechanism and other institutions which facilitated exchange. Exchange also involved the creation of additional utility or, to be more specific, time, place and possession utilities as distinct from utility which arose out of production. The implications of this distinction for marketing were not properly understood until a great many years later. Distribution, as defined by the traditional economists, had no connection with the modern meaning of the word which has to do with the physical movement or conveying of goods from the producer through wholesalers and/or retailers and thence to the final users. Distribution, in their sense, was considered to be part of production. As used by them, the term was concerned with the allocation of the proceeds of production among the four original factors of production, namely land, labour, capital and entrepreneurship (or management). It enquired into the ways in which these shares were determined and apportioned in the form of rent, wages, interest and profit. Lastly, consumption was the final act of using up goods and services to satisfy wants.

[1] L. Robbins. *The Nature and Significance of Economic Science*. 1935. p. 64. By permission of Macmillan & Co.

The Place of Consumption in Classical Economics

It is not by accident or default that consumption comes last in practically every economic textbook written during the past two hundred years. This, according to their writers, is where it belonged and where, in fact, it stayed in relative obscurity for the greater part of this period. McCulloch, alone among the Classical economists, gave it more than a passing reference. He devoted a whole chapter to the subject of consumption, saying that 'it is, in fact, the great end and object of industry'.[1] Yet seventy years later Alfred Marshall was claiming that the proper study of economics was the organisation of production and credit and was only indirectly concerned with consumption.[2]

The neglect of the study of consumption has been well summarised by Kyrk: 'It is true that a survey of English Classical treatises shows that a place co-ordinate with production, exchange and distribution, is often assigned to consumption. . . . These early writers and their latter-day followers recognised consumption as the *raison d'être* of production, but once having pointed out this obvious fact . . . economic enquiry ceased. Formally, the consumers' existence was recognised: they were always there, a sort of bottomless pit into which a continuous and ever-increasing stream of commodities must be kept flowing.'[3]

The viewpoint of the orthodox economists that consumers were mere users of goods, rather than choosers of goods with particular preferences, purposes and propensities which were open to influence and manipulation, is all the more surprising in the light of their exhaustive treatment of the division of labour. For it was precisely the growth of specialisation and exchange which widened the gap between the manufacturer and the consumer, as between the time and place of production on the one hand and the time and place of consumption on the other. This separation was eventually to give rise to the whole complex of distribution, salesmanship, trade marks, branding and advertising by means of which manufacturers aimed at favourably predisposing consumers towards their products in order to increase their sale. But attempts by manufacturers to influence consumers' choices in the former's own interests, as opposed to merely consulting the market, were slow to develop. It was some time before business men began to realise that 'profits lie not in opposing but in seeking out consumer impulses and interests and satisfying them'.[4]

Consumption involves the problem of choice and of valuation by the consumer who has an income to spend and goods to choose from among a number of competing alternatives in the market-place. It involves a marketing process the success of which depends on the consumer's skill in handling the market mechanism and upon the adequacy and efficiency of the

[1] J. McCulloch. *Principles of Political Economy*. Adam & Charles Black. Edinburgh 1825. p. 488.

[2] Alfred Marshall. *Principles of Economics*. 8th Edition. Macmillan & Co. 1920, p. 712.

[3] H. Kyrk. *A Theory of Consumption*. pp. 12–13.

[4] Ibid. p. 107.

manufacturer's and distributor's own marketing methods. In other words, consumer choice is a function of the chooser's own past experience and of other direct influences affecting him at the time his choice is made, e.g. advertising, the conspicuous availability of the product, size of income, amount of discretionary spending power. Marketing not only extends the range of consumer choice but makes the business of choosing more efficient in terms of time and in terms of the total satisfaction gained in exchanging a given income for a given assortment of products and services.

Classical theory stopped short at the very point where marketing proper begins, that is, with the study of the consumer and problems of demand-creation and with the analysis of demand-influencing factors. It failed to recognise the basic fact that demand has generally to be created. Instead, the Classical economists saw the adjustment of supply and demand purely in terms of the automatic operation of the price mechanism. If the supply of a commodity was increased the price level would fall and consumers would automatically buy more. Conversely, if the demand for a product increased, the price would rise in response and manufacturers would raise their output to take advantage of the higher price. J. S. Mill carried this argument to its logical conclusion: 'All sellers are inevitably, and by the meaning of the word, buyers. Could we suddenly double the productive powers of the country, we should double the supply of commodities in every market; but we should, at the same stroke, double the purchasing power. Everybody would bring a double demand as well as supply; everybody would be able to buy twice as much because everyone would have twice as much to offer in exchange.'[1]

It was left to J. M. Keynes, when he published his *General Theory of Employment, Interest and Money* in 1936, to expose the fallacy of this argument and to stress the overriding importance of consumption and the real possibility, discounted by the Classical economists, of a deficiency of demand, due to the effect on the rate and patterns of spending of changes in the rate of income and of a host of psychological factors which influence consumer behaviour—the desire to save for a rainy day or to meet unforeseen contingencies, to provide for changing needs such as old age, education and maintenance of dependants, to forgo current spending in order to enjoy a larger real consumption later, to emulate others, to secure higher status, etc. These motives to spend or not to spend vary according to the institutions and organisations of our economic environment according to habits formed by class, religion, education, convention and current modes of conduct, according to present expectations and past experience, and according to the prevailing distribution of income and the established standards of living. Thus, the propensity to consume, which expresses the relationship between a person's income and what he will spend on the consumption of various goods and services—and it is with this relationship that the marketer is primarily concerned—is seen to depend

[1] J. S. Mill. *Principles of Political Economy*. Longmans, Green and Co. 1909. Book III. Ch. XIV. p. 558.

partly on the actual amount of his income, partly on other objective factors such as the rate of change in his income, his future income expectations, government policies and taxation, and partly on the mixture of psychological needs and motivations which affect us all in greater or lesser degree.

Up until the publication of Keynes's *General Theory* the weight of economic doctrine was on the side of the self-regulating economy in which all adjustments on one side or the other were solely a function of price. Production would always expand to take advantage of high prices leading inevitably to a state of over-supply which, in turn, would cause prices to fall again. According to this theory the system would tend towards equilibrium with supply equating demand at a given price. Nowhere was any attention given to factors other than price. Non-price influences on supply and demand were considered unimportant and represented market 'imperfections' which, although known to exist in real-life competition, could safely be ignored. But marketing problems exist precisely because of the uncertainties caused by imperfections of the market.

The Theories of Perfect Competition and Pure Monopoly

The neglect of consumption by the Classical economists meant inevitably that their theories took no account of manufacturers' efforts to influence demand or of consumers' responses to various marketing stimuli. They were unable to follow through the distinction they drew between production costs and selling and other marketing costs because the latter were irrelevant and unnecessary in a situation where all costs were incurred to meet a given demand (as under conditions of perfect competition) or where a single supplier was already in possession of an entire market for a product (as under conditions of pure monopoly). And herein lies the major fallacy of Classical economic doctrine. These two mutually exclusive systems, of perfect competition on the one hand and pure monopoly on the other hand, were taken as being typical of prevailing market conditions and followed as a direct and logical consequence of their disregard of the real life imperfections of the market—imperfect knowledge of manufacturers as to the conditions of demand, as to the plans of competitors, and as to their own marginal costs and long-range profit-maximising prices, and imperfect knowledge of consumers as to the existence of products to satisfy their known wants, as to the various alternatives available to them for satisfying a given want and as to the ability of specific products to provide maximum satisfaction.

The concept of perfect competition assumed a market for a product in which the given level of demand was predetermined, in which there were a large number of buyers and sellers, none of whom could individually exercise any influence on the actions of others or on the general price level, in which the product was completely homogeneous and non-differentiated, in which price was the only basis of competition, and in which all buyers and sellers had instant and perfect knowledge of available alternatives and of market conditions generally. Under these circumstances there could be no basis for consumer preference since the product was identical from any source of supply and the price the same wherever the product was bought.

At the other extreme, pure monopoly postulated a single seller in control of the total supply of a product and able to set his price at the level which would maximise his profit. Clearly, there is no such thing as pure private, as opposed to public, monopoly since every product competes to some extent with every other product and most goods and services have substitutes to a greater or lesser degree. Even if there were no income limitations on spending there is a limitation on the individual's capacity or propensity to consume goods and services.

This polarisation of economic theory, elaborated and refined over almost two centuries, probably did more to retard the development of marketing theory and to obscure the real significance of marketing in the economic process than is generally realised. As J. M. Keynes was at pains to point out, 'the postulates of the Classical theory are applicable to a special case only and not to the general case and the characteristics of the special case assumed by the Classical theory happen not to be those of the economic society in which we actually live with the result that its teaching is misleading and disastrous if we attempt to apply it to the facts of experience'.[1]

The Theories of Imperfect and Monopolistic Competition

Later economists, observing the growing disparity between the facts of everyday business life and the assumptions underlying prevailing economic doctrine, attempted to take account in their theories of the 'imperfections' of the market-place. As one of the most eminent of these economists observed: 'Economic literature affords a curious mixture, confusion and separation of the ideas of competition and monopoly. On the one hand, analysis has revealed the differences between them and has led to the perfection and refinement of a separate body of theory for each. On the other hand, the facts of intermixture in real life have subtly worked against the complete theoretical distinction between competition and monopoly which is essential to a clear understanding of either.'[2] The great economic changes which took place in the latter part of the nineteenth century and, in particular, the economic aftermath of the First World War, finally gave the lie to the theory of the self-regulating automatic market system which had hitherto dominated English economic thought.

A reappraisal of traditional theories led to the formulation of a new set of theories which better fitted the more uncomfortable facts of economic life. This new family of theories attempted to blend the older theories of

[1] J. M. Keynes. *The General Theory of Employment, Interest and Money*. 1936. p. 3. By permission of Macmillan & Co.

[2] E. Chamberlin. *The Theory of Monopolistic Competition*. Harvard University Press. 2nd ed. 1936. Chap. IV.

competition and monopoly contending, with Keynes, that these theories represented special cases at each end of the economic spectrum and which in no way approximated to prevailing market forms. The prevalent market structure was seen to contain both competitive and monopolistic elements —hence the designations 'imperfect competition' and 'monopolistic competition' given to these theories. These developments have been of great importance to marketing since they represented the first attempt to establish an integrated theory to fit the facts of experience. That they failed to provide a completely integrated system which would accommodate all the relevant facts does not detract from their significance as the basis of modern marketing theory and practice.

The theory of 'imperfect' competition enunciated by Joan Robinson,[1] for instance, while representing a major advance on earlier economic models, still assumed a homogeneous product and no monopoly control over supply except in relation to a commodity which was virtually co-extensive with the whole industry. Thus the theory did not achieve a true synthesis of competitive and monopoly elements. The theory explored the possibilities of increasing efficiency and reducing waste and exploitation through the elimination of market imperfections.

The theory of 'monopolistic competition' first expounded by Edward Chamberlin recognised the fact that any body of doctrine purporting to explain the workings of our competitive economic system must incorporate and take account of the following conditions hitherto specifically ignored.[2]

1. Products in competition are not normally identical but differentiated, that is to say adapted to differences in taste and requirements of consumers. Individual manufacturers differentiate both the products themselves and the brands and packages to provide a basis for distinguishing their product from those of competitors so that it is preferred by the consumer. The basis may be real or fancied so long as it is significant to the consumer.
2. Consumers do not ordinarily have perfect knowledge and a definitely known demand. Their knowledge is imperfect and their demands are subject to influence. Thus, manufacturers adopt aggressive selling efforts aimed at inducing consumers to buy merchandise because of improvements in quality, convenience or other special features rather than solely on the basis of price reductions. Chamberlin distinguished between selling costs and production costs by saying that those costs which adapted the product to the demand were costs of production and those that adapted demand to the product were costs of selling. In fact, trading-up or up-grading the market in terms of price is a strategy which commends itself to more and more manufacturers. Competition, in such circumstances, calls upon advertising,

[1] J. Robinson. *The Economics of Imperfect Competition*. Macmillan & Co. 1933.
[2] This section is adapted from N. H. Borden. *The Economic Effects of Advertising* (Richard D. Irwin Inc. Chicago 1944). pp. 159–60.

display, personal selling, sales promotion, product quality claims, service guarantees and other non-price forms.

3. In place of markets with a large number of sellers, none of whom can exert an appreciable influence on price, we have markets which may be dominated by a small number of large concerns, each of which is big enough to affect prices, if it so wishes. Price leadership and association agreements on pricing policy are not an uncommon phenomena in a number of closely integrated industries. Under such circumstances, the individual concern does not have to accept an impersonal price established in the market-place on a take-it-or-leave-it basis: on the contrary, it may decide to exercise its 'monopolistic' control and sell a lower output at a higher price. Nevertheless, it is assumed that the tendency of management in manufacturing or in distribution is to maximise profits in the long-term and, so far as possible, to adopt pricing policies which will achieve this.

4. Manufacturers and traders in their pricing frequently operate without knowledge of their costs or long-range profit-maximising prices, of the pricing activities of competitors, or of the conditions which determine the demand for the products they make and sell.

Two aspects of the theory of monopolistic competition lack precision. First is the assumption that manufacturers will adopt pricing policies to maximise profits in the long-term. It is questionable whether, in practice, any individual manufacturer can ever maximise his profits except by accident or by deliberate trial and error, for it depends upon his knowing in advance the quantity of product that the market will take, which means (a) knowing what his competitors will do and how much of the market their products will take, (b) knowing his own marginal costs (i.e. the incremental cost of producing and selling an additional unit of output) and (c) freedom to fix and get a price for his product which will equate his marginal cost with his marginal revenue. Moreover, a marketing strategy that provides a reasonable expectation of maximum profits might, at the same time, involve the greatest risk of maximum loss. There may even be a greater probability of making a large loss than of making a large profit by following a particular strategy and the relative probabilities of making certain rates of loss or profit as a result must enter into a manufacturer's calculations. A wiser course of action might be to maximise the expected value of profits so as to ensure the greatest protection against large losses, in other words to settle for that rate of profit which is consistent with minimum risk of loss. A going business concern must be basically concerned with survival and with protecting its continued existence on a profitable basis. Thus, a firm may deliberately forgo the highest attainable profits in the short-term if this either avoids reduced profit possibilities or increases profit potential in the future. An 'average' but continuing rate of profit is preferable to bankruptcy due to subsequent larger losses.

It seems likely, however, that in most real life business situations, the maximum or optimum long-term rate of profit is not discoverable as a basis for policy-making. Druker has suggested that 'the guiding principle of business economics is not the maximisation of profits; it is the avoidance of loss'.[1] According to this view there is a minimum level of profit for each firm which is vital for its survival, but this does not imply any compulsion to maximise profit. Firms may deliberately avoid maximum or optimum profits for several reasons, such as fear of attracting new competitors, fear of being charged with unreasonable profiteering and the abuse of excessive market power, fear of damaging the company's public image and fear of antagonising its workers and the trade unions.

The second aspect of the theory of monopolistic competition which lacks precision arises from the juxtaposition of these two words. Indeed they are, in a sense, a direct contradiction in terms. Monopolistic means a single seller in control of an entire market. By definition therefore competition is impossible. Firms engaged in 'monopolistic competition' are not in *exclusive* control of the market. The only sense in which an individual firm can be said to exercise a monopoly influence is in regard to its exclusive control over the supply of a unique product, differentiated in some significant way (to the user, that is) from all competitive substitutes. But it is stretching the use of language a bit far to say that because one firm produces an expensive car which no other firm can make, it is therefore in a monopoly position. It has to compete with other expensive and uniquely designed cars, with smaller cheaper cars and with other forms of personal and public transport.

(b) TOWARDS AN INTEGRATED THEORY OF MARKETING

An appreciation of the nature and significance of marketing was precluded for as long as economics was primarily concerned with the problem of allocating supplies of what had already been produced rather than with catering for people's tastes, interests and even impulses; for as long as manufacturers concerned themselves with the problems of their factories and of production rather than the growing and changing needs of their ultimate customers; for so long as the general standard of living was such that the mass of the people had little call for things other than basic necessities and little or no discretionary income to make selections of products.

Pre-1900, the problem was how to produce goods in sufficient quantities, first to meet basic needs, then for a growing complexity of wants. During and following the war of 1914–18 production capacity in America, in Great Britain and on the Continent of Europe was greatly expanded and gave rise to the problem of excess capacity in relation to what could be

[1] Peter F. Druker. *The Practice of Management*, Harper & Brothers. New York 1954. p. 46.

profitably sold. The over-development of production (or the under-development of markets) led to much more aggressive selling, branding, advertising and price-cutting in order to develop markets for the greatly increased supply of goods made possible by large-scale production technique. Before 1900, the basic business risk was the possible destruction or loss of goods before they could be sold. From the 1920's onwards the greatest risk became the inability to find a market for the goods produced.

The problems of marketing have been and are essentially economic problems. Both are concerned with what goes on in the market-place and with the allocation of scarce resources among alternative uses so as to maximise results in some way or other. But the economist and the marketing man has tended to approach these basic problems from two different directions. The economist, on the one hand, started out by studying the whole national economy and only in fairly recent times—say the last fifty years—has he extended his field to include the problems of the individual firm. The marketing man, on the other hand, had to start with the problems of the individual firm in his search for practical solutions to specific and concrete marketing problems, including the detailed processes of moving goods to the consumer and of creating and influencing demand. Again, the economist made certain assumptions as to market organisation whereas it was the marketing man's task to try to organise and change the market in ways advantageous to the individual firm.

The advancement in economic theory has tended to set the pace for economic practice in many sectors of public and business policy. In marketing, however, business men have put principles swiftly into practice in advance of academic exploration into the subject. Where the development of marketing theory has been left to the academic economist the result has tended to reflect an excessive degree of abstraction. The marketing practitioner, for his part, has never been able to hide his impatience with propositions which do not yield precise and reliable methods of solving marketing problems in all circumstances. This is a situation which is changing as marketing men become increasingly aware of the complex nature of buying and selling. More and more, they are turning to the economist and other behavioural scientists for technical advice and assistance as the business man's practical wisdom, intuition and hunch give ground to 'scientific method'.

With the advantage of hindsight, it might be argued that marketing theory could not have developed at a faster rate than in fact has been the case. Nicholas Stacey and Aubrey Wilson, in a recent book, put the view that 'the process of rethinking marketing as a function in its own right as a specialist skill could not be contemplated before the need for it arrived'.[1] It is possible to imagine a medieval market-place or those of the eighteenth and nineteenth centuries, but hardly the marketing of those

[1] N. Stacey and A. Wilson. *Industrial Marketing Research; Management and Technique.* Hutchinson 1962. p. 48.

periods. Marketing is a phenomenon of our times brought about by the pressures of mass production and increased spending power. The advancement of marketing theory and practice has paralleled the advancement of the mass consumer economy in which people found themselves with a growing margin of income to make selections of products beyond the bare necessities of food, shelter and clothing and with a widening range of tastes and interests to be satisfied. It has also paralleled the advance of technology which has created unprecedented rivalry in the marketing of new inventions and innovations.

Kendall[1] has gone so far as to express the following view: 'It is technology, not inspiration, that dictates the pace of progress, even in the sciences, and even, I would contend, in philosophy. Imagination and vision are as important as ever they were to provide the initial ideas and the motive force; but to work out their consequences requires an adequate technical equipment.'[1]

The implication of this idea for marketing is that only in the last ten or fifteen years have we advanced far enough, technically and methodologically, to begin to develop an integrated theory of marketing. No body of sound principles can be built up unless enough facts are known about marketing processes and an adequate information technology exists for collecting, handling, ordering and interpreting the known facts.

Group Behaviour in Marketing

Particularly important in marketing is the study and analysis of group behaviour whether it be groups of manufacturers or distributors, buyers or sellers or consumers. The problem for the marketing man becomes the same as for other investigators of group behaviour—the psychologist, sociologist, anthropologist and politician—namely, how to reduce the individual behaviour of possibly millions of people into some sort of order which will serve as a basis for practical action aimed at influencing such behaviour in a given direction. For so long as the means of observing and measuring individual patterns of behaviour were absent, little progress was possible in any of the social sciences in contrast to the physical or natural sciences. Kendall[2] summarised the major difficulties facing the investigator in any field of study to do with the group behaviour.

1. Group behaviour systems are complex with an enormous amount of interaction between the component parts.
2. In order to quantify it is necessary to observe and measure. A great deal of the system may be either theoretically unobservable, or, in practice, unobserved, and the problem of measurement is itself of quite a different order of magnitude from that in the physical sciences.
3. It is difficult to test hypotheses experimentally.

[1] M. Kendall. *New Prospects in Economic Analysis. Stamp Memorial Lecture.* The Athlone Press, University of London. 1960.

[2] Ibid.

4. The conditions which determine the motion of the system may change, relatively rapidly.
5. The human minds which understand the system, or think they do, are themselves part of the system and use their knowledge to alter it.

Examining each of these points in turn: *first*, as regards marketing behaviour (and group behaviour in general), the phenomena to be dealt with differ in kind from those of the physical sciences and the technique needed to study them are likely to be different from existing methods. As Bursk[1] has observed, buying and selling involve a 'subtle, fluid interaction, with actions on each side affecting actions on the other'. The number of possible combinations of actions by a seller or a buyer is very large. General economic conditions are continually changing the marketing environment and obscure the effects of firms' marketing policies, and competitors' initiatory actions and responses also help to cloud marketing results. In other words, observable behaviour in marketing is influenced by a large number of variables with the result that it is extremely difficult to isolate the effects of any one variable or combination of variables. Moreover, whereas relationships between events or phenomena studied by physical scientists tend to be stable over fairly long periods of time, human behaviour is essentially dynamic, that is, it varies over time. Cause and effect are distributed over time with varying degrees of lag which can be quite critical for the operation of the system. Physical systems can claim a number of constants of general application—gravitation, the boiling point of water, the velocity of light and so on—but not so human behaviour systems. There are no physical constants or fixed relationships in marketing. Hence there is no exact *science* of marketing as such. Marketing is an area for the application of scientific methods.

Second, quantification in human behaviour systems involves formidable problems of measurement. There are a great many quantities of interest to marketing which are not easily susceptible to existing measuring rods, e.g. standards of living, advertising effectiveness, consumer attitudes, and the strength of consumers' desires, motivations and expectations. Many critical measurements in marketing are concerned with rates of change as distinct from absolute magnitudes, particularly in the areas of consumption, market growth, pricing and profitability. How does the business man assess the various uncertainties confronting him, involving possible changes in price and cost structure, profits, consumer demand and economic conditions generally, in terms which will enable him to calculate and thereby reduce the element of risk or error in his marketing operations? Can the marketing behaviour of literally millions of consumers be reduced to quantitative terms which will serve as a basis for marketing planning and action by the manufacturer?

These questions are not easily answered. The difficulty and cost of

[1] Edward C. Bursk. *Text and Cases in Marketing. A Scientific Approach.* © 1962. By permission of Prentice-Hall Inc. Englewood Cliffs, New Jersey. pp. 6–7.

gathering accurate and usable data are considerable. Nevertheless, techniques of observation, analysis, evaluation and measurement are being improved all the time, through better sampling technique, questionnaire design, motivation research methods, and the use of mathematical models.

Third, experimentation in the behavioural field presents many problems not present in physical systems. Whereas in the physical sciences practically every step forward is the result of experiment under controlled conditions, the subject matter of human behaviour does not lend itself to such treatment. The medical student dissects a dead body before he operates on a living one. The mechanical engineer constructs a working model from a blueprint and tests it before building a prototype. Unfortunately, for the marketing man the application of this kind of experimental technique, as yet, is very limited. Unlike the medical student he cannot ask for another cadaver and unlike the engineer he has to operate, by and large, without benefit of wind-tunnel or water-tank. At the same time, significant progress has been and is being made in the development of experimental procedures which promise to give new insights into the workings of and relationships between various marketing phenomena. The techniques for pre-testing of products, selling and distribution methods, and advertising under relatively controlled conditions have advanced considerably over the last ten years or so. Mathematical model-building, business-game theory and decision theory are among the principal developments that have taken place in the search for some methodological breakthrough in the investigation and analysis of business behaviour.

Fourth, the chief characteristic of any behaviour system is its dynamic nature, by which is meant that it varies over time and that the conditions which determine the direction and velocity of the system can be subject to relatively rapid change. In this regard, technology is a prime mover. It is only necessary to compare our present technology-based society with the society of fifty years ago to realise how much the pace of living has changed and how much material progress has been telescoped into a comparatively short period of time when measured against our life span. For the business man this means that accepted ideas, materials and methods are being rendered obsolete at a quickening pace. Better communications are increasing the articulateness and responsiveness of the system and facilitating change. Developments in manufacturers' selling and distribution methods, advertising, merchandising and marketing research provide specific examples of more effective communications in the field of marketing.

Finally, the people who are themselves an integral part of the system use their knowledge to modify it in ways that are deemed to be advantageous either to the system as a whole, or those sections of it which are of special concern to them. Manufacturers, individually and collectively, seek to influence and modify the markets for their products in ways advantageous to themselves. Similarly with the wholesale and retail distributive trades. Government agencies have spheres of influence and use their powers to alter certain aspects of the system in the general interest. The

Treasury, Board of Trade, Department of Economic Affairs, National Economic Development Council and National Board for Prices and Incomes are all working to change the environment within which business must function. Monopoly and restrictive trade practices legislation, merchandise marks legislation, resale price maintenance legislation, officially sponsored consumer education and protection measures, all impinge directly on business operations. Government intervention in the economic field takes many forms and seems likely to increase rather than diminish in view of the general desire to create and maintain conditions for sound planned growth. Employers' federations and the trade unions are also working to change certain key interrelationships within the system. Then there are the efforts of unofficial groupings seeking to promote special interests—manufacturers' and traders' associations, consumer movements and the like. There are thus a considerable number of organised sub-groups working within the total system each with its own set of objectives.The attainment of these objectives must affect other parts of the system. Any study of group behaviour must take account of these sub-group activities.

The Requirements of Good Marketing Theory

The aim of marketing theory is to comprehend what is known and to derive a set of principles or action-guides to enable businessmen to manage their affairs better. Marketing theory may never advance to the stage where risk and uncertainty are entirely eliminated from business decisions but the progressive reduction of risk and error must be the desirable aim of any body of theory. Good theory must also explore the unknown, suggest hypotheses and occasionally, therefore, stick its neck out. Scientific method requires that if the facts, when they subsequently become known, are at variance with an hypothesis, then it is the hypothesis which must be rejected. If too many hypotheses based on the same theory are rejected in this way, then the theory itself must be suspect.

The requirements of good marketing theory, then, are as follows:

First, it should provide the means of classifying, organising and integrating information relevant to the factual world of business. The mere accumulation of facts is no more the basis of good theory than a pile of bricks is the basis of a well-built house; what matters is the way the facts are arranged and put together to form some kind of logical structure.

Second, it should provide a technique of thinking about marketing problems and a perspective for practical action. Adapting Keynes's dictum, marketing theory cannot furnish a body of settled conclusions immediately applicable to policy. It is a methodological approach rather than a doctrine which helps its possessor to draw correct conclusions as a basis for action.

Third, it should make available an analytical tool-kit to be drawn on as appropriate in the solution of marketing problems. Many such tools already exist, mainly borrowed from techniques used in other fields such as statistics, sociology, psychology and economics. The further application of scientific method to marketing will call for new special-purpose tools, the precise nature of some of which cannot be foreseen at this time, although it seems likely that they will be derived from or draw heavily on recent developments in computer technology, operations research and biology.

Fourth, it should provide a basis for the explanation, prediction and perhaps even the control of marketing processes and events. Explanation means interpretation not only of the facts or events but of the relationships between them. The right facts wrongly interpreted can lead to bad decisions. Prediction calls for the exercise of foresight, forecasting ability, planning and evaluation. Control involves the determination of goals and objectives, and the setting up of control procedures and of the organisation to implement them. Control, of course, is a relative term and although it may be difficult to achieve in marketing, most business managements strive hard to secure some measure of it both internally and externally in relation to the markets for their products.

Fifth, good marketing theory should, in time, permit the derivation of a number of general principles, possibly even laws, of marketing behaviour.

The few principles enunciated in marketing, by and large, have been derived or taken over from economics, the only other discipline dealing with market phenomena. The principle of the division of labour as it applies to marketing has already been mentioned. The principle of diminishing returns originally applied to production must hold equally for a large part of marketing activity. Thus, increased marketing effort is undertaken in the expectation that more output will be sold. Up to a certain point higher marketing expenditure leads to rising sales, but at a decreasing rate; beyond that point higher marketing costs will not increase sales further.

A practical example would be the consideration as to whether it would be worth while for a manufacturer to add another salesman to his sales force. If the increase in sales revenue resulting from the addition of one extra salesman was not more than or less than his salary and associated selling costs then the point of diminishing returns for that particular form of marketing expenditure would have been reached. This principle can be re-stated as the 'diminishing marginal productivity of marketing', where the increase in sales resulting from a unit increase in total marketing costs is called the marginal productivity of marketing. The principle may apply to any component of marketing costs such as field selling, distribution, advertising and display. Management may not recognise it as such but the principle can be seen at work when a manufacturer sets minimum order levels, or minimum turnover rates for his customers, or eliminates unprofitable sales territories, salesmen or customers.

The principle of diminishing marginal utility as applied to the consumer of goods and services simply states that the more a person has of something the less he will want more of it at the same price; the more he adds to his stock of a particular product the less urgent his demand for still more of it and the more he is likely to spend income on other things he wants more. The principle of comparative advantage postulates that an individual, a firm, or a nation will gain by specialising in doing or producing those things in which its comparative cost advantage is greater.

Two of the most important principles, having their origin in economic theory, have been put into practice by marketing men. These are the principle of 'market segmentation' and the principle of 'differential advantage'. The principle of market segmentation arises from the fact that marketing tries to individualise consumption by the process of product differentiation, whereby each product variation is designed to match, more precisely than any standardised product could, the particular needs and preferences of groups of consumers who make up the total market for the type of product in question.

Product differentiation is both a cause and an effect of the segmentation of the market. On the one hand, manufacturers try to find preferred combinations of product attributes, real or fancied, in order to create new market segments and retain the loyalty of existing segments. They try to identify market segments based on locational, physical or psychological characteristics, which will serve as a basis for advertising and promotion, packaging, product differentiation, etc. The principle of market segmentation applies particularly where the opportunities for product differentiation are relatively limited and where the basis of consumer selection rests more heavily on the particular brand image put across in advertising and other forms of promotion. However, product differentiation carried to excess, in an attempt to cover the whole spectrum of consumer requirements, can be a source of trouble to the manufacturer if it means foregoing the economies of scale and the benefits from standardised production.

The principle of differential advantage, first put forward by the American economist J. M. Clark, arises out of the very nature of business competition. Chamberlin's theory of monopolistic competition was the take-off point for Clark, who saw competition taking the form of 'independent action by business units in pursuit of increased profits, or avoidance of reduced profits, by offering others inducements to deal with them, the others being free to accept the alternative inducements offered by rival business units'.[1]

The Principle of Competitive Differential Advantage

According to this principle, competition is seen as a complex of interactions in which a business firm's operations are affected not only by its own actions but by the actions or strategies of competitive firms, and involving a sequence of initiatory moves by one firm and counteracting responses by those with whom it deals (including not only customers, but also its own workers and suppliers) and by its competitors. It is assumed that business units attempt to find some distinctive feature that will set them off from their competitors, and carve a niche for themselves in the market. To this end, they will exploit whatever comparative advantages

[1] *Monopoly and Competition and their Regulation.* Macmillan & Co. 1954. Edited by E. H. Chamberlin. pp. 326–8.

they possess over competition, and will constantly be seeking new competitive advantage and the widening of their existing advantages.

Thus, a manufacturer may offer his customers a lower price, a better quality, or more selling support in the expectation of increased sales volume at the expense, wholly or in part, of his direct competitors. His competitors will retaliate in order to minimise the loss of sales or to redress the balance of sales. In other words, competitors will seek to counteract or neutralise the initiating manufacturer's advantage by offering the customer inducements as good as, or better than, the initiator and obtaining a sales-increasing advantage for themselves.

The actual outcome of this never-ending cycle of initiatory move and counter-response in respect of any individual firm operating within the market will depend upon the relative speed and timing of the initiating firm's actions and competitors' responses. The time lag between action and counteraction can be a matter of days or of years. Instantaneous neutralisation usually happens only in the case of reductions in the prices of homogeneous or very closely competitive products. This can happen with some consumer goods, e.g. ice-cream, chocolate, confectionery, but is much more widespread in the durable goods and industrial products fields, especially where there is a relatively small number of large sellers, e.g. industrial chemicals and metals. But whereas the advantage gained from a price differential can quickly be neutralised by competitors, a firm may enjoy a substantial 'time lead' where new production processes or products are difficult to duplicate, particularly if extended patents or secret processes are involved. Between these two extremes the outcome will vary quite widely, depending upon the relative timing and speed of the different movements within the system which, in turn, depend upon the nature of the differential advantages open to a manufacturer and his competitors. The anticipated length of time before neutralisation takes place must be sufficient to allow the initiating firm to recover the estimated costs of innovation if it is to be undertaken at all. In practice, most firms expect some continuing residual advantage from innovation.

The theory of monopolistic competition holds that firms seek to differentiate or distinguish themselves from their competitors in some respect, that each firm is, in this sense, unique and that this stems in the first instance from the uniqueness of its products or services through differentiation. Such differentiation may be located in the product or service itself based on quality, convenience in use, design, styling or other special features; or it may reside in the style or convenience of packaging, in trade-marks or brand-name reputation. To the extent that a firm offers the market a product or service that is significantly different from all other products or services in the same general category, it enjoys a limited monopoly control over its supply. In markets where differences between products based on considerations of technical performance and efficiency are slight, or at any rate are not demonstrable to the consumer, non-product forms of differentiation become specially important.

Opportunities to create a differential advantage for an individual firm may exist in the brand image of the product as presented in advertising and display; in distribution, such as door-to-door selling; in technological developments in production and marketing methods; in geographical location (whereby a local manufacturer may be in a specially strong position due to ties with regional customers and suppliers); in the degree of control that the firm is able to exercise over *its* customers and suppliers; in its financial bargaining power and status with the banks and other financial institutions; in the disparate skills of management and in its ability to act with a higher degree of certainty, or a smaller degree of uncertainty, than its competitors. Probably the most important of these areas of opportunity, from the viewpoint of the consumer at least, is represented by the brand image of a product which Harry Henry, a pioneer and leading authority on motivation research in Europe, has described as perhaps the key concept to have emerged in the whole history of advertising.

The brand image, as defined by Henry, is 'the total personality of the product which consists not only of its chemical composition and formulation but also of all the *ideas* which the public has about it. It consists, in other words, of the picture which the consumer has in his mind of the qualities inherent in it, real or imaginary (frequently the latter), the sort of people who use it, the sort of circumstances in which it is appropriate, the sort of person he will demonstrate himself to be if he uses it, and so on.'[1] The brand-image concept, he goes on, 'enables one to explain why, for example, when two brands of petrol are barely distinguishable in chemical analysis, and totally indistinguishable in performance in any ordinary car, one brand should be regarded as particularly appropriate to gay and sporting types and the other as particularly appropriate to the solid citizen. It also enables one to explain why it is that certain types of people tend to buy one brand rather than the other.' Here, explicitly stated, are the factors which underlie the principle of market segmentation.

According to the principle of competitive differential advantage business competition consists, in the main, of identifying and specifying such differential advantages and of maintaining, developing and extending them. These differential advantages can be the critical factor in a company's ability to earn profits now and in the future. Take, for example, a firm which secures a differential advantage in production due to the introduction of a new cost-reducing process; other things being equal, the firm's profits will rise and management is free to put these extra profits in its pocket or plough them back into, say, product research and development, or use them to strengthen the firm's competitive market position through increased promotional expenditure.

It might be argued that if the neutralisation of a firm's competitive advantage is likely to take place before it has recovered the costs of developing and exploiting this advantage, then there will be no incentive to innovate. On the other hand, if the firm has a permanent advantage

[1] H. Henry. *Motivation Research.* Crosby, Lockwood & Son Ltd. 1958. p. 59.

which no competitor can neutralise, then the innovator would exercise a limited monopoly over the supply of his product or service. According to Clark 'the desirable case lies somewhere between too prompt and too slow neutralisation . . . neutralisation needs to take time enough to leave the innovator incentive that is adequate, but not more, and then diffuse the gains as promptly as is consistent with their being ample gains to diffuse'.[1]

The Case for a Functional Approach to the Study of Marketing

There are, as yet, few accepted scientific principles on which business men can rely as does the engineer, physicist or chemist. Business has developed largely on a pragmatic basis, learning from the past and taking decisions on an amalgam of hunch, rule-of-thumb, judgment and inspiration. The last two qualities will always be necessary, and the difference between success and failure of marketing policies will, in many instances, continue to be due to the degree to which the men chosen to carry them out possess these attributes. A number of so-called marketing principles have been adumbrated, but together they do not constitute a central theory of marketing for the practical guidance of business executives.

What approach to the study of marketing appears to be likely to lead to the development of a consistent body of principles, that will provide a perspective for practical business action? There are three basic approaches to the study of marketing—the commodity approach, the institutional approach and the functional approach.

The *commodity approach* studies the marketing of different types of commodities, in particular, the nature and conditions of supply and demand, distribution processes, selling and promotional methods, and pricing policies. This generalised approach tends to be purely descriptive of the similarities and differences, with emphasis on the latter, between agricultural produce, mineral products, industrial goods and manufactured products.

The *institutional approach* examines and analyses different marketing agencies or institutions. It sets out to explain the place and purpose of retail institutions, wholesalers, brokers, etc. in the marketing system and the significance of changes in the patterns of distribution, and in the relative importance of the various facilitating agencies which aid and supplement production and distribution operations, e.g. financing, purchasing and accounting. It deals also with legal institutions that have helped to shape the business environment.

The *functional approach* breaks down the marketing system into a number of separate but interrelated functions, the nature and significance of each of which is considered singly and in relation to the whole. It takes account of all types of commodities, institutions and firms, or applies to one particular commodity, institution or firm after another. It attempts to put each function in its right perspective in relation to all the other marketing functions and in relation to the total business function. It is essentially

[1] Ibid.

an analytical rather than a descriptive approach. Of these three approaches to marketing the last-mentioned, the functional approach, has proved the most fruitful to date.

The development of operational research and analysis can probably be regarded as having the most practical results for marketing. Operations research may be defined as the application of scientific method to the analysis of the structure of problems with the object of providing a quantitative basis for their solution and for assessing the consequences of different courses of action leading to their solution. As applied to business problems it aims to provide executives with quantitative information as a basis for decisions regarding the functions under their control. It can be used to improve the performance of a particular function (e.g. allocation of factory resources, warehouse and depot location) or of a total operating system viewed as an integrated whole and comprising many interrelated functions, e.g. a business organisation. Developed largely in a military context during the last war to assist in solving strategic and tactical problems, operations research moved into business and industry after the war.

Its military origin is an interesting one in the light of what has already been said in relation to the concept of competitive differential advantage. The war involved the interplay of new technical measures (initiatory moves) and opposing counter-measures (counteracting responses by rivals). For example, the German U-boats had to revise their tactics and equipment when the Allies began to use radar and anti-submarine aircraft. The Allies, in turn, had to modify their tactics and radar equipment to counter their changes. In this seesaw of techniques, the side which countered quickly before the opponent had time to perfect the new tactics and weapons, had the decided advantage.

Operations research, by bringing together a team of scientists to analyse the technical impact of measures and counter-measures, made it possible to speed up the reaction rate in several critical cases. The essence of operations research is the mixed-team approach involving scientists drawn from different disciplines—perhaps an engineer, a chemist, an economist, a physicist, a mathematician and a psychologist. This approach is based on the assumption that no single mind can match a 'team-mind' in relation to the potentially useful scientific information and technique that can be brought to bear on a particular problem. The inter-disciplinary character of operations research seems likely to be of the greatest significance for marketing, since it can be the means of bringing together and turning to practical account the findings and techniques of a number of different sciences—sociology, economics, mathematics and psychology—in an attempt to construct a comprehensive theory of business behaviour. The functionalist is interested in the interactions between organisational structures, their external environments and the individuals within the organisations. He is concerned with the technological, economic and social milieu in which an organisation or operating system has to function and with the effects of group behaviour on the internal and external workings of the system under changing conditions.

The functional approach in marketing is considered by the author to be the most relevant to present problems and needs. Marketing functions are carried out by executives working within an operating system, that is to say, a business firm, as members of various related organised groups. These executives seek to influence the behaviour of other organised groups—salesmen, trade customers, suppliers and consumers—in ways advantageous to the furtherance of the aims of the system. In so doing, they have to compete against rival operating systems each seeking to turn the balance of competitive advantage in its favour.

A dynamic functional approach is essential in the training of future marketing executives because there are, as yet, no hard and fast rules of universal application to be learned in marketing, no guarantee that results will be as predicted since the outcome is always dependent on how competitors or other interested parties such as suppliers, distributors, investors and government agencies act or react.

The potted success stories which typify so many case studies are of limited value in themselves to students of marketing. The study of the pathology of business is every bit as important to the marketing student and practising executive as is the study of human pathology to the medical student and practitioner. Cures to business ills will not be discovered purely on the basis of the study of healthy organisms. The marketing practitioner, operating on the business organism, has to learn to live with his mistakes just as the surgeon operating on the human organism has to do.

2
The Marketing Perspective

(a) THE MARKETING CONCEPT

IT IS necessary to distinguish between marketing as a concept and marketing as a group of activities that executives carry out, between marketing as a 'thought-process' and marketing as a 'doing-process'. Marketing must start as a concept which defines the purpose of marketing operations rather than as a description of the operations themselves. For when a company has embraced the marketing concept there are many different ways in which the marketing functions can be organised according to the particular circumstances and environment in which the individual company finds itself. There is no universal formula for mobilising and organising the marketing effort and no single mould for casting a firm's marketing structure. There is, indeed, no universally accepted definition of 'marketing'.

The American Marketing Association defines marketing as 'the performance of business activities that direct the flow of goods and services from producer to consumer or user'. As it stands this definition is purely factual and descriptive. It emphasises activity rather than effective accomplishment. It does not provide an adequate explanation of which goods or services in what quantities and with what characteristics ought to be produced or of the importance of planning and integrating these and related activities concerned with the movement of goods and services from the producer to the consumer. Marketing does not merely take over where production leaves off, but is concerned with determining the nature and scale of production and with profitably exploiting a firm's capacities and technological know-how in relation to market opportunities. In other words, marketing decisions precede production decisions and investment decisions. The economics of large-scale production and returns from long-range investment cannot be realised unless the output can be sold and the added capacity resulting from investment fully utilised, at least for most of the time. There is nothing so wasteful as doing with great efficiency that which should not have been done at all. Finally, the above definition places the consumer or user at the tail-end of the production-marketing sequence.

According to the British Institute of Marketing and Sales Management, marketing is 'the creative management function which promotes trade and employment by assessing consumer needs and initiating research and development to meet them; it co-ordinates the resources of production and distribution of goods and services; determines and directs the nature and scale of the total effort required to sell profitably the maximum production to the ultimate user'. This definition is more explicit than that used by the American Marketing Association since it makes specific reference to the research and development responsibilities of marketing, to the key co-ordinating role it plays between the linked processes of production, selling and distribution. According to this definition marketing is nothing more nor less than the *total business function* of producing a saleable product.

Business firms in competitive markets must abandon the historical approach of manufacturing what they want to sell and instead manufacture what their customers want to buy. However, this does not mean that through market research customers can provide the manufacturer with a fairly detailed specification of the product they want. In practice, consumers cannot demand products not already in existence; they are not very articulate when it comes to specifying their particular requirements; they have difficulty in visualising the precise product features they would like to see incorporated in the design; they can only give vague guidance as to what the product should look like and what they expect it to do for them. The basic idea for a product comes from the manufacturer, arising out of his detailed knowledge and understanding of consumer needs, and his ability and ingenuity in translating, in technological terms, a specific need into a workable product at a price which the consumer is prepared to pay and which gives the manufacturer sufficient profit to make it worth his while to market it.

Thus, management decisions and the policies based on them are taken in the fullest possible knowledge of market factors and awareness of the effects of those decisions and policies on the market. This should not be taken to imply that *all* management decisions are reached in this way but simply that, in the final analysis, management has the responsibility for making a profit through supplying a marketable output. Out of a company's technological facilities and know-how will come workable products but it is the company's marketing know-how that creates saleable products. Production and investment plans, raw material procurement and employment programmes can only be based on confidence in what can be sold.

J. H. Buck, a Unilever food marketing specialist, has given his organisation's definition of marketing as 'the planning and execution of all aspects and activities of a product so as to exert optimum influence on the consumer to result in maximum consumption at the optimum price and therefore producing the maximum long-term profit'.[1] The key element in this definition is 'maximum consumption at optimum price resulting in maximum long-term profit'. A company must first establish the benefits of its products to the prospective purchaser and these benefits must be saleable at a price at least sufficient to cover the cost of initial product development and of getting them across to the purchaser or user. Further, the bundle of benefits represented by the product must be recognised by the potential

[1] *Institute of Marketing and Sales Management*. Published Paper No. 128. April 1962.

purchaser as value for the money he is asked to pay. At this stage, marketing aims to ensure that the quality and performance of the product, its price and the advertising, all combine to give the most effective appeal to the consumer within the profit objective set by the company. This definition of marketing goes further than most in emphasising the profit objective. It is right and proper that this should be so since one of the major criteria by which a company's performance is judged is the profits earned in relation to capital employed in the business.

Allowing for varying degrees of generalisation and emphasis, most of the foregoing definitions are broadly in accord. The danger to be avoided, of course, is ending up with a definition which sacrifices precision for the sake of generalisation. What is required is a precise and concise definition which is both meaningful to the individual firm, and, at the same time, is applicable to all types of business in the consumer and industrial goods and services fields. Therefore, marketing can be defined as *the primary management function which organises and directs the aggregate of business activities involved in converting customer purchasing power into effective demand for a specific product or service and in moving the product or service to the final customer or user so as to achieve company-set profit or other objectives.*

The term 'customers', in the foregoing definition of marketing, means not only the ultimate consumer or user of the product but the manufacturers' own customers—importers, retailers and wholesalers who must be induced to stock, distribute and give active selling support to the product if the final user is to be able to buy it. Effective demand means demand at a price the customer is both able and willing to pay and at a profit that makes it worth while for a company to make and supply the product. By 'specific product or service' is meant a product or service which by virtue of its differentiation, real or imaginary, can be readily distinguished from competitive or substitute products or services. The differentiation, whether a characteristic of the product itself, of its packaging or pricing, of its advertising and promotion, must be significant enough to form the basis for preference by the potential customer.

A very large part of the marketing effort of most companies and an ever increasing share of marketing expenditures, is taken up with keeping the company's products on the move between the factory warehouse and the final customer. The whole of the company sales effort, through personal selling and advertising, as well as the logistics of supply—warehousing, depot location, stock control and shipment—represent a major component in marketing costs. Whenever products stop moving for any reason on their journey towards the ultimate user, they accumulate cost—for warehousing and storage, insurance, stock-handling, order processing and packing, stock obsolescence and deterioration, working capital tied up in unsaleable or slow-moving stocks, etc. It is the responsibility of marketing management to look for greater efficiency and lower costs in the physical distribution and stock-handling.

Ideally, marketing aims to secure the optimum rate of movement of products from factory to final user, that is to say, that rate which combines the most profitable rates of sale and stockturn and the minimum level of investment in stocks consistent with providing adequate service to customers. This last point can be critically important in the case of certain goods subject to cyclical or seasonal supply and demand. Where it is necessary to hold strategic reserves of a particular commodity or product then the accumulation of cost by holding heavy stocks may be less than the accumulated cost of frequent or irregular short-run production.

Finally, in our definition no assumption is made as regards the profit-maximising or cost-minimising goals of the company. In any given set of circumstances, the profit objective is not the sole measure for judging a company's performance over a given period of time. Factors such as building up the company's prestige or status in the industry, the fear of attracting new entrants to the market, the fear of government intervention and regulation, the desire to steer an 'average-rate of-profit' course between the highest attainable short-run profits and the greatest risk of maximum losses are other legitimate objectives or considerations. However, it is fair to say that every company goal, regardless of the language in which it may be couched, has an economic dimension.

The Responsibilities of Management

The major responsibilities of general management are to establish marketing objectives; to make policy decisions and communicate those decisions to the managers of the operating (or implementing) divisions of the company; to establish standards for measuring and auditing the overall performance of the company. The responsibilities of operational or line management are to plan programmes, methods and procedures and implement the decisions necessary to achieve the stated objectives; to organise and co-ordinate the activities and resources necessary to carry out the programmes; and to see that operating results conform as nearly as possible to agreed plans and standards of performance.

The production division is responsible for the manufacturing aspects of marketing—organising men, materials, machines and time to produce specified products in the requisite qualities and quantities at specified times and at a designated cost to meet market requirements and sales forecasts. Quality control, production programming, raw materials procurement are included here.

The financial or accounting division of the company is concerned with the financial aspects of marketing—budgetary control, standard costing and profit planning. Business is based on the rigorous discipline of money and a major criterion of performance, but not necessarily the only one, must be profit earned. Nothing that a company produces makes money for the company until it is sold and paid for.

The marketing division is responsible for the sales, market research, product planning and development, distribution and promotional aspects of marketing, for the detailed implementation of marketing and advertising plans and programmes and for achieving designated marketing goals. In some companies the sales and distribution functions are separated from the research, product planning and promotion functions—the latter group sometimes being designated as 'marketing services'. This does not matter so long as *both* the sales division and the 'marketing services' division are co-ordinated by the same individual, irrespective of the latter's title, i.e. Marketing Director, Sales Director or Commercial Director.

Finally, the Personnel and Administration Division of the company, if this is separated from general management, is responsible for those aspects of marketing dealing with job evaluation, selection and recruitment, executive training and general administrative procedures laid down in company policy.

The line-up of top management and the four basic operating divisions of a company as described above is depicted in Chart 1.

The Marketing Process

Marketing is nothing more nor less than the profitable matching of total company resources against market requirements and opportunities. Production requirements are dependent upon the solution given to this commercial equation; in other words, a company should make what can be profitably sold. When a product is made there is no certainty that it will yield a profit. What is absolutely certain is that if it remains unsold, it cannot yield a profit. In the past, the business function has been more concerned with matching total company resources against production requirements, that is to say, the company has attempted to sell what it wanted to make. The task of marketing management is to identify, assess and realise market opportunities and potentials.

Marketing management is responsible for creating customers by persuading them through advertising and personal salesmanship that the company's products or services match their indicated needs and preferences more closely than competitors' offerings, by developing products and services through technical and market research which appear to offer profitable sales opportunities, and by making these products or services available in a form, and at a price, time and place the customers want.

The key elements in the marketing of any product or service are illustrated in the flow-chart (Chart 2).

The marketing process starts with knowledge of the customer and his needs and ends with a customer purchase and the satisfaction of those needs. Through technical product research and customer research, generalised needs are translated into specific product sales opportunities. Product planning identifies and specifies the particular product-price-package combinations to exploit these opportunities. Products are engineered or formulated [a number of variations of a single prototype may be made up], screened and tested with customers for overall acceptance and performance. Final decisions have to be taken on packaging design, pricing

CHART 1. THE RESPONSIBILITIES OF TOP MANAGEMENT AND THE FOUR OPERATING DIVISIONS OF A COMPANY

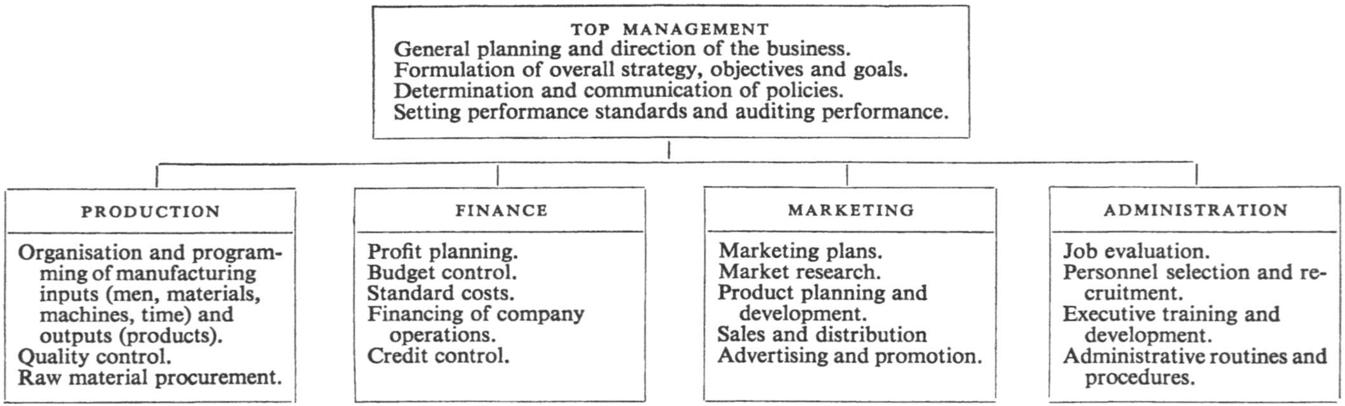

CHART 2. THE MARKETING PROCESS

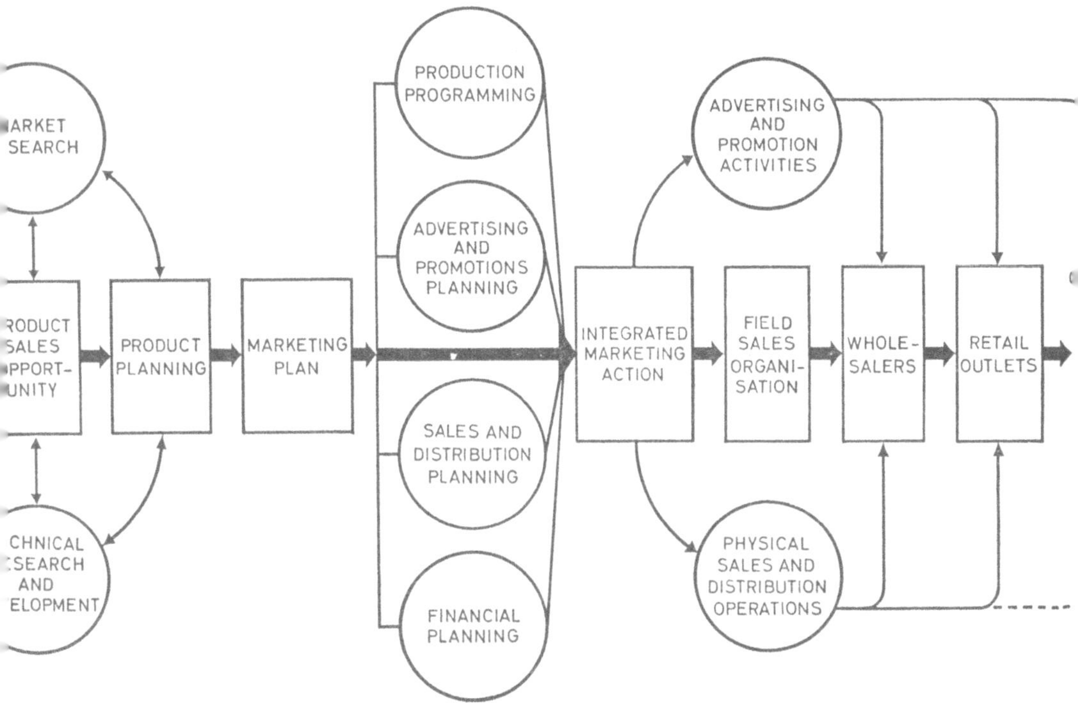

and trade terms. Assuming that one product stands out as eminently suitable in all *major* respects, the next step is to prepare a marketing plan, in writing, setting down all the relevant facts about the product, the market, and the competition, the company's marketing objectives and sales goals and the means by which they are to be achieved.

The marketing plan is the key document which sets down precisely who is to do what, when, where and how. There must be liaison with production to determine product requirements and scheduling; ample stocks of the product must be available at the times required by the sales organisation. The advertising and promotional programme must be worked out in detail —the amount of money to be spent, the media to be used, the kind of advertising to be run. What is to be the basis of the advertising appeal, to reach what kind of audience with what degree of frequency and impact? Are there to be any introductory consumer offers, coupons, premiums or competitions? On the sales side, distribution and product sales targets must be set, by sales territory and by individual sales representative. Physical distribution facilities have to be organised, delivery schedules worked out and so on. The financial people have to provide costings and profit estimates based on proposed expenditures and forecasted sales volumes. Every part of the marketing plan has to be costed out and budgets prepared.

The next stage is the implementation of the paper plan through the coordination and integration of the physical field selling and distribution effort and the company's advertising and promotional activities. The functions of the former are to see to it that the company's distribution and sales targets are met, that wholesale, retail and direct customers are efficiently serviced and at all times carry adequate stock to meet their anticipated requirements, and that customer information is fed back regularly to sales management in the form of daily, weekly or monthly reports. An efficient field intelligence system is of the utmost importance in keeping headquarters appraised of the latest situation and expected developments in the market and in checking and controlling actual field performance against planned performance.

Advertising and sales promotion activities run parallel with the physical selling and distribution operations, and include advertising and display material aimed directly at the consumer or user; trade and technical press advertising to distributors, trade buyers, professional groups, etc.; direct mail, trade receptions, and planned sales presentations to trade buyers, committees or associations; consumer and trade incentive schemes, such as special offers, bonuses, competitions, premiums, etc.

(b) THE NATURE OF MARKETING PROBLEMS

Any marketing problem involves a situation requiring a decision to act, or not to act, in the face of uncertainty. The major sources of uncertainty are the difficulties of trying to anticipate and influence the future course of events, in determining the interactions of cause and effect, in allocating limited resources among competing ends, of choosing between different courses of action, and in obtaining accurate and reliable information. The existence of uncertainty and, therefore, the necessity of taking risks—and a decision not to take action can involve as great a risk, if not a greater degree of risk—is a characteristic of all problems. Decisions to alter the price of an existing product or service, to introduce a new product, to increase the level of advertising for a product or to discontinue advertising for a product, all involve uncertainty and risk as to their probable outcomes in terms of achieving company objectives.

Seen in this light, problem-solving means finding ways of progressively reducing uncertainty and risk in business judgments, assumptions, decisions and actions, at least to more tolerable limits.

The scientific approach to problem-solving involves the basic steps shown in Chart 3.

The ability to identify and assess a particular problem is related to the quantity, accuracy, relevancy and timeliness of the information available, and to how well the information is analysed and interpreted.

The setting of objectives and goals and the selection of the particular course of action to follow are related, on the one hand, to management's ability to forecast or anticipate events over which it either can or cannot exercise some degree of control and the probable outcomes of its own and other's actions; on the other hand, it is also related to management's capacity for perceiving the possibilities and potentialities in a given or expected situation, not apparent at first sight, and what can be made to happen by purposeful action.

Planning and control relate to the organisation and allocation of limited sources to a particular course of action, chosen from a number of possible alternatives, and to the evaluation of the results achieved by such action against planned performance. If at the end of this sequence of steps the original problem remains then the cycle must start again in the hope of coming closer to the final solution through successive approximations and corrections. The original as well as any new information, including the results yielded by the previous plan of action, must be reappraised; assumptions, conclusions, objectives and goals must be critically re-examined and either reaffirmed or changed in the light of newer or more accurate knowledge; a fresh course of action must be embarked upon and its results evaluated.

Some Recent Developments in Problem-solving

A very wide range of marketing problems requiring quantitative solutions have only been tackled with great difficulty in the past due to sheer limitations in computational power. Many problems just took too long to solve using the traditional and very time-consuming hand computational methods. Moreover, their solutions frequently called for a degree of mathematical knowledge and expertise not possessed by the average

CHART 3. THE SIX BASIC STEPS IN PROBLEM-SOLVING

STEP 1. THE IDENTIFICATION OF THE PROBLEM

Isolation of the key determining factors and areas of decision

prior to

STEP 2. THE EVALUATION OF RELEVANT INFORMATION

Gathering, processing and analysing all relevant information and drawing conclusions

relevant to

STEP 3. THE SETTING OF OBJECTIVES AND GOALS

Distinguishing between generalised aims (objectives) and specific quantified targets (goals)

which will determine

STEP 4. THE SELECTION OF A PARTICULAR COURSE OF ACTION

Representing the most favourable balance of risk, effort, timing and expected results

necessitating

STEP 5. THE PLANNING AND CONTROL OF ACTION

Specifying who does what, to whom, when and how

leading to

STEP 6. THE EVALUATION OF THE ACTION TAKEN

Measuring the effectiveness of the action taken in terms of the complete or partial solution of the original problem or total failure to solve the problem. Comparing actual operating results against planned performance

marketing executive. The behavioural sciences, mathematics, statistics and electronics have combined to produce better methods of gathering and processing information of all kinds—a good deal faster, in fact, than the users' abilities to put the resulting data to work effectively.

Together, the development of the high-speed computer and of a new family of analytical tools, based on a few relatively simple mathematical procedures, have brought an increasing range of problems within the compass of the average business executive and materially shortened the time period required to arrive at workable solutions. These latter techniques, largely developed by operational researchers, employ scientific methods to identify problem situations and to analyse the nature and structure of business problems involving alternative courses of action. It is questionable whether progress in developing these analytical tools could have been made to anything like the same degree in the absence of the technical 'hardware' and know-how—epitomised by the electronic computer—with which to handle and process enormous quantities of data at tremendously high speeds.

Among the most widely used techniques with immediate or potential application to marketing problems are the following:

Linear Programming—A mathematical technique for selecting the most favourable or desirable course of action in terms of least cost, highest profit, least time or least effort from among a number of alternative courses of action, using limited resources. Programming means planning activity to achieve a given objective through the optimum use or allocation of available resources. Programming is linear when there is a straight-line relationship between the variables as when a change in the number of calls a salesman makes brings a proportional change in the number or value of orders he collects. A non-linear relationship would exist where a change in the former produces a less than or more than proportional change in the latter. The very large number of computations usually called for in all but a limited range of linear programming problems makes access to a computer almost essential and this represents a major limitation on the extension of the use of the technique at this time. The sort of marketing problems that linear (and non-linear) programming should help to solve include determining the most profitable combination of products to be made from limited resources, determining the optimum location of warehouses and depots to minimise transport and delivery costs, determining the optimum stock levels to meet sales requirements at least cost [taking into consideration production capacity and flexibility and delivery commitments], planning salesmen's journeys and customer-calling cycles so as to maximise sales revenue or profit or to minimise sales costs.

Business Games—These are competitive business situations which have been reduced to highly simplified 'models' of real and urgent situations for training purposes. Competing teams of 'executives'—each executive is usually assigned responsibility for a particular function, e.g. manufacturing, marketing, finance—have to make decisions aimed at ending up in a more advantageous position in relation to the others than at the start. The games can be operated to determine the best strategy or the winning pattern of initiating moves and counteracting responses. The effects of decisions taken are calculated, frequently with the aid of a computer, and fed back to the teams as a basis for taking further decisions. A business game usually follows certain rules which the 'players' must adhere to, depending on the nature of the particular model on which it is based. Further advances in the technique lie in extending the range of competitive situations which can be realistically dealt with and in building increasingly complex and sophisticated models that approximate more closely to real-life business situations.

Queuing Theory—A technique concerned with relationships involved in waiting in line and progressing on a sequential basis. It involves determining the number and frequency distribution of demands on a particular service or arrivals at a particular location, the length of time required to provide the service or dispose of arrivals, the number of service channels or locations available and queue behaviour patterns, e.g. random or planned, regular or spasmodic, etc. Queuing theory has been applied to solving telephone line congestion, loading and unloading ships, the movement of freight wagons, the handling of aircraft waiting to land or take-off at airports, servicing equipment awaiting maintenance or repair and airline booking systems. Of greater importance to marketing will be the application of the technique to such problems as customers waiting to be serviced, order processing, delivery scheduling and stock control. The technique aims at improving the speed and efficiency of service and minimising queues or delays that waste time, cost money, tie up facilities and effort that could be put to more profitable use.

Model-building—Models describe, usually in mathematical form, a set of known or assumed relationships between events, activities or processes. They attempt to simulate the conditions and relationships found in the real world so that the effects of induced changes in selected variables can be observed and measured.

Models can be physical in structure, e.g. a wind-tunnel for testing the design and performance of aircraft, a test-market launch of a new product in a limited area and under controlled conditions, or an electrical circuit model used to evaluate the effectiveness of communication and information flow. Alternatively, they can be theoretical structures involving the use of mathematics. Econometric models are adding greatly to our knowledge and understanding of how certain economic quantities and relationships within the national economy are determined and interact. Such methods, applied as yet on a limited scale to marketing systems, can be expected in time to provide fresh insights into the workings of such systems. Some experimental work has already been done using mathematical models to determine the optimum size of advertising appropriation in relation to other marketing outlays and the effects of changes in size of appropriations on market share, sales turnover, net profit or some other criterion in relation to competitors.

Among the types of marketing problems to which model-building would appear to have particular application are (i) the analysis of information and communication flows in business organisations, (ii) determining the optimal size and allocation of various forms of marketing expenditures such as advertising, sales promotion, field selling, transport and delivery, (iii) determining optimal marketing strategies in terms of initiatory moves and competitors' counteracting responses, and (iv) the analysis of certain problems in industrial dynamics, i.e. the effects of changes in one part of the system on other parts of the system in terms of time, magnitude and velocity. For example what would be the effects of a 20% fall in customer demand for a product on the level of factory and depot stocks, and on factory production levels? How long would it take for the initial falling away of demand to work its way through the system and what would be the magnitude of the changes at each subsequent stage? Alternatively, how quickly could production levels, factory inventories and distributors' stocks respond to a 20% rise in customer demand? Answers to these kinds of questions would help to improve production programming, distribution planning and stock control through the avoidance of bottlenecks and critical lags at various stages of the marketing process.

Communication Theory—As its name implies, this theory originated in the electrical communications field and is concerned to evaluate the effectiveness of the flow of information and communication within a given system. Consequently, many problems in communication theory can be translated into models. One branch of the theory, cybernetics, deals with self-regulating and control mechanisms and has provided greater insight into the workings of human behaviour systems. The study of the mechanism of 'feedback' has been of particular importance to communication and control theory, for control of an operation involves reporting back whenever it goes outside certain specified limits so that corrections can be made. When a human being, sensing that he may fall, corrects his balance, he is making use of a built-in, self-regulating, information feedback control process. Industrial automation is one practical commercial result of the theory of cybernetics.

The application of this principle has obvious advantages for those aspects of the marketing process which are capable of being automated such as stock control [the problem of balancing stocks-in and stocks-out] and production and sales control [matching production capacities to sales requirements]. The application of communication theory to complex business organisation structures should provide the means of improving such structures to permit more effective co-ordination and control through better information and communication flow.

Network Analysis—This technique uses mathematical programming and statistical methods to plan and control sequential or dependent activities. Basically what it involves is the detailed analysis of a particular project, breaking it down into the smallest individual tasks and estimating the time needed to complete each separate task. In constructing network diagrams[1]

[1] An example of a network diagram applied to product planning appears on p. 105.

an 'activity' represents the performance of work necessary to complete an 'event' or specific accomplishment in the programme. No event can be accomplished until all the preceding activities leading to it are concluded and work on a succeeding event cannot begin until the preceding event is completed. When the network is finalised estimated duration times are put in against each actitity and, by addition, the longest, shortest, or most likely time paths can be calculated. These paths represent the overall time needed to execute the project on different assumptions. The most optimistic completion time assumes that everything goes right in the shortest possible time. The most pessimistic completion time assumes the worst that is likely to happen. The most likely completion time represents the most reasonable forecast made in the light of previous experience. The longest path is called 'the critical path' since any delay in any activity along this path will cause the whole project to fall behind schedule.

The two best known applications of the network principle are PERT (Programme Evaluation and Review Technique) and CPM (Critical Path Method). The PERT technique was developed as a method of planning and controlling the co-ordination of the Polaris Fleet Ballistic Missile Programme for the Special Projects Office of the U.S. Navy's Bureau of Ordnance. Several thousands of contractors and agencies involved in the programme had to be integrated and as a result of the use of PERT the completion date is reported to have been advanced by more than two years. Both PERT and CPM have found their widest application to date—outside of military uses, that is—in the programming of constructional and installation work.

J. S. Pickup and D. A. Thwaites[1] have summarised the main advantages of these network techniques as follows: (i) they record all the activities necessary for the completion of a project; (ii) they display the reasoning behind the forecasting of completion dates; (iii) they enable potential trouble areas to be foreseen; (iv) they pin-point responsibility; (v) they save time and money by simulating changes in cost variables; (vi) they define objectives; (vii) they provide a good communication medium; (viii) they permit management by exception whereby only significant deviations from planned or standard performance, abnormal situations and trouble spots are brought to the attention of management. The authors conclude: 'One of the greatest benefits of drawing up networks is improved communication throughout an organisation horizontally and vertically. The necessity to analyse in detail the activities and events of a project not only brings out the relative "time" importance of interrelated activities, but forces people to think and discuss with others the sequence in which operations are done and the associated problems which emerge. Management by exception is a natural outcome of using networks, for by concentrating control on the critical path activities, time is not wasted by progressing

[1] J. S. Pickup and D. A. Thwaites. 'Networks: A Path to Success.' *The Manager*. December 1962. pp. 31–7.

other activities which could not shorten the overall length of the project.'[1]

The application of network analysis to marketing operations is still in the experimental stage. Its use in planning new product development, test marketing planning and the co-ordination and scheduling of selling and advertising plans and programmes can be expected to become much more widespread during the next few years. Networks can give the marketing executive a better planning perspective in which the relative importance of time, costs and profits can be taken into account. Operating management is concerned with two basic problems. On the one hand, activities must be organised, scheduled and co-ordinated. On the other hand, limited resources must be assembled and allocated to various tasks at the time and place and in the quantity necessary so as to maximise or minimise some magnitude of importance to management. It is not enough to merely allocate resources to ensure a successful and efficient plan. Although the simultaneous optimisation of all phases of a project may be desirable, in some cases it is usually necessary for the different parts of the programme to be optimised in a particular sequence. But there is always a danger that the whole programme is actually weakened rather than strengthened by making one part more efficient in isolation from or at the expense of others. For example, spending a sum of money on advertising too far in advance of the sales force's capacity to obtain the minimum level of distribution necessary is a common error of marketing policy.

(c) APPLYING THE MARKETING CONCEPT

The marketing concept is applicable to all business organisations irrespective of size or nature of the goods and services marketed. Differences in the types of goods supplied, in the size and characteristics of the consumer or user markets for the various classes of goods, in the purposes for which they are acquired and in the methods by which they are distributed, do not invalidate the universal applicability of the marketing concept to business operations.

As between large and small firms, and as between producers of consumer goods and producers of industrial goods, there may be differences in the permissible scale of marketing effort and in the specific types of marketing techniques that are appropriate to the particular industry or market. A far more fundamental difference, irrespective of size or type of business, is the attitude of mind of management. The following chart attempts to highlight some of the major differences that might be expected to be reflected in business operations according to whether management tends to think in terms of production or in terms of marketing.[2]

[1] Op. cit.

[2] F. F. Mauser. *Modern Marketing Management: An Integrated Approach.* McGraw-Hill Book Co. Inc. 1961. p. 10–11. The chart has been adapted from the author's original compilation.

CHART 4. THE BASIC DIFFERENCES BETWEEN PRODUCTION-ORIENTED AND MARKETING-ORIENTED ORGANISATION

Business Function or Activity	*Company Perspective*	
	Production	*Marketing*
Top Management	Technological considerations predominate. Production and engineering personnel in highest level executive positions.	Customer considerations paramount. Marketing personnel in highest level executive positions.
Objectives	Internal influences predominate. Business objective is to match total company resources against production requirements. More emphasis on technical efficiency and method. Want to be known for technical or production know-how.	External market influences predominate. Business objective is to match total company resources against market requirements and opportunities. More emphasis on market strategy and planning. Want to be regarded as style and market leader.
Manufacturing	Production less flexible. The company sells what can be made.	Flexibility in production so as to match product sales opportunities. The company manufactures what can be profitably sold.
Marketing	Aims to fulfil existing needs and develop workable products to meet these needs. Company's future bound up with markets already supplied, and products already in existence. Marketing function not considered to be as valuable as manufacturing, engineering or finance.	Seeks to create markets and develop saleable products. Company's future bound up with markets yet to be identified and developed, and with products not yet in existence. Marketing considered to be co-ordinate with manufacturing, finance and other major business functions.
Financial	Emphasis on cost rather than selling price; greater concern with how to do things cheaply and well. Budgets based on financial or production requirements rather than marketing considerations.	Greater attention to what the customer will pay, to how pricing can be used as a marketing weapon and to how competition will react. Budgets based on marketing requirements and funds are allocated on the basis of marketing tasks to be accomplished.
Research	Leads in technical and scientific research. Market intelligence system relatively undeveloped.	Leads in analytical and marketing research. Market intelligence system well developed.

Business Function or Activity	*Company Perspective*	
	Production	*Marketing*
Product Planning	Based on technical research —suggestions for new or improved products stem from functional performance and cost improvements. Performance and applications are prime considerations. Engineering considerations tend to predominate.	Based on market research— suggestions for new or improved products stem from research into customer needs. Performance and applications are prime considerations. Styling and design considerations regarded to be almost as important.
	Laboratory testing more prominent than sales or market testing.	Sales and market testing an integral part of planning.
	Packaging viewed as a shipping and protective device. Chief concern is engineering, materials handling and packaging machinery.	Packaging viewed as a sales tool in terms of its user-convenience and advertising and promotional effectiveness.
Sales Organisation	Salesman regarded as an order-getter for the factory.	Salesman regarded as an order-maker who keeps the factory running and provides employment to production workers.
	Salesman lacks the professional status of the engineer, chemist, lawyer or accountant. Less likely to be promoted to top management.	Salesman accorded high status in the company and more likely to be promoted to top management position.
	Salesman lacks formal training. Tends to get left to his own devices as the man 'out there'. Motivation of the salesman minimal.	Salesman given formal and continuous internal and on-the-job training. Motivation of sales organisation given high priority. Chief sales executive regarded as part of the management team.
Advertising and Promotion	Emphasis on cost rather than on the value of its contribution to the total selling effort. Advertising and promotion regarded as an extra cost not a basic cost like machines, raw materials, research laboratories, etc.	Advertising and promotion is an integral part of the company's marketing effort and a basic cost.
	Not regarded as one of the skills required to run a modern business successfully.	Outstanding advertising and promotion considered to be as equally important to the successful running of a business as outstanding manufacturing technique, technical research ability or financial and legal skills.
	Advertising and promotion not looked upon as an important source of competitive differential advantage.	Advertising and promotion regarded as a potential source of competitive differential advantage, particularly when the differences in own and competitive products become less and less distinguishable.

It is not suggested that all production-minded managements think and act along the lines indicated any more than all marketing-minded managements do. But it is a good deal more likely that managements will view the various business functions and activities in the ways indicated depending on their traditional perspective.

To change one's fundamental viewpoint or methods of operation is not an easy thing to do at the best of times. It is, however, all too easy to change the organisational structure, without a corresponding real change in underlying mental attitude or approach. Changing the title of the Sales Manager to Marketing Manager or of Sales Director to Marketing Director does not change anything unless the adoption of the marketing concept is supported and acted upon by top management and seen to be supported and acted upon by them down the line. Unless this is done, confusion, misunderstanding and disenchantment are likely to follow.

Behind any changes in the organisation charts lie a number of critical personnel and personal relationship problems—problems of explanation, communication, re-education and staff training—which management has to deal with successfully if a different way of doing things is to be made acceptable to all concerned. An organisation chart is like a pre-printed electrical circuit. All the guide lines, power and communication channels are there; but it requires a power source and an electrical current or dynamic impulse to make the thing work properly. Applied in the right way and hooked up to the main source of power, i.e. top management, the marketing concept can be the dynamic impulse needed in business organisation.

Problems of the Small Firm

It is sometimes asserted that 'marketing is all very well if the firm is large, but a small firm has neither the men, the money nor the time at its disposal to be able to do very much about it', or words to that effect.

While conceding that the size of a firm largely determines the degree of management division of labour or specialisation which is feasible, the facts remain that (a) marketing problems do not disappear simply because a business firm does not have the personnel or resources to deal with them, (b) the marketing functions must be carried out to a greater or lesser degree implicitly, if not explicitly, by someone either within or outside the firm and (c) the causes of small business failure seem to have a good deal less to do with size, availability of capital and product engineering skill than with basic management and planning weaknesses, in particular, poor product and marketing planning due to inadequate records and insufficient or inaccurate information, unbalanced management experience, and poor financial planning and control.[1]

But accepting the fact that the problems remain and have to be dealt with as best the firm can, how can the smaller firm get over the limitations

[1] For a fuller discussion of the reasons for small business failures see J. C. Denyer. *The Manager*. January 1963. pp. 23–4.

imposed by size, or its inability to employ the necessary marketing skills? Assuming that there is no one individual with the time, experience and knowledge to co-ordinate the basic marketing functions, then there are two ways of meeting the difficulty. One way is to come to some joint association arrangement with another firm or group of other like-minded firms to finance and carry out certain centralised marketing services. Group market research projects, product testing facilities and information services, group advertising and promotion and reciprocal trading and purchasing arrangements—these are just a few areas in which greater co-operation should be possible.

The second method by which the small firm can partially overcome the size problem is the use of outside consultants. Numerous expert organisations in research and information, product planning, market testing, selling, advertising and public relations, are available to the individual firm or groups of firms on either an *ad hoc* or continuing basis.

Industrial versus *Consumer Goods Marketing*

Again, it has often been said that the techniques used with success in consumer goods marketing are not applicable to the marketing of industrial goods, that the marketing problems faced by industrial goods producers are quite different from those met with in the consumer goods field.

The marketing differences between industrial and consumer goods are fairly clear, if not always appreciated.

1. Industrial goods are destined for use by producers of other goods and services and include raw materials, buildings, equipment, supplies, fabricated materials and industrial services. The customers of industrial goods manufacturers are firms, factories, mines, farms, contractors and other service industries, institutions and government agencies. Consumer goods are normally for personal or household use without further processing. By way of illustration, the biscuit manufacturer makes a product for consumption by individuals and families in the home mainly. He must plan his marketing so as to make his product known and available in the areas where his consumers live and purchase their requirements. An assortment of industrial goods manufacturers will have supplied, among other things, the equipment with which the biscuit manufacturer makes, packages and distributes his products to the ultimate consumer. By comparison with most consumer goods and services, the demand for industrial goods can be intermittent and change abruptly.
2. Channels of distribution for industrial goods tend to be shorter than for consumer goods. Industrial goods suppliers and purchasers are very often in direct contact or use a few highly specialised middlemen. The biscuit manufacturer mentioned above may have to sell direct and/or through wholesalers to something like 150,000 retailers before his final consumers can buy his product. He has three tasks—to

persuade the trade to stock his product, to persuade the consumer to try it and to keep on reminding people about it so that they will keep on buying it.

3. There are relatively fewer customers for industrial goods than for consumer goods, although the former have far greater purchasing power at their command. For many industrial goods manufacturers, the total number of buyers is determinable and a small proportion of major buyers may account for the bulk of a company's output.

4. The criteria for purchasing industrial goods are primarily technical in nature, i.e. efficiency of performance, economy, durability, effects on productivity and profitability. The customer is normally the user and an expert purchaser; the actual purchase is usually subject to multiple influences, both technical and commercial, within the customer organisation and to lengthy negotiation. Many industrial goods are supplied on a tendering basis, which raises special problems of estimating and pricing.

5. The industrial goods salesman is usually primarily concerned with finding the right people to influence—specifiers, contractors, technical experts, commercial buyers—with paving the way for his own technical experts. The consumer goods salesman, on the other hand, usually completes the sale to his wholesale and retail customers.

6. The demand for industrial goods tends to fluctuate much more widely with the ups and downs of the general economy. This is primaily due to the relative durability of such goods (hence it is easier to postpone purchases and extend the useful life of existing equipment) and to the fact that the demand for industrial goods and services is dependent upon the demand for consumer goods and services and upon the state of business confidence about the present and future economic situation.

7. Industrial purchasers buy products for their companies not for themselves. Having several different sources of supply is a sound buying policy. Consumers, on the other hand, may spread their purchases among a number of different brands or sources of supply, but more from inquisitiveness and a desire to experiment than from the desire to protect their sources of supply.

Thus, in terms of the purposes for which they are bought, the markets to which they sell, and the methods by which they are marketed, industrial goods can involve more complex and widely differing marketing patterns than in the case of most consumer goods which tend to follow a common pattern. A British Institute of Management study group on industrial marketing, however, reported that 'Within the field of industrial goods, the type of product and the nature of the market vary greatly. Despite this, it soon emerged from the discussions that there is a surprising amount of common ground. An initial reaction, that the problems of the various industries in the group were too different to allow useful comparison, quickly disappeared. The sugar manufacturer, for instance, found that his problems were unexpectedly similar to those of the electrical engineer.'[1]

The differences between industrial and consumer goods and their respective markets in no way invalidates the applicability of the marketing concept to industrial goods. Indeed because of the high value of unit sales and unit purchases of many industrial goods and because of the longer manufacturing cycle and high cost of building and maintaining stocks associated with a wide range of such goods, the importance of the marketing concept may be even greater than for consumer goods to the extent that the consequences of being wrong—through bad business and sales forecasting, faulty product planning, inadequate or inaccurate information, failure to identify, contact and follow-up sales prospects with well-conceived sales promotional activity—can be a great deal more costly. This is not to say that the marketing techniques developed and refined by consumer goods manufacturers are immediately transferable to the industrial field. The use of such techniques unadapted to the specific needs of industrial markets and without taking account of the real differences that exist between industrial and consumer goods marketing is doomed to failure.

Much of the disillusionment among many industrial goods manufacturers with the so-called marketing concept, stems from the undiscriminating use of methods ill-adapted to deal with the peculiar problems met with in industrial marketing or applied in completely the wrong circumstances. But this is a matter of detailed application. The point at issue is not whether some of the techniques used in consumer goods marketing are adaptable to industrial goods marketing. New techniques are being developed in both fields and the cross-fertilisation of ideas and methods is by no means one-way. The argument put forward here is that manufacturers of industrial goods have something to gain by taking a marketing perspective of their commercial operations, by looking at their businesses first and foremost in terms of customers and markets rather than in terms of production engineering and industrial processes.

The principles of competitive differential advantage and market segmentation apply with at least as much force to the marketing of industrial goods as to the marketing of consumer goods. So far as differential advantages are concerned, technical patents are a much more common source in industrial goods than in consumer goods. This can be of critical importance because of the necessity to recover the high cost of research and development, tooling-up and other investment costs associated with a large number of industrial marketing projects.

Again, the number and spread of markets or market segments supplied or capable of being supplied by an industrial goods manufacturer can be greater even than those of many consumer goods manufacturers. The more highly specialised the industrial product, of course, the less is this likely to

[1] *Selling to Industry*. British Institute of Management Marketing Services Report No. 2. June 1957. p. 2.

be the case. A walking drag-line, for instance, has a highly specialised use and its markets are clearly predetermined. Paint, on the other hand, is not only used in the home by 'do-it-yourselfers', professional builders and decorators, but also by a myriad of secondary users producing an infinite variety of consumer goods or other industrial goods. Thus, industrial goods manufacturers may have to tackle a much wider variety of markets with diverse requirements and different buying and selling conditions.

Accurate business and market forecasting is of major concern because (i) an industrial goods manufacturer's future is bound up to a much greater degree with that of the industries he supplies, (ii) the impact of technological innovation can be very much greater and more abrupt in industrial markets, and (iii) it takes longer and, in general, requires a larger investment to undertake any major expansion or change of direction. Manufacturing, viewed as a single activity, makes use of a variety of technical skills and facilities according to some central plan or objective. Likewise, marketing should be regarded as a single activity making use of a variety of research, selling and communication skills and facilities which is also based on a central plan or objective. And yet, according to a recent survey carried out by *Metalworking Production*, 'A high proportion of industrial goods manufacturers must still be regarded as production-biased, managed by engineers and technologists (hardly ever by sales- or marketing-oriented executives) and with little attempt being made to integrate all the related marketing functions in an effective manner.'[1]

The same survey of the buying and selling techniques used by machine-tool builders, who can probably be taken as representative of a fairly wide section of the engineering industry, reports that fewer than one out of every two manufacturers approached properly integrate selling and promotional planning. Only one in ten had someone assigned to marketing research. The report concluded: 'With few exceptions they (*the manufacturers*) undertake no market research. As a result, the majority are unable to draw up a really effective sales plan or apportion the necessary promotion expenditure in terms of reaching their market potential. It becomes quite clear that even the simplest of market research, designed to delineate their major prospects, which would enable companies to see to it that all buying influences were covered by suitably planned promotion strategy, is not being carried out.'[2]

(d) MARKETING ORGANISATION

There will usually be a number of transitional stages through which a business enterprise will pass from being a production-centred organisation to being a marketing-centred organisation. The following three-stage

[1] *Buying and Selling Techniques Used in the British Engineering Industry*. Special Report prepared by the Research Department of Metal-Working Production (a McGraw-Hill publication). May 1963.

[2] Ibid. p. 20.

transition—pre-marketing organisation, sales-oriented organisation and marketing-centred organisation—illustrates the process.

CHART 5a. PRE-MARKETING ORGANISATION

The main point to note in this chart, which is not untypical of many organisations as they were or as they exist today, is the absence of co-ordination between and integrated control of sales, information and research, order processing, sales forecasting, product planning, advertising and public relations. While it is true that each of these activities is the responsibility of one or other of the management team, they are not grouped on a functional basis, and are not under the control of one co-ordinating executive. How competent is financial management to make market and sales forecasts and budgets? Since when was personnel management a repository of advertising expertise? How accurate and objective are the findings of sales and market research carried out by interested parties with a stake in the outcome?

Chart 5b shows what the line-up might be after certain changes have been made to give greater emphasis to the selling function.

There has been a noticeable increase in the responsibilities of sales management and in the number of supporting staff needed to carry out the duties now assigned. The transition reflects the development of a sales-directed approach to the firm's problems. Certain activities previously carried out by some other individuals or departments have been regrouped and are now overseen and co-ordinated by one responsible sales management

CHART 5b. SALES-ORIENTED ORGANISATION

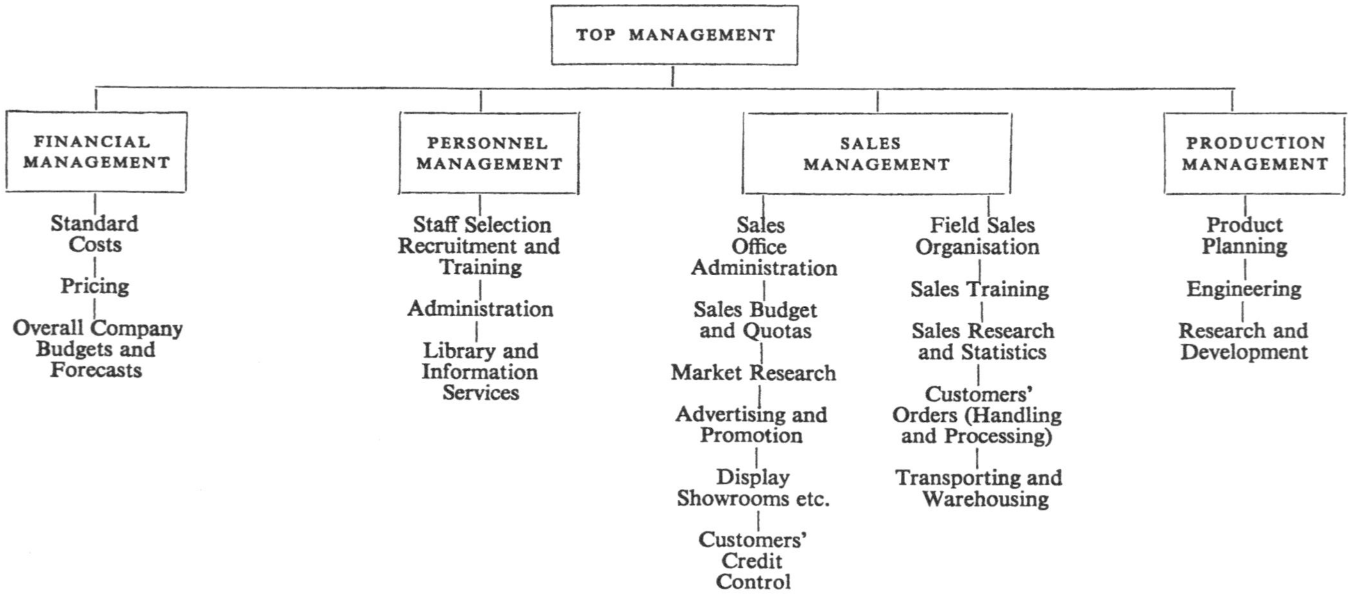

executive. However, not all of the key marketing activities have been brought together under a single management executive. The responsibility for information services remains with Personnel and product planning responsibility with Production. At the same time Sales Management is still held responsible for researching its own activities and auditing its own performance.

The transition to a fully fledged marketing organisation is shown in the following chart.

CHART 5c. MARKETING-CENTRED ORGANISATION

The marketing function is now co-ordinate with production, finance and personnel. Marketing management is finally responsible for co-ordinating and integrating the sales and distribution, information and research, advertising and promotion, market and product planning functions of the business. Marketing management in these circumstances is responsible for the administration and control of the company's total marketing effort, for initiating marketing research and the preparation of marketing plans, and for presenting to and obtaining the approval of top management for all plans and proposals to meet agreed objectives.

(e) THE PRINCIPAL MARKETING FUNCTIONS

A marketing function may be defined as a major specialised activity or group of activities performed in the marketing of goods and services. Although the performance of a specific function may be inescapable, it is frequently transferable, in other words it has to be performed by someone regardless of his official title and responsibilities. Another characteristic of a function is that whereas its purpose may be unchanging, its content, in terms of the number and kinds of activities involved, may be subject to constant change. Newer and better ways of doing things and of carrying out traditional functions are continually being developed.

Traditionally, some seven or eight so-called marketing functions have been listed and normally include (a) the exchange functions of buying and selling, (b) the physical distribution functions of transporting, warehousing and handling goods between producer and customer, (c) what are usually

CHART 6. THE PRINCIPAL MARKETING FUNCTIONS

SPECIFIC FUNCTION	ACTIVITIES INVOLVED
Marketing Information and Research	Economic, business, trade, industry, consumer, user, product, sales and advertising research and analysis. Information handling and data processing. Marketing operations research. Competitive intelligence.
Product Planning	Determining and developing the company's product mix. Matching the products' specifications, packaging, pricing, performance and servicing to customer needs through product and service improvements and new product development.
Sales and Distribution	Field selling. Selection of Distribution Channels. Warehousing. Transport. Sales Reporting. Sales Analysis. Sales Forecasting. Sales Budgets and Quotas Merchandising. Sales Communications.
Advertising and Promotion	Advertising to the customer or user in all media (press, television, cinema, radio, outdoor posters, etc.). Consumer Promotions directed at the customer or user, e.g. reduced price offers, banded pack offers, premiums, competitions, couponing, etc. Point-of-purchase display material. Trade Promotions, e.g. incentive schemes, display competitions, sales contests.

described as the 'facilitating' functions which take in product standardisation and simplification, commercial and market information, financing and risk-bearing. (It is questionable whether risk-bearing, in the true entrepreneurial sense of committing one's own resources to a speculative venture, really belongs in any list of marketing functions. Risk-taking is a responsibility jointly undertaken by the managers of a business or solely by the chief executive.)

This kind of analysis is inadequate as a description of modern marketing activities since it fails to distinguish clearly between major functions and the specialised activities which comprise the different functions. Under the modern marketing concept there are four principal functions—marketing research and information, product planning, selling and distribution, and advertising and promotion. Chart 6 sets out these major functions and the specialised activities involved in each.

The next section considers each of these major specialised functions and their organisation in detail.

PART TWO

MANAGING THE MARKETING FUNCTIONS

3

Managing the Marketing Information and Research Function

(a) MANAGEMENT INFORMATION NEEDS

MANAGEMENT'S job is to decide what needs to be done, to specify who is to do it, to see that it gets done and to evaluate how well it was done. Business operations run on facts and the effectiveness with which these are carried out depends on the intelligent and purposeful use of the reporting process which, in turn, determines the quantity, quality and relevance of the information available for planning and control purposes. The lack of essential information, the use of irrelevant or inaccurate information as well as the misuse of any information can seriously impair a firm's competitive performance.

Any executive at any level—headquarters' staff, divisional, territorial or departmental—is, to a greater or lesser extent, a receiver and user of information. How good an executive he is and how well he carries out his assigned tasks will depend, firstly, on how much, how relevant and how good his information is and, secondly, on how well he interprets and acts upon it. In a situation requiring a decision to act or not to act in the face of uncertainty, every executive has the dual problem of determining the nature of the problem he has to deal with and of predicting the outcome of his action or inaction. Each decision to follow a particular course of action entails the risk either that it will be the wrong action or, at least, will not be the best possible action or that no action at all would have been preferable. Furthermore in committing himself to one particular course of action the executive blocks his ability to move in other directions, and it is this that constitutes the real difficulty in taking decisions.

Seen in this light, the executive's ability to take better decisions means finding ways of reducing the uncertainty and risk associated with following one particular course of action, and of improving his power to act in the right direction. The sources of such improvement lie in the methodical selection, collection, processing, analysis and communication of relevant information and in the ability to formulate sound assumptions as a basis for making more accurate forecasts and planning decisions.

However, although information of some kind is necessary in order to arrive at any decision, information alone does not automatically lead to the right decisions. Information has to be interpreted and translated into decisions.

It will be recalled that there are four basic decision-areas confronting management executives in any problem-solving situation: (a) decisions that relate to the nature of the problem situation itself and the key determining factors in it; (b) decisions that relate to the kind of information that will be relevant to the problems of setting objectives or targets; (c) decisions that relate to the selection of one of several possible alternative courses of action and to the actual plan of action to be put into operation; (d) decisions that relate to the control and evaluation of the particular course of action followed.

Every company has to make some rational attempt to project its business into the future, to identify its overall business aims and objectives and the specific problems and opportunities which present themselves in its chosen sphere of activity. It cannot avoid making forecasts inasmuch as all decisions, because they are related to future expectations or outcomes, involve forecasting, either implicitly or explicitly. Planning is necessary if problems are to be anticipated, overcome or avoided, and if advantage is to be taken of available opportunities in a rational way. Results must be evaluated to find out if everything went according to plan or, if not, what went wrong, and how the same mistakes can be avoided in the future. Furthermore, plans must constantly be re-evaluated for changing conditions. If conditions change when the original plan has only partly run its course, the necessary information must be fed back to the decision-makers and planners so that the remainder of the programme can be adjusted for better results. The more quickly accurate and relevant information is made available about changing conditions, the more room there is for management to manœuvre and take advantage of change *vis-à-vis* their less well-informed, more inflexible and slower-reacting competitors.

In Chart 7, information needs of management are drawn up as they relate to the three basic elements of the business process outlined above; these are planning, execution and control.

For planning purposes, there are three basic sources of information—internal operating data, marketing research data and environmental data. Internal operating data comprises all the measurable quantitative information that comes out of the operational divisions of the company—financial data in respect of past, present and forecasted sales, costs and profits; production data covering volume, capacity, manpower, raw materials, productivity, stocks, etc.; marketing data in respect of sales organisation and manpower, promotional and advertising expenditures and budgets, distribution levels, delivery schedules, trade terms, pricing, etc.; personnel data in terms of organisation charts, numbers, responsibilities, promotability and so on.

Marketing research information includes the findings of product research, consumer or user market research, sales operations and distribution research, advertising research and special project studies, e.g. distribution cost analyses, warehouse location studies.

Environmental data covers social, political, economic and business

CHART 7. THE INFORMATION FUNCTION

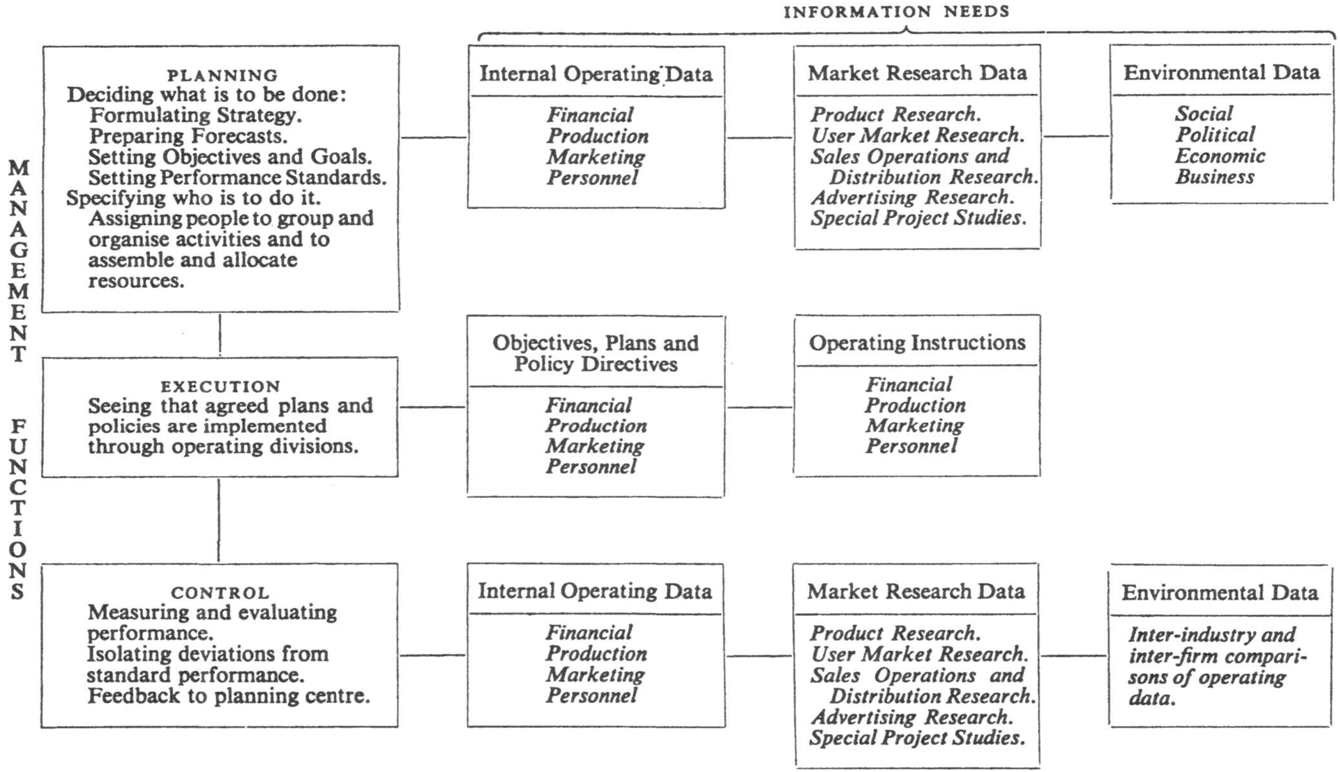

trends of significance to the company's operations such as population, spending habits, price trends, overseas trade, government planning policies, business controls and regulations, legal developments, taxation, production and consumption trends, etc. It also includes information about competitors' activities—their past, present and future plans, organisational structures, and relative strengths and weaknesses—and inter-industry and inter-firm comparisons of operating data.

Information required for the implementation of plans obviously includes the specific directives and goals laid down for each of the operating divisions of the company. The financial division prepares profit plans based on income and expenditure forecasts; the production division programmes its output of products to meet stipulated volume requirements at specified times; the marketing division is responsible for achieving certain sales and distribution targets, for meeting delivery schedules, for implementing promotional plans, and for controlling advertising expenditures, etc.; the personnel division is responsible for manpower recruitment, training and development. Detailed operating instructions must designate who is to do what, when, where and to whom in order to achieve all the agreed targets.

For the purpose of control, the responsible executives must be in possession of all the internal operating data necessary to the proper evaluation of the particular standards of performance set. Additionally, they should have access to any relevant data comparing standards of performance *vis-à-vis* competitors such as volume or value of sales and share of market. The chief instruments of control are an early warning system which isolates and identifies significant deviations from planned performance, in terms of either inputs (budgets) or outputs (results), and a feedback mechanism which relays these variations back to the planning centre so that timely corrective action can be taken.

So far the information function has been looked at from a total company standpoint. Particular consideration must now be given to the role of marketing research, for it is this aspect of the information function, more than any other, which has had the greatest significance for the development of the 'marketing perspective'. Internal operating data and operating instructions tend to flow more easily to the job than marketing and external environmental information—at least this is likely to be so in medium- and small-sized companies where lines of communication are not too extended and where the number of levels of management and the physical number of executives involved are relatively small. As companies increase in size and extend their operations into other markets and countries, serious problems of communication and information can and frequently do arise. But the organisation of marketing research and the manner in which its results are fed into the planning and decision-making system raises special problems. A survey of current marketing research practice will serve to highlight some of these problems and the present inadequacies and shortcomings of research activity in Great Britain.

(b) SURVEY OF MARKETING RESEARCH IN GREAT BRITAIN

An indication of what marketing research should cover has already been given. The definition used by the British Institute of Management in the first survey of its kind ever undertaken of marketing research in Great Britain[1] is 'the objective gathering, recording and analysing of all facts about problems relating to the transfer and sales of goods and services from producer to consumer'. In other words, it covers the investigation and analysis of each and every facet of the marketing process—the product itself, the market for the product, channels of distribution, selling methods, sales promotion, merchandising, advertising and other related marketing activities. As distinct from pure market research which is, traditionally, concerned primarily with the consumer market for the product, marketing research covers the totality of the process from the time that a manufacturer has an idea for a product which he thinks customers might buy to the time it is consumed or used by the final customer.

The B.I.M. Survey questionnaire was sent out to 265 companies of which eighty-six, or about one in three, were returned. Of those returned, three quarters were from manufacturers of industrial or consumer products, and the remaining quarter were from advertising agencies. In its report on the findings, it was observed that the unusually low response to the survey reflected the uncertainty which, as recently as 1961, many manufacturers still had about marketing research and the limited use made of it. Because of this low response rate, figures must be treated with caution and may be regarded as indicative only of British industry taken as a whole.

According to the survey, marketing research expenditure by all the firms reporting totalled 0·7% of turnover. The industrial goods producers' ratio of expenditure was 0·04%, the consumer goods producers' ratio 0·08% and the advertising agents' ratio 0·82%. Generally speaking, firms with a turnover of less than £10 million in either the industrial or the consumer goods sectors, spent a higher proportion of turnover on marketing research than firms with a turnover of more than £10 million.

The explanation suggested by Stacey and Wilson[2] that 'smaller firms tend to use marketing research more extensively because they want to become better established or because this is one way in which they hope to counter competition from larger firms', seems a reasonable one. There is also the fact that the costs of comparable marketing research are the same for large or small firms so that even assuming the research carried out by the smaller manufacturers was no more extensive than that carried out by the larger ones, it would cost more as a percentage of the former's turnover.

Firms in both the industrial or consumer goods sectors with at urnover of under £1 million attempted little organised marketing research of any

[1] *Survey of Marketing Research in Great Britain.* British Institute of Management Information Summary No. 97. January 1962.

[2] Ibid. p. 82.

kind. In summary, the survey shows that marketing research, generally, is of fairly recent origin in Great Britain. In the companies reporting, only eight had a marketing research department by 1939 and none of these belonged to industrial goods producers. In the decade 1940–50 nine more departments were set up; between 1950 and 1960 another forty were established—more than 80% of them since 1956. In these four years more than twice as many marketing research departments were set up than in the previous thirty years or more. Moreover, since the mid-fifties three times as many marketing research departments have been set up by industrial goods producers as by consumer goods producers.

Even so, in 1961 only 58% of industrial goods producers reporting had a central marketing research department compared with 77% of consumer goods producers and over 82% of advertising agencies. This is, of course, a generalisation. For example, against the figure for industrial goods producers with a marketing research department or marketing research officer must be set the evidence of the survey of the machine tool industry quoted earlier[1] to the effect that only one company out of every ten had an executive permanently assigned to marketing research.

As regards the types of marketing research undertaken by firms, the survey's general finding was that out of thirty-seven marketing research activities the types of work most frequently done, i.e. by at least 60% of all the companies reporting, were in connection with:

Acceptability of new products
Product testing
Research on competitive products
Determination of market characteristics and changes in the market
Development of market potentials
'Share of market' analyses
Sales analyses
Short- and long-range sales and business forecasting
Studies of business trends.

Types of marketing research work done least frequently, i.e. less than 40% of all companies reporting, were in connection with:

Studies of sales incentives
Distribution cost studies
Premium and other promotions research
Plant and warehouse locations
Export market research (products, sales, advertising and business trends).

Comparatively speaking, the work done on export marketing research (covering product, market, sales, advertising, business and economic research) was described as 'dangerously small'.

Two further findings from the B.I.M. study are worth noting. Although

[1] See p. 66.

it might be expected that the logical outcome of any marketing research project would be to make appropriate recommendations to management, only 74% of marketing research reports contained actual recommendations and only about half of these were acted upon by management. Even making allowance for the difficulty in answering this type of question, the replies indicate a disturbing attitude of mind towards research and its use by management.

Marketing research is still, it seems, having to prove itself to business managements. As it succeeds in gaining the confidence of management in its findings and its practical applications, it will be brought more and more into the councils of management and looked to to make contributions to management thinking and policy-making. The stature of research, the scope of its authority and the degree of encouragement given to research executives to interpret their findings and make their own recommendations to management will be in direct proportion to its practical contribution to management problems.

The role of the marketing research executive is not an easy one, for he must often present findings and recommendations which are contrary to management's own experience, opinions or beliefs. Lack of knowledge and, in some cases, suspicion and misunderstanding of research techniques inhibit acceptance of research findings, particularly in firms where marketing research is an innovation. The effective use of marketing research is only possible in an atmosphere of mutual co-operation and understanding between top management and the marketing research department. Top management must put itself out to give marketing research a chance to prove its value. It should divest itself of any prejudices and preconceptions, and approach research with open-mindedness. It should clearly define the problems on which it expects research help and guidance and pinpoint the information needed to take decisions.

At the same time, marketing research managers and executives have responsibilities towards top management. They must 'sell' management on the value and uses of research in dealing with problems of immediate concern to management, e.g. keeping in touch with its markets, reducing waste in marketing methods, developing new sources of company growth and profits through new products, new uses for existing products and new markets, insuring against unexpected changes in the market and against product obsolescence.

An appropriate epitaph for a great many research reports would be 'Here lies Marketing Research which died from poor presentation and bad communication technique'. Marketing research *must* have an action-perspective and speak to management in management's language and not in the professional gobbledygook of the research specialist. Explanations of sampling technique, methodology and statistical formulas should be kept to the absolute minimum sufficient to give management confidence in the research results, conclusions and recommendations. Management is interested in results and applications, not methodologies.

Types of Marketing Research

The main types of marketing research needed for management planning and control purposes are outlined in Chart 8.

Product research takes in (i) the screening of new products; (ii) tests on the acceptability of new or improved products, own and competitors', in terms of their inherent physical properties (flavour, smell, colour, size, design, quality), their performance in use (durability, convenience, speed of operation, trouble-free operation), or their psychological attributes (product name, prestige, conferred status, exclusiveness, etc.); (iii) comparison tests of new or existing products versus competition on a blind (concealed identity) or open basis; (iv) packaging tests covering physical characteristics, design, visual appeal and impact, product identification, convenience in use, after-uses (ornamental or functional); (v) product line simplification studies to eliminate superfluous and uneconomic variations in styles, colours, sizes, qualities, etc.; (vi) product range completeness studies to ensure that the company is adequately represented, *vis-à-vis* competitive products, in all major product and user-market sectors; (vii) after-sales service studies, particularly important for industrial products whose installation and running-in may take some months from the time that the actual sale has been completed.

User market research includes (i) assessment and analysis of size and trends of the market and its seasonality; (ii) assessment and analysis of market potentials in terms of existing and new products for existing or new markets; (iii) analysis of changes and trends within the market in relation to style, colour, taste, size, price, quality, convenience and other revealed preferences of different types of users; (iv) analysis of user characteristics in terms of age, regional location, social class, sex, family composition, purchasing and usage habits, or any other relevant criteria, with particular regard to actual or anticipated shifts in market composition; (v) analysis of user attitudes, opinions, motivations, expectations and desires so as to take competitive advantage of such knowledge in formulating product, sales and advertising policies; (vi) analysis of sales and share of market in terms of geographical location, demographic characteristics, type of distributive outlet, type of user-industry, turnover size and price groups in order to determine strengths and weaknesses in market position.

Sales operations and distribution research covers (i) the effectiveness of the sales force as a whole and of individual salesmen in the performance of their selling tasks, e.g. organisation of calling sequence, number of calls made, number of orders taken, ratio of orders to calls, size and value of orders, time spent waiting for buyers, time spent face to face with buyers, effectiveness of sales presentation, use of visual selling aids, handling of complaints, display material placed, quality of reporting, time spent filling in reports for head office, expense control, etc.; (ii) the establishment or

CHART 8. TYPES OF MARKETING RESEARCH

revision of sales territories, the analysis of territorial potentials and variations in territorial results; (iii) the analysis of channels of distribution in terms of their relative importance, particularly changes in their effectiveness as outlets for the company's products, and of the best method of servicing them; (iv) the analysis of distribution costs by type of distributor in order to reveal and eliminate unprofitable products and services, customers, orders and sales territories; (v) trade or distributor attitude and opinion studies in connection with the image of the company and of its competitors, their products, pricing policies, selling methods, distribution policies, advertising and promotional policies, etc.; (vi) distribution and sales audits, i.e. the regular physical counting and recording of the number of stockists of the product, distributors' purchases, stocks and sales to customers over a specified period of time; (vii) the analysis of company sales statistics by product type, trade customer classification, order size, sales territory, salesmen, etc.; (viii) the preparation of sales forecasts by product, customers and territories and of sales quotas for individual salesmen; (ix) the study of individual salesman's and group compensation to determine the most effective combination of salary, commission, bonus payments and other special incentives; (x) the study of trade incentive schemes (special bonuses, thirteen-to-the-dozen and other 'free goods' deals, wholesaler and/or retailer contests, etc.), to determine costs in relation to results achieved, preferred forms of incentive, and improved methods of operating trade incentive programmes.

Communications research includes (i) the testing of press, television, cinema, radio or poster advertisements before and/or after they have been seen, read or heard by the particular audience for whom they are intended; (ii) research on the effectiveness of public relations and company image-building campaigns; (iii) the study of different media and combinations of media, in relation to their effectiveness and comparative cost in reaching defined audiences of potential customers for the company's products; (iv) the analysis of the effectiveness of sales communications—sales conferences, trade receptions, exhibitions, demonstrations, direct mail, catalogues, trade brochures, trade sampling, salesmen's presentation material and visual selling aids and trade advertising—in terms of number of enquiries received, orders placed and other measurable criteria.

Special project studies. Many investigations, by their very nature, usually cannot be anticipated or planned for. It may be possible to assign such *ad hoc* projects, as and when they arise, to the executive or group of executives specialising in the particular field concerned. On the other hand, rather than interrupt the normal flow of research activity, it is sometimes more convenient to assign an individual executive or small task force to work on a special project.

The types of problems which are often best handled in this way include (i) special measurement or quantification problems, e.g. measuring the sales or other results from a particular advertising campaign; (ii) research on the effectiveness of *ad hoc* trade and consumer promotions and special point-of-purchase displays in terms of distributor support, consumer interest, analysis of shop traffic, quantities of merchandise sold, impulse versus planned purchases, etc.; (iii) information handling and data processing problems, e.g. the introduction of computers into certain fields of marketing activity presents difficulties of integration and adaptation if their use is to be maximised; (iv) research into possible new developments in marketing ideas and techniques as a means of widening a company's competitive differential advantage, e.g. new and more efficient methods of selling and advertising, new ways of organising the marketing functions within the firm, new methods of stock control; (v) the study of opportunities for company diversification into related fields from internal resources or through external acquisition or merger; (vi) research into 'research' and how it can be integrated more effectively into the planning process.

Economic and business research may, or may not, come under the jurisdiction of the marketing research manager, or indeed, of marketing management at all. It is still fairly common practice for general information or economic intelligence departments to be responsible directly to top management or general management. The actual line of responsibility is not of critical importance provided that marketing management and marketing research personnel are kept fully informed and have direct access to the department concerned.

The greater part of the general information or economic intelligence department's work in most companies is likely to be concerned with the gathering of economic and business information (mainly, though not exclusively, from 'desk' sources) of particular importance to marketing management. The integration of this source of information with the other sources at its command will be made easier by placing the department under the direct control of marketing management.

The kind of information provided includes (i) general economic trends and forecasts for the major sectors of the economy, both short- and long-range, e.g. population, industrial production, domestic consumption, prices, incomes, manpower resources, overseas trade; (ii) business trends and forecasts, both short- and long-range, for different types of business, e.g. motor cars, man-made fibres, refrigerators, carpets, canned soup and so on, with particular reference to the key economic factors affecting sales and profitability in the business concerned and the general climate in which the company operates or is likely to operate in the future; (iii) political trends and forecasts of relevance to business planning, i.e. present and future government attitudes and policies towards business, government planning policies, regulations and controls, taxation and investment policies, business legislation, e.g. monopolies, restrictive practices, merchandise marks, sale of food and drugs; (iv) social trends and developments of importance to the business; for example, the growing articulateness of the consumer through official and independent consumer organisations and associations, changes in living and leisure habits, housing and amenity developments; (v) competitive intelligence covering past results, present and future plans and expectations, company balance sheets, reports of shareholders' meetings, management changes, organisation changes, acquisition, mergers, research and development activity, advertising effort and expenditures and so on; (vi) company searches, i.e. information obtained at the instigation of management from the Companies Registration Office and other published sources in connection with possible acquisitions and mergers or for competitive reasons.

Positioning the Marketing Research Department

It will be self-evident that the positioning of the marketing research department within the company's organisational structure is critical if it is to be an effective tool of marketing management and an integral part of the marketing function. The whole basis of product and marketing planning rests, under the marketing concept, on the firm foundation of marketing research knowledge. The survey carried out by the British Institute of Management throws some interesting light on how, in practice, marketing research is positioned over a wide range of businesses. It reveals that about half of all the marketing research departments in the seventy-four firms reporting were responsible to marketing or sales management. 24% reported directly to top management, i.e. the chairman, or managing-director, and a further 22% reported to general management. 4% came under engineering and development and 2% under financial management.

The location of management responsibility for the marketing research function showed some interesting differences between industrial goods and consumer goods manufacturers:

Table 1. Management Responsibility for Marketing Research Departments[1]

Reporting to:	Industrial Goods Manufacturers	Consumer Goods Manufacturers	Advertising Agencies	Total
	%	%	%	%
Top Management	10	29	48	24
Other General Management	31	25	14	22
Marketing or Sales Management	52	37	38	48
Engineering and Development	7	4	—	4
Financial	—	4	—	2
Total	100 (29 firms)	100 (24 firms)	100 (21 firms)	100 (74 firms)

Whereas 52% of departments in industrial goods companies reported to Marketing and Sales Management only 37% of departments in consumer goods companies did so. Conversely only 10% of industrial goods

[1] Ibid.

marketing research departments reported to top management as against 29% of consumer goods departments and 48% of advertising agency departments. This latter comparison is perhaps the most revealing one so far as integrating the results of research into basic planning and policy is concerned.

Whilst the direct responsibility of marketing research to senior marketing management may reflect good management practice, it is only as effective as the status and influence of marketing management *vis-à-vis* top management will allow. In other words, if marketing management does not carry the necessary weight and authority in the councils of top management then it is preferable for marketing research executives to report directly to the latter.

The existence of a titular marketing manager does not necessarily mean that the marketing function is being properly carried out by the person holding that office or that the company is paying anything more than lip-service to the marketing concept. Few business titles lend themselves to greater misrepresentation than that of Marketing Manager. It is necessary to go behind the title and analyse what the executive does, how his functions and responsibilities have been defined and what authority he commands.

Sales management is not marketing management unless it has full responsibility for and authority over a broad range of activities including marketing research, advertising and public relations, sales promotion and merchandising. Indeed, a very strong case exists for making certain that the marketing research department does not report to sales management using the latter in its traditional sense of managing the sales office and field selling organisation. The dangers inherent in making sales management responsible for researching its own activities have already been commented upon. Marketing research must be free from the influence of those whom its investigations and recommendations affect.

It is interesting to note as a final comment on the foregoing table that a similar survey undertaken in the United States in 1959 covering 661 firms[1] showed certain striking comparisons with Great Britain.

Across all types of business (in the U.S. study retail and wholesale businesses, publishing and broadcasting were also included as separate categories) the proportions of all marketing research managers reporting to top management and marketing and sales management were practically identical. An interesting difference was that British industrial goods producers conformed much more closely to the American practice in this respect than did consumer goods producers in the two countries. In the latter case, the percentage of U.S. consumer goods research departments reporting to marketing and sales management was very nearly double the U.K. percentage, confirming perhaps the more rapid adoption of the marketing concept in the consumer goods field in the United States.

[1] *A Survey of Marketing Research.* American Marketing Association. Chicago 1959. p. 22.

The Use of External Research Services

Another aspect dealt with by the B.I.M. survey was the allocation of marketing research work as between outside firms, the marketing research department and other departments. A little less than half of all consumer goods producers' expenditure on marketing research went on external research carried out by independent market research organisations or advertising agencies—compared with only about one-fifth of industrial goods producers' expenditure. In other words, consumer goods manufacturers spent, as a proportion of total marketing research expenditure, more than twice as much as industrial goods manufacturers on external research. This reflects to a large extent the differing nature of the markets and marketing problems that need to be researched in these two sectors.

The markets and the sort of problems that have to be investigated in the fast-moving mass consumer goods field present a very different order of magnitude from those met with in the much more technical and specialised industrial goods industry. Industrial goods producers may have comparatively few customers, each of whom is important and each of whom is a highly knowledgeable, experienced and articulate buyer. The breakfast cereal or soap manufacturer, on the other hand, is not in direct contact with the many thousands and possibly millions of users of his product, the majority of whom tend not to be particularly knowledgeable or articulate about the products they buy and use.

Some research projects by their nature or their size and scope are often beyond the ability of the manufacturer's own staff to handle, due to other work and time commitments, even where they have large research departments of their own. The use of properly qualified outside marketing research organisations, both in the producer goods and consumer goods fields, can have a number of advantages.

First, they can offer facilities for large-scale field operations with greater economy covering the hundreds or even thousands of interviews often necessary in mass consumer goods marketing. Second, they may have access to specialised skills not normally available within the company—this is particularly necessary in motivation and other highly specialised forms of research. Third, they will normally have all the necessary staff and 'hardware' to process masses of data, e.g. computers and their programmers, punch-card operators and electronic sorters, tabulators, etc. Fourth, they can provide their clients with anonymity and complete objectivity. Fifth, by serving many clients in many different markets and from experience of handling a wide variety of marketing problems, they have access to a pool of research know-how and experience which few clients could match, or, indeed, which it would be economical for them to build up for themselves.

Due to the large amount of research work placed with outside agencies it is important, therefore, to know the different types of organisation that exist and to investigate closely the various services they offer, their relative strengths and weaknesses, reputation for objectivity, and so on. Outside organisations exist to carry out national consumer market surveys, industrial market surveys, motivation studies, retail shop audits, product and package testing and advertising research. In addition most major media publish statistical and consumer survey data as a means of selling advertising time and space.

(c) ORGANISATION OF THE MARKETING RESEARCH DEPARTMENT

There is no 'ideal' organisational structure for a marketing research department which will fit all cases. The internal organisation of the department must be tailored to the individual characteristics and needs of the particular firm and this, in turn, will depend upon (1) the size of the firm, (2) the markets in which it operates, i.e. type of business, (3) the degree of centralisation or de-centralisation of its activities, (4) the anticipated volume and continuity of the research programme and the extent to which it will be placed in the hands of outside organisations.

Generally speaking, the smaller the company the greater the tendency for the marketing function and, therefore, marketing research activity, to be centralised. Larger companies selling a wide range of diverse products are more likely to be administratively decentralised with marketing and research responsibility carried at the divisional level. Research departments, therefore, may be organised in any one of the following ways:

(a) A central department serving the requirements of all operating divisions.
(b) A centralised department with specialised sections serving the needs of various product, industry or regional divisions.
(c) Divisional departments working independently from one another.
(d) Separate divisional departments working under central control.

According to the B.I.M. Survey, the first and last methods were the most common.

Table 2. Organisation of Marketing Research Departments[1]

	Industrial Goods Manufacturers		*Consumer Goods Manufacturers*		*Advertising Agencies*		*All Firms*	
	No.	%	No.	%	No.	%	No.	%
Central Department only	18	47	17	65	18	82	53	62
Central and Divisional Departments	4	11	3	12	—	—	7	8
One person only	7	18	4	15	3	14	14	16
None	5	13	1	4	—	—	6	7
Other Arrangements (subsidiary research companies, trade associations, etc.)	4	11	1	4	1	4	6	7
Total	38	100	26	100	22	100	86	100

[1] Ibid.

Thus, the predominant arrangement for all types of firms was a central marketing research department or single executive but less so in the case of industrial goods firms than in the others. About one firm in ten had both central and divisional departments.

One-man marketing research operations, as expected, were considerably more common among the smaller firms—just half of all firms with a turnover of under £1 million. Understandably, large marketing research departments are uneconomic for the smaller firm. Too rapid a build-up of the research department can bring demoralising cut-backs later on. In such circumstances, it is preferable to place the responsibility for marketing research in the hands of a single competent executive and to farm out the research assignments to independent outside organisations.

The balance of argument for most, but not all, firms would appear to be in favour of centralising marketing research activities principally because the best specialised research talent can be brought to bear on any particular marketing problem, and the results can be more easily communicated to marketing management and integrated into top management thinking and planning.

Ideas on how research can be more effectively integrated, operationally, into the business process can be expected to change and may well have to be adapted to new information systems in the future. The degree of research specialisation that can be introduced into the research department again depends on the criteria mentioned earlier. The question of whether the research executive should be a full-time specialist in one particular type of research [e.g. psychological or motivation research, consumer panel research] or should get involved in all types of research and move from one project to another can only be answered in terms of the particular needs of the individual company. The following examples represent different ways in which particular companies have organised the research and information function:

CHART 9. ORGANISING THE RESEARCH FUNCTION

Medium-sized producer of plastic materials and components for industry—mainly food, drink and chemical manufacturers

The Market Research Manager with a staff of four reports directly to the Managing Director.

The Product Analyst is concerned, in effect, with analysing existing potential markets in relation to the company's manufacturing capabilities, for finding new uses for present products, new and improved products for existing and new uses.

CHART 10. ORGANISING THE RESEARCH FUNCTION

Large manufacturer of edible oils and related products for industrial and domestic uses.

The Marketing Research Director reports to the Director of Marketing who sits on the main board. The research function is split into Industrial Products and Packaged Consumer Products. The Marketing Development Officer's function is to find new industrial markets for the company's products and new industrial products for existing markets. He has two field investigators to help him, both of whom are qualified engineers.

The Packaged Consumer Goods Research Manager is responsible for new product research, development and test marketing, consumer market research and the operation of the test kitchen and home economics service (recipes prepared by this department are featured on the packages and in the advertising of the company's consumer products). All consumer research is placed either through the company's advertising agency or directly with independent outside organisations.

An Information and Statistical Services Department consisting of a Librarian, two Information Executives and two Statisticians, also reports to the Marketing Research Director. No sales analysis or forecasting is undertaken by the Marketing Research Department, these being the responsibility of the General Sales Manager. However, the statistical services of the Information Department are available to him for special analyses.

The broken lines are lines of communication only.

CHART 11. ORGANISING THE RESEARCH FUNCTION

Large multi-product manufacturer serving pharmaceutical, household products and toiletries markets

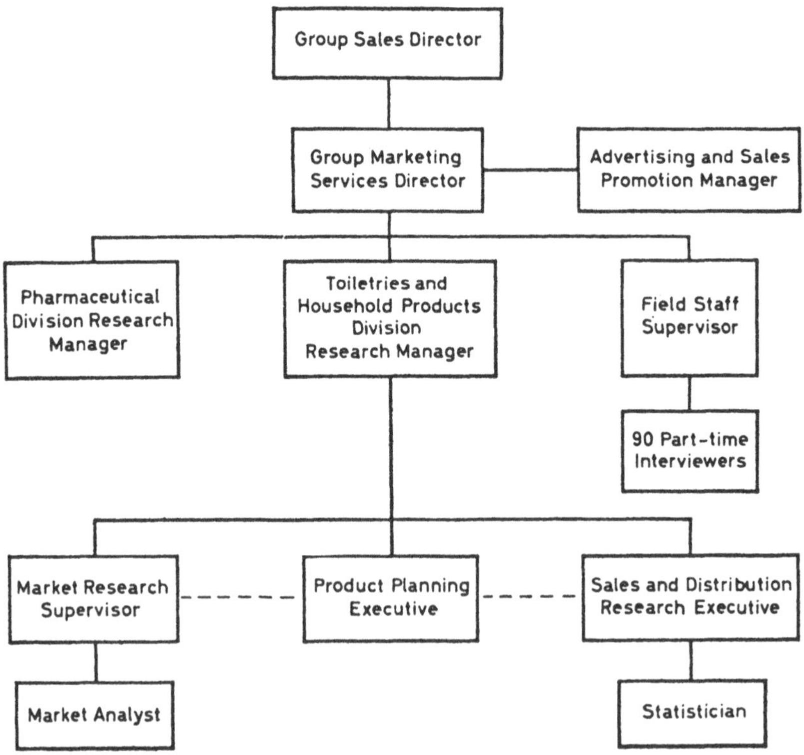

This company operates two separate sales divisions, the Pharmaceutical Division distributing products almost exclusively through chemists, and the Toiletries and Household Products Division distributing mainly through grocers, hardware stores, department stores and chain stores, e.g. Woolworths.

The sales managers of both divisions report to the Group Sales Director. A Group Marketing Services Director is responsible to the Group Sales Director for all matters in connection with market research, advertising, sales promotion and product planning. He has no direct responsibility for the sales organisation or field selling operations. Each division is headed by a Research Manager who, in turn, has under him a Market Research Supervisor, a Product Planning Executive and a Sales and Distribution Research Executive. A Field Staff Supervisor controlling ninety part-time interviewers also reports directly to the Group Marketing Services Director. A Research Co-ordinating Committee consisting of the Marketing Services Director, his two divisional Research Managers and the Field Staff Supervisor, meets at regular intervals to review plans, programmes and the availability and allocation of field interviewing time to divisional research projects.

Within each research division there is a Market Research Supervisor, assisted by an analyst, who is responsible for planning, scheduling and reporting on assigned projects. The Sales and Distribution Research Executive plans and undertakes sales statistics analysis, sales forecasting, distribution studies and distribution cost analyses.

The Product Planning Executive is responsible for the preparation of product recommendations to meet market requirements—investigation of new product ideas, product conception, product specification in consumer terms, product testing and test marketing. It is his job to liaise with the Technical Research and Development Division to develop prototypes for testing purposes.

He must recommend when would be the best time to introduce a new product, and how it should be distributed. He must prepare sales estimates and profit forecasts based on a recommended price for the product, a recommended weight of advertising expenditure and a realistic allocation of selling and other expenses. He must be a fountain of information about the product and its market so that he can brief the company's advertising, promotion and sales executives. To carry out this function the Product Planning Executive must work closely not only with his own research colleagues in the market research, sales and distribution areas but also with the Advertising and Sales Promotion Department, the Sales Department and the Commercial and Economic Intelligence Department.

The latter department is a centralised group information service with a full-time business economist as director-in-charge, who reports directly to the Group Managing Director.

CHART 12. ORGANISING THE RESEARCH FUNCTION

A large advertising agency with some 30 major national clients primarily in the consumer goods sector

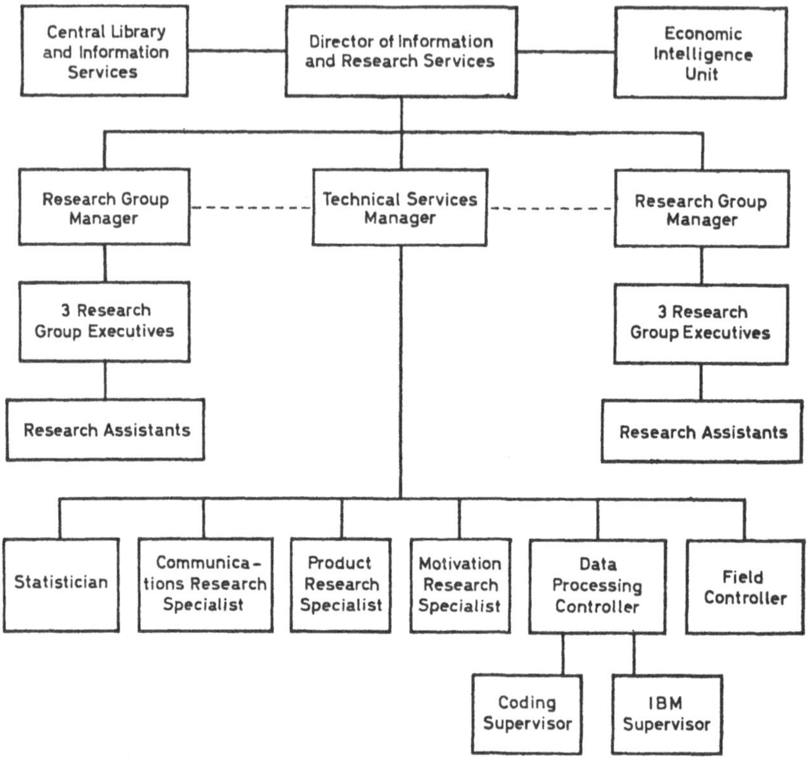

The Director of Information and Research Services is responsible for the total marketing research operation of the Agency. The Central Library and Information Services division and an Economic Intelligence Unit specialising in economic and business research report to him. The Marketing research function is managed by two Research Group Managers, each of whom has three executives in charge of the continuing research programmes of a group of the agency's clients. No attempt is made to make each research executive a specialist in a particular product field, e.g. food products or toiletries, but rather to give them all-round experience, so that they become interchangeable and can apply research experience in one field to the problems in other fields. Each executive has an assistant.

The Research Group Manager is responsible for initial contact with the client, day-to-day liaison thereafter being left to the responsible executive concerned. The Research Group Manager is responsible for client presentations on all assigned projects. The Technical Services Manager is concerned with techniques and facilities rather than products. He has responsibility for advising the Research Group Managers and executives on various forms of specialised research: (a) communications research covering advertisement testing and packaging research (where the use of highly specialised equipment is involved), (b) product research covering product testing, taste tests, etc., (c) motivation research into people's attitudes, how and why they have come to hold them, and their inner basic urges and motivations.

In addition, the Technical Services Manager carries responsibility for field control of a staff of 250 part-time interviewers through a Field Controller, for data processing control through a Data Processing Controller in charge of coding and IBM staff, and for statistical services (sampling and analysis). The total permanent staff including secretaries, clerks, coders, checkers, and analysts is forty-five.

(d) INTEGRATION OF MARKETING RESEARCH

The problems of integrating marketing research into a business organisation are of two kinds. The first group of problems are those associated with the difficulties or obstacles in the way of introducing marketing research into the company structure for the first time. The second group of problems are concerned with the difficulties of integrating the use and the results of marketing research into management thinking and planning. The incidence of marketing research departments in British businesses, as revealed by the B.I.M. Survey, is, unfortunately, no guide to the quality of the marketing research work done or of the effective application of research to business problems.

Setting up a Marketing Research Department

The first group of problems is concerned with fitting marketing research into the organisation, developing awareness of what marketing research is and what it is able to do (and, equally important, what it cannot do) and communicating effectively with operating management. Generally speaking, fitting marketing research into the organisation will be easier in those companies which already have central marketing departments or are applying the marketing concept in their day-to-day operations. Under these circumstances, the role of marketing research will almost certainly have been discussed. Top management will have been exposed to such discussions and the need of research for planning purposes recognised. Therefore, the ground is likely to prove more fertile and the nature of the resistances to the setting up of a research department, at any rate, understood, if not overcome. Thereafter, the use to which marketing research is put will depend upon practical and measurable benefits of first and subsequent applications.

Selling the idea of marketing research to management will be more difficult in firms which have no marketing departments or to whom the application of the 'marketing concept' is something of a mystery. It is in such circumstances that the barriers to research go up as management and other executives see 'all this marketing and research business' as a potential threat to their security, status and authority.

People's fear of the unfamiliar is perhaps the major obstacle—fear that they will be made redundant or moved to other and perhaps less congenial jobs within the firm, that their position and authority will be undermined by the slide-rule experts, that the change will be taken as a criticism of their past ways of operating and managing, that their functions will have to change and new modes of thought and technique will have to be learnt, that their freedom of action and judgment will be curtailed and so on. These are all genuine fears and misgivings and will not disappear by being overlooked.

Executive acceptance and use of marketing research [and this applies to any management innovation] will be in direct proportion to how well they understand it, how it is likely to affect them, and the degree to which they are kept in the picture as to what is going on. It is imperative that anyone connected with or likely to be affected by its operation and use should be so informed and have explained to them how it will benefit them and the company as it has benefited others. It is as well to recognise at the very outset that there will be a problem of communication regardless of whether there is a marketing-minded management or not.

Where top management is sold on the idea of marketing research but anticipates great difficulty in its introduction and application it is sometimes helpful to call on the services of consultants to determine whether and how a research department should be set up, what information it should provide, how it should be staffed and how it should be 'presented' to management and executive personnel. Some consultants are able to advise on the selection of research managers and executives and to prepare job descriptions and executive specifications. Furthermore, independent consultants are frequently able, by virtue of their wide experience of company research problems in diverse fields and of the varying degrees of management sophistication in research, to recommend a marketing research set-up tailored to the particular needs of the company, bearing in mind such factors as the existing organisation structure, the type of products and markets with which the company deals, its methods of distribution and selling, breadth of marketing perspective, and internal political factors. They can arbitrate between what is the desirable 'ideal' and what is practically attainable. The advice one gets from those who do not exercise executive responsibility within a firm is necessarily but honourably different from that given by those who share or are affected by executive responsibility for decision and action.

The integration of a newly formed marketing research department is likely to be easier if it is under some form of central control, preferably a top or marketing management executive, who is sympathetic to its development within the company. Not only will such an arrangement afford status and importance to the work undertaken by the department, but, being under the wing of senior management, it is more likely to be used on longer-range problems and applications of importance to senior management and, thereby, better able to prove itself during the early and, in many ways, most critical stages of its development.

The Closer Integration of Established Marketing Research Departments

The second group of problems are concerned with the integration of an already established marketing research operation into management thinking and planning so as to ensure smoother and more effective working co-operation between the marketing research department and other departments and operating divisions of the business. The main problem areas are the same as those that must be faced when setting up a marketing research department for the first time, namely organisation obstacles, determining what management's problems are and how marketing research can best contribute to their solution and communicating effectively with management.

Even in the most mature marketing organisations where major organisational defects appear to be absent and where marketing researchers work closely and continuously with management executives and, therefore, presumably know and understand their problems, the problem of communication remains. The problem is a two-way one. On the one hand, there is the difficulty arising from the professional jargon used by many specialist research executives which other executives in the business do not understand and in terms of which they are not accustomed to thinking and talking. On the other hand, the research man, equally unfamiliar with business management and accounting terminology, may be hard put to it to express himself clearly and convincingly in management language.

With the growing number of specialists engaged in business—economists, psychologists, sociologists, mathematicians, statisticians, operations research workers and so on—the problem of communication assumes new dimensions. The problems of putting these specialists to work effectively in the business world, of understanding how and when to employ their techniques and of coping with the flood of information they can make available, are now urgent.

How then can the communications gap be bridged and a common language be developed that will enable these diverse activities to be related and directed towards a common end? Meetings, training programmes, management and executive development schemes designed to familiarise people with the ever-increasing flow of new ideas and techniques for researching, planning and controlling business operations will help, of course, but it is not the whole answer to the problem.

Clearly, there is a growing need for Marketing Research Directors and Managers to be generalists (to distinguish them from research specialists) with specific responsibility for:

1. Studying and learning about the resources of other intellectual disciplines which would be of assistance to general and marketing management.
2. Developing satisfactory working relationships and communications between general and marketing management.
3. Developing a thorough appreciation of management problems and to initiate and plan a programme of research that will help towards their solution.
4. Ensuring that the right internal and external technical specialists are called into action, individually or as members of a team, at the most appropriate time and on the basis of a precise and agreed brief.
5. Liaising between general and marketing management and research technicians during the carrying out of the research programme.
6. Helping general and marketing management to understand research and its uses, its strengths and its limitations.
7. Preparing budgets for and controlling the costs of the total company marketing research effort including the purchase of external services.[1]

The discipline of money applies with no less force to marketing research as to any other business activity. Hence, the research budget is the main instrument of control. The Marketing Director or Manager must estimate what scale of research effort is required to meet the company's needs and must seek approval of his estimates. In this, he must usually allow for the costs of unplanned or unexpected projects. It is advisable for management to allocate a definite budget for a programme of research providing for future needs, first, to ensure that research costs do not exceed a certain authorised amount, and second, to avoid having to justify costs on a day-to-day basis. Most research cannot be justified on such a basis—it may be some while before the return on a research programme is realised and it may not even be measurable in financial terms.

Buying outside research services is no different from buying any other product or service externally. The onus is on the buyer either to prepare a job or product specification which the contracting supplier undertakes to meet at a specified cost or to accept the supplier's quotation based on his own specification of the job to be done. Once the contract has been signed, the specification should only be changed by written agreement by both parties. Complete mutual confidence is necessary if the work is to be brought to a successful conclusion.

As a leading industrial marketing researcher has commented: 'Unless the marketing research agency is aware of the purpose behind the research—particularly in the complex field of industrial marketing research—it cannot contribute to the identification of the buyer's real, as opposed to apparent, problems. In the pursuit of research, much more material is

[1] This list is adapted from J. Newman. 'Put Research into Marketing Decisions.' *Harvard Business Review.* March/April 1962.

acquired than is subsequently used. If the marketing researcher is not a confidant of management, he can unwittingly throw out the baby with the bath-water by not being aware of the relevance of some of the information he has obtained.'[1]

[1] A. Wilson. 'No Bargain Basement for Marketing Research'. *The Director*. May 1962.

4

Managing the Product Planning Function

(a) THE ELEMENTS OF PRODUCT PLANNING

PRODUCT PLANNING, in general terms, comprises those planning activities involved in selecting what products the company will make and sell and in matching the specifications of these products and their performance to the needs of the user. Marketing research provides the knowledge about user needs, desires and preferences. Product planning is the catalytic process that converts this knowledge, in the light of technical, cost and profit considerations, into acceptable saleable products. Product planning is a continuous process which goes on throughout a product's life from the day that the 'idea' for a new product is conceived until the day it is withdrawn from the market-place.

The main elements or phases of product planning are as follows:

1. Determining customer needs, present and potential, and analysing usage and buying habits in the market concerned.
2. Assessing existing competitive products in relation to (1) above.
3. Critically appraising the company's present products in relation to (1) and (2) above *from the customer's sta'.dpoint.*
4. Determining what products should be added to or eliminated from the existing line of products for reasons of profitability, obsolescence, competitive developments, etc.—and whether to diversify into other lines of products beyond the existing range.
5. Screening ideas for new products, for improvements in existing products, and for new uses for existing products.
6. Preparing customer specifications for new or improved products.
7. Carrying out of product feasibility studies by technical research and development personnel of short-listed new or improved products covering price, cost and profit investigations.
8. Undertaking product tests for customer acceptance in all major relevant respects, e.g. flavour, colour, quality, design, appearance, durability, convenience, performance-in-use, name, packaging, price, value for money.
9. Formulating specific product recommendations in respect of quality, design, name, price, packaging, after-sales service, etc. as

confirmed by, or modified in accordance with, product test findings.

10. Preparing product marketing recommendations covering the timing and phasing of the new or improved product's introduction, the scale of initial introduction (i.e. test towns only, a regional development area or a national launch), selling and distribution plans and the advertising and promotional programme.

11. Evaluating and reviewing the total programme.

The Product Planning Function

One marketing research commentator[1] has described a product as an input-output device which translates a customer proposition in terms of value into a manufacturer proposition in terms of profit, and vice versa. Adapting this concept, the product planning function can be visualised in the following way.

CHART 13. THE PRODUCT PLANNING FUNCTION

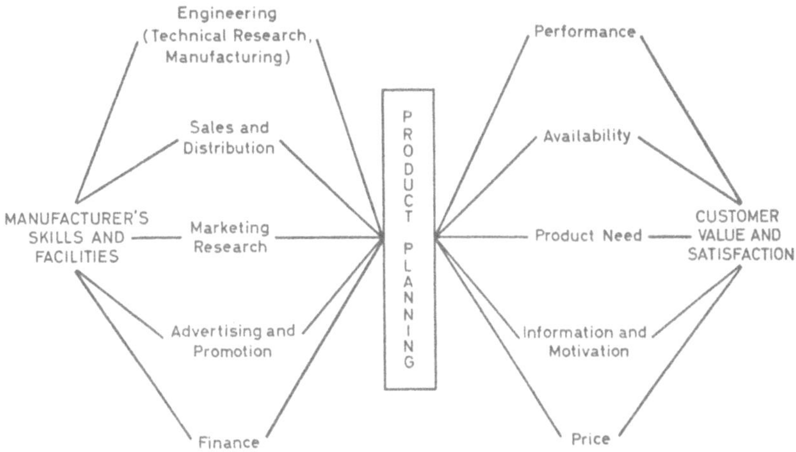

The skill in product planning lies in converting a manufacturer's inherited or acquired skills and facilities into products and services yielding customer value and satisfaction at a profit. Customers do not buy 'products' as such but rather what it is that the products will do for them. Thus, consumers do not buy domestic oil-fired boilers—they buy the convenience and comfort of central heating. They do not buy washing machines—they buy the capability to do the wash more quickly and more easily. A manufacturer does not buy a fleet of forklift trucks—he buys a transport and mechanical-handling facility.

In other words, every manufacturer is involved in creating and satisfying

[1] G. Leman. *New Product Development and the Development of a Product Range.* Market Research Society Commentary No. 8. Summer 1962. p. 8.

customers and not in merely producing goods. Every company has certain technical and selling skills and know-how. It is the job of product planning to convert these skills and facilities into customer satisfying values. Product planning is concerned with those *values* that make customers exchange purchasing power for product satisfaction.

Many companies tend to regard the products they produce as representing the business they are in. A spokesman[1] for one leading marketing-oriented organisation, British Nylon Spinners, has provided some interesting examples of commercial enterprises that have managed their operations from a market perspective rather than a product perspective.

For instance, the National Coal Board's job is not just one of digging up coal and selling it to industrial, commercial and domestic consumers. The customer 'has no particular love for its heat or power to be provided in the form of black, hard material dug up from the earth and its conversion into gas, steam and hot water but is only concerned with his heating or power requirements, and the consumer will compare the efficiencies and cost and convenience with which the National Coal Board can meet such wants as against alternatives offered by competitors such as the electricity and oil industries'. Hence the Coal Board is in the heating and power business and must concern itself with the nature, efficiency and even aesthetics of the appliances produced by other manufacturers to convert the Coal Board's raw material into the things the consumer wants. Research into clean, smokeless, more efficient fuels, into automatic gravity-feed domestic fuel loading systems, and into small bore piping systems are very much its concern also.

Again, British Nylon Spinners is not just a producer of nylon filament yarn or fibre—which few customers would recognise in its raw form. The basic raw material can be processed many different ways to produce a wide range of consumer or user values in the form of carpets, knitted jumpers, brassières, fishing nets, conveyor belting, or aircraft and car tyres. In other words, British Nylon Spinners is not merely in the chemical business using raw materials derived from coal by-products—it is in the domestic textile and apparel business and, on the industrial side, it supplies various needs of the aircraft and car industries, the fishing industry, the materials-handling industry and so on.

The product planning process starts either with a recognised customer need or with a basic product idea established through market research or other sources. Regardless of the pedigree of the product idea—it may originate from a salesman, a customer, the company's advertising agents, the technical research and development department, the suggestions box or the chairman's wife—market research should be used at some stage, to determine whether it meets a known or as yet unrealised need. Marketing research will help to establish (a) the existence or otherwise of a real or latent need, (b) the dimensions and trend of the market (the number of

[1] E. Sharp. *Productivity is a Marketing Problem.* Institute of Marketing and Sales Management. Published Paper No. 130. May 1962.

potential customers, their desires and preferences, where they are located, their purchasing power and buying habits, whether the market is expanding, static or shrinking in size and so on), (c) the competitive state of the market and (d) the standing, with the customer, of competitors' and the company's own products.

If a new or improved product is indicated and if it fits into the company's present product line as an addition to the line or as a replacement for an existing product, the next step is a preliminary evaluation of the idea or ideas on the basis of the marketing research findings (the problems of diversifying into new fields outside the company's immediate experience and know-how are considered later). If one or more ideas emerge as promising, product specifications based on consumer or user requirements are drawn up. When approved these are passed to the manufacturing or research and development division which make prototypes and carry out preliminary checks on the feasibility of producing them, taking into account existing capacity, techniques and know-how, new materials or facilities needed and so on.

If preliminary costings indicate an acceptable margin of profit then a small quantity will be produced for testing with potential users. At the same time, the production division will obtain some experience of manufacture and, it is hoped, any major snags exposed and corrected. Simultaneously, the marketing division prepares tentative sales and advertising plans and budgets to see if the product looks like being a worthwhile marketing proposition to the company. The findings of the product tests will have indicated whether any modifications are necessary prior to the product being placed on the market.

With this background of testing and evaluation, the marketing division must then decide whether or not the product is viable and stands a reasonable and calculable chance of being a successful and profitable addition to the line.

Assuming a favourable outcome, product and marketing proposals are submitted for management approval, setting out in detail how, when, where and at what cost and profit the product is to be introduced. A series of sales-test towns may be recommended to find the answer to certain unresolved questions on pricing, packaging, advertising, etc. Alternatively it may be proposed that the product be launched piecemeal in one region of the country at a time so that developments can be progressively watched and plans modified and improved before moving into each successive area. Or it may be decided that the product should be introduced on a national basis right away because of the threat of early retaliatory action by a competitor.

Whatever course of marketing action is recommended it should be based firmly on a realistic assessment of the risks involved and the potential gains or losses that may follow from the particular course selected. The outcome will depend upon the company's own strengths and weaknesses *vis-à-vis* those of its competitors, i.e. its differential advantages in terms of products, selling ability, advertising, marketing research and other communication skills, and its ability to act more quickly, more decisively or more flexibly than its competitors.

The final approved recommendations are embodied in a written marketing plan which forms the basis for integrated action by all the departments concerned. Operating instructions are issued to implement the various parts of the agreed plan. The progress made in implementing the plan should be constantly reviewed and evaluated to see how and where future improvements can be made.

Product Planning Activity Analysis

An adaptation of the technique used in network analysis may help to clarify the dependent activities involved in product planning. The following highly simplified activity analysis diagram shows a typical product planning cycle from the time that a new product idea is first conceived to the time of its national launch after test marketing.

What it attempts to demonstrate is the sequential product planning activity involved in bringing a new product to market and the time taken to complete the various phases of product planning previously outlined (the time periods are illustrative only). It will be seen that each subsequent phase is dependent upon the satisfactory completion of the previous phase or phases. The shortest possible time for completion of the entire programme is the path represented by the thick line connecting the longest sequence of phases. The programme cannot be completed in any less time except by the application of special effort or the taking of certain decisions at one of several critical points along the path.

The sequential accomplishment points in the diagram are represented by circles and are called 'events' and the passage of time between specific events are represented by arrows and called 'activities'. An event, which is a specific point in time, may depend on one single prior event or on a convergence of several inter-related events. No event can be accomplished until the prior activities leading to it have been completed.

The events depicted in the diagram are as follows:

Event No.	*Event*
1.	Product idea originates from Marketing Director.
2.	Marketing research plan is given approval to go ahead.
3.	Marketing research findings are presented.
4.	Product specification is drawn up on basis of research findings.
5.	Decision is taken on product feasibility.
6.	Production prototype is completed by engineering (research and development).
7.	Production of a small test batch for product testing purposes is completed.
8.	Product test plan is given approval to go ahead.

CHART 14. PRODUCT PLANNING ACTIVITY ANALYSIS DIAGRAM

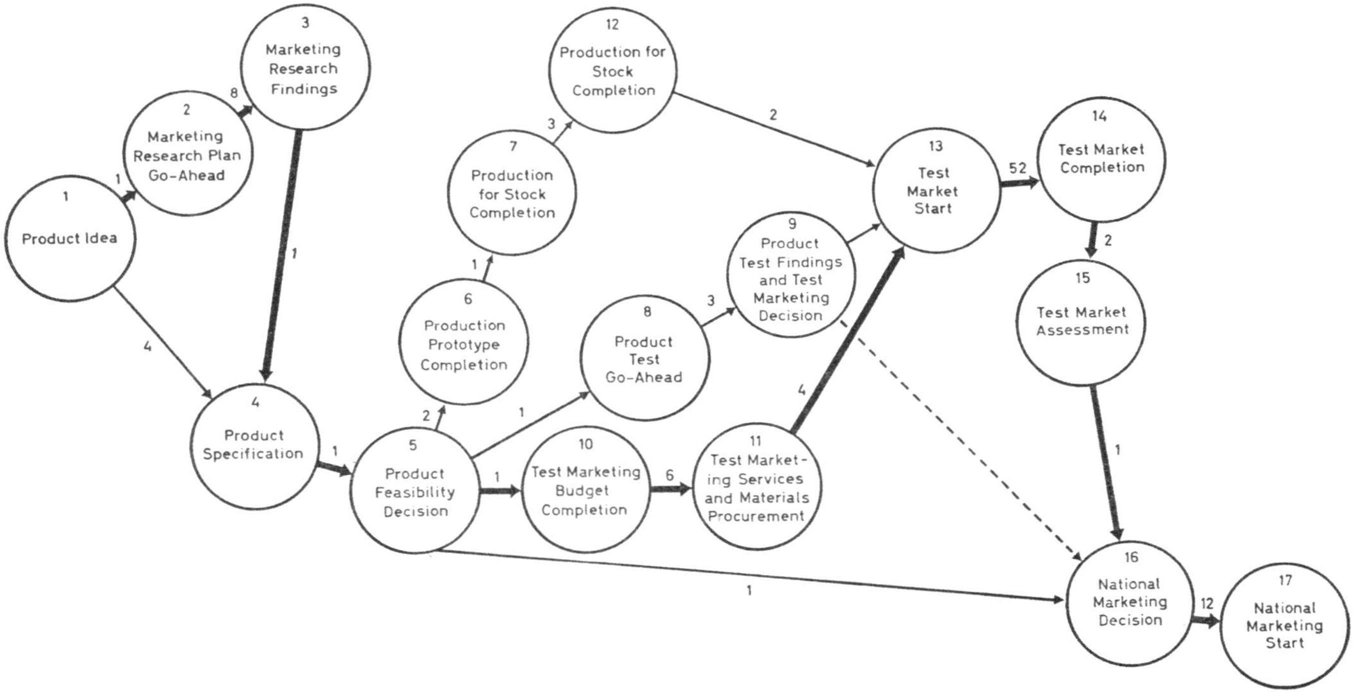

Event No.	*Event*
9.	Product test findings are presented and decision whether or not to test market is taken.
10.	Test marketing budget is submitted and approved.
11.	Marketing services and materials are scheduled for test market.
12.	Production of test market product requirements are completed.
13.	Test market starts.
14.	Test market ends.
15.	Test market results are assessed from market research findings and sales analysis.
16.	Decision is taken whether or not to market the product nationally.
17.	National launch starts.

The activities involved are as follows:

Between Event Nos.	*Activity*
1–2	Marketing research proposals covering customer market analysis, competitive product comparisons and product line analysis are drawn up and submitted for approval.
1–4	Decision is taken not to carry out consumer market study but to develop product specification from internal sources.
2–3	Market research fieldwork, tabulation, analysis and presentation.
3–4	Interpretation of research findings in terms of customer specifications for product. Translation of customer specifications in technical engineering terms.
4–5	Examination of feasibility of product specifications in the light of existing or required manufacturing technique and know-how, resources and facilities, and of price, cost and profit considerations.
5–6	Prototype manufactured and subjected to technical tests.
5–8	Product testing proposals, covering representative sample of users, are drawn up and submitted for approval.
5–10	Preliminary test market budget is drawn up incorporating estimated sales revenue, manufacturing, marketing and selling costs and profit (or loss).
5–16	Decision is taken not to carry out any product testing or test marketing but to commence national marketing at earliest possible date.
6–7	Manufacture of a small batch of product for consumer testing purposes.
7–12	Manufacture of sufficient stock of product to meet initial and 'going' test market requirements.
8–9	Product test fieldwork carried out and results tabulated, analysed and interpreted.

Between Event Nos.	*Activity*
9–13	Waiting time from decision to test market to actual start of test market due to time required to manufacture sufficient stock, to make distribution arrangements and to prepare and schedule sales and advertising plans.
9–16	Decision is taken not to proceed with test market but to go straight to a national launch of the product.
10–11	The requisition and organisation of marketing services (sales force time, distribution and warehousing facilities, advertising and promotion) and materials (display materials, sales aids, etc.) in line with budget authorisation.
11–13	Selling in to the trade in the test market. Waiting time before advertising breaks in the test area.
12–13	Shipment of product stocks to regional warehouses, depots or temporary pick-up points to meet sales force requirements.
13–14	Time allowed for test market operations. (This should be long enough to enable repeat purchasing pattern to become established and annual sales forecasts to be made.)
14–15	Time needed to assess findings of the test market, to project test market results on a national basis and prepare recommendation as to whether or not to go ahead with national launch.
15–16	Marketing recommendations considered by management and decision taken whether or not to go ahead with national launch.
16–17	Buying in and awaiting delivery from raw material and packaging suppliers; acquiring and training additional factory personnel; installing additional equipment; setting up cost and quality control systems; build-up of factory, warehouse and depot stocks to meet national sales requirements. Preparation and approval of detailed sales estimates, marketing budgets, selling and distribution plans and advertising schedules. Issuing of instructions to operating divisions.

As will be seen from the diagram the longest path in the product planning cycle is eighty-nine weeks. This represents the time taken by the manufacturer from the moment the new product idea is conceived till the product is marketed nationally provided *all* the phases of product planning activity are observed in strict sequence. A delay in any activities along this path will cause the whole project to fall behind schedule, whereas the earlier completion of those activities which lie off the 'critical path' will have no effect on the final completion date.

At a number of critical stages—events 3, 5, 9 and 15—the manufacturer may, on the evidence, decide not to proceed further. Or he may elect to forgo the precautions of product testing and test marketing and decide to go ahead with a national launch of the product without further delay. For instance, he may decide for competitive reasons that he cannot afford to wait nearly two years before the new product is on the market across the country; or, for reasons of pride and prestige, that he must be in the market first even if he cannot be the best. Later evidence will show that, in general, the success of new product introductions lies heavily in favour of those manufacturers who follow a systematic product planning procedure and that the penalties of short-circuiting these procedures can be very great.

Suffice to say that although the maximum length of time in the example is eighty-nine weeks, the manufacturer could be in national distribution with a new product within eighteen weeks, the sequence of events in this case being 1, 4, 5, 16 and 17. It is possible to adapt this simplified example of network analysis as applied to product planning, so as to allow for different time estimates for each activity, i.e. for the most likely completion time, the most optimistic completion time and most pessimistic completion time.

Product planning activity analysis diagrams have several uses. First, they enable management to determine how long it will be from product conception to national marketing according to strict product planning sequence. The total time taken can only be reduced by bringing more resources and effort to bear during one or two critical phases along this path, say at the market research phase, or at the test market stage.

If, for example, the company's own market research resources are fully committed, then such work may be placed with an outside organisation in order to overcome temporary bottlenecks. Conversely, idle resources can be used in other directions during waiting time, e.g. research facilities, selling capacity. For instance, as will be seen from the diagram, there are three possible paths from the product feasibility stage to the test market stage requiring 11, 8 and 4 weeks, respectively, for completion. Resources employed in various phases on either of the two shorter paths would be left idle waiting for other activities to be completed.

Second, management may decide for reasons of profit, due to falling sales of the company's major established product, or to knowledge of competitor's plans, that it must have a successful new product on the market in fifteen months' time at the very latest. By re-working the activity analysis backwards, from right to left in the diagram, a path can be plotted indicating whether such an objective is feasible, which of the various phases may have to be omitted altogether or have special resources and effort brought to bear on them in order to allow completion by the required date.

Third, such diagrams are useful in reviewing progress and controlling the programme. The effects on the total programme of any changes in actual or estimated times of the different phases can be assessed and the programme re-scheduled accordingly.

Planning for Existing Products

It should not be thought that product planning is something that applies only to new products. While the introduction of new products is unquestionably of great importance to the future growth and profitability of any business concern the extension of the profitable life of existing products must also be planned for. In most cases new product development must be financed out of the sales proceeds of current products which the company has been selling for many years past and which it hopes will continue to be sold for some years more on a profitable basis.

The search for new uses and new markets for existing products is necessary to provide a more secure basis for the company's operations. Persuading people to serve ice-cream all the year round as a dessert after a main meal instead of in summer or on outings provides one instance. Other examples in the consumer field include getting people to use aluminium foil for wrapping or cooking foods, to use linoleum, carpets and other floor coverings in all rooms instead of just one or two, to use paper towels in the home as well as outside it, to use portable fire extinguishers in cars and in the home, and so on. Examples in the industrial field include the application of aluminium and plastics for packaging and unit load bulk materials handling and of computers and automatic data processing equipment to banking and insurance.

The finding of new uses for by-products of a manufacturing process is also in many industries a key factor in overall company profitability. Whole new industries have grown up as a result of finding new uses for by-products, e.g. industrial solvents, synthetic rubber, pet-foods, dye stuffs, synthetic fibres. As well as product innovation many companies seek innovations in the way in which existing products are marketed. New marketing ideas related to the way in which the product is presented and made available to the consuming public can open up new areas of potential growth in both sales and profits, e.g. pre-packed bolts and screws, self-lay linoleum and vinyl floor tiles, soft-drink and milk dispensers, vertical refrigerated food display cabinets, selling nylons and paper-back books in chemists', supermarkets or automatic vending machines. Plant and equipment leasing, the hiring of computer time at special centres and cash and carry wholesaling are examples of innovations in the marketing of industrial goods and services.

(b) THE CONCEPT OF THE PRODUCT LIFE CYCLE

It is helpful, for product planning purposes, to think of products in terms of their life cycles. The basic concept is certainly not new, and it has many antecedents. Students of economics will be familiar with the trade cycle of boom and recession, and the monetary cycle of inflation and deflation. Industries pass through long-range cycles of invention, growth, maturity and decline. Family life goes through a cycle or series of structural changes which have important implications for firms marketing both consumer and industrial goods and services since consumption patterns and demand-determining factors are often directly related to these different structural states. The consumption of durable consumer goods such as cars, houses, furniture, record players, bedding, kitchen equipment and of services, like life and property insurance, banking, education, laundry and dry-cleaning, hairdressing, medical and funeral services depend greatly on changes in the family life cycle. A typical cycle might be—young and single, young married home builder with no children, young and married with children, older and with established family, older and married without children, older and single again. Quite clearly people's needs, desires, expectations and attitudes change as they pass from one stage to the next.

Similarly, products go through a series of stages or phases which together constitute some form of life cycle. The principle is perhaps seen in its most dramatic form in fashion goods, since these come and go sometimes with startling rapidity. Three stages are discernible: (1) The exclusive or distinctive stage set by the leaders of new creations in the main fashion centres, e.g. Paris, Rome, London and New York. At this stage there are no immediate direct competitors although there will always be plenty of substitutes. Here the choice is between using or not using one particular exclusive product. (2) The simulation stage where other manufacturers follow the leaders, and where deviations from the original tend to be in minor features only. (3) The mass production stage where all competitive products become more or less interchangeable. Products at this stage may use cheaper materials and demand for them is usually very responsive to price changes. Lower prices bring many more consumers into the market who can now afford to buy the products previously bought by the fashionable style-setting Joneses. Eventually, such products may have to be sold off at bargain prices.

It will be apparent that virtually every product goes through a similar sort of cycle. Different types of products obviously have different life cycle patterns, particularly as regards their overall length, the duration of each of the various phases within the cycle and the way in which the cycle itself develops. Therefore, although it is probably safe to generalise that every product or every service that is marketed has some kind of life cycle, and that there are a number of identifiable phases in this cycle, further generalisation becomes extremely difficult. For example the life cycle of a suite of furniture may be thirty years while that of the latest 'pop' record may only be thirty weeks or even thirty days.

Chart 15, therefore, is intended merely as a pictorialisation of the concept of the life cycle of a product and should not be taken as being typical of any particular industry or class of product.[1]

In this chart, sales revenue or profit earned is represented on the vertical axis, the passage of time on the horizontal axis. The area above the horizontal line indicates the value of sales to the company or the profit made on those sales, whereas the area below the line represents costs or actual losses incurred. The relative durations of the phases of the cycle are purely notional. In practice, they will vary for each product.

[1] See also Jay W. Forrester 'Advertising: A Problem in Industrial Dynamics.' *Harvard Business Review*. March/April 1959.

CHART 15. CONCEPT OF PRODUCT LIFE CYCLE

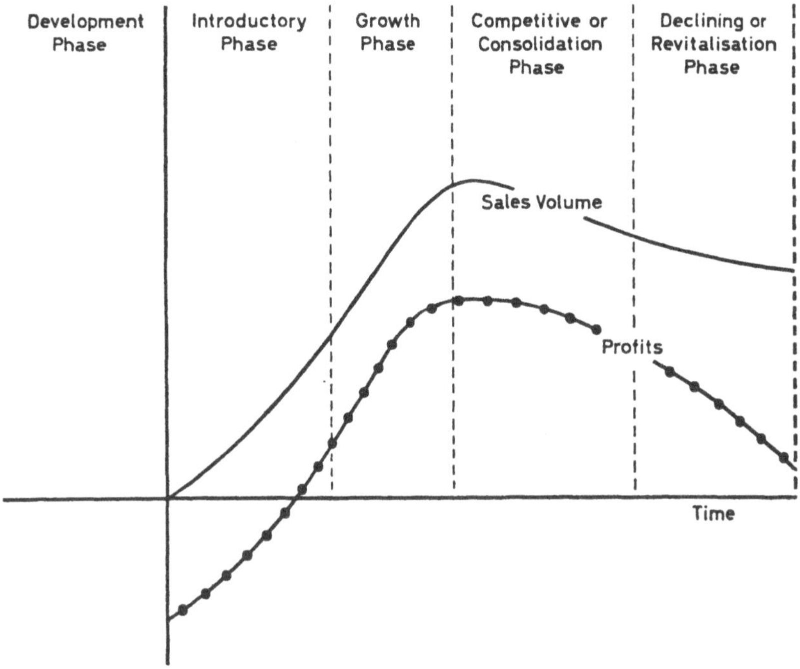

The Development Phase

The development phase is probably the most important in the whole of the product's life. The product's likely success or failure will be determined here prior to the time it ever reaches the market-place, whether it be on a test-market basis or a full-scale national introduction (referring back to the Product Planning Activity Analysis diagram shown earlier, this development phase is completed at Event 13 or 17 whichever the case may be). It is during this phase that the company incurs whatever development costs are involved in bringing the product to market. It is a period of investment which must subsequently be charged to the product's future earnings or written off altogether if the product is abandoned before it reaches the marketable stage.

The Introductory Phase

The second stage, the introductory stage, covers the period of initial launching of the product in a test-area or nationally. The product will not begin making a profit for the company until the profit curve crosses the horizontal line. This point will occur some time after the product has been on sale, the actual time necessary being a function of the level of investment incurred for initial development and marketing and the level of actual sales achieved.

It is during this stage that the company is likely to enjoy the greatest competitive differential advantage. While the product is moving into distribution and customers are getting to know about its existence, its advantages and uses through advertising, sales publicity and display, sales rise fairly gradually. For a great many fast-moving consumer goods in the food, detergent and toiletries fields particularly, sampling and couponing can be highly effective ways of inducing first-time trials of a new product among the great majority of households in the country.

The Growth Phase

The third stage may be described as the growth phase. The product is in established distribution after months of selling effort by the sales force and is becoming better known after months of advertising and display activity. The emphasis is now on rapid market penetration. Competing firms will begin to take counter-measures against the new entrant by bringing out similar, or preferably superior, products, by increasing their advertising and other promotional activity, by strengthening field selling effort or by other means. Advertising will tend to stress the relative merits of the different products on the market and it is at this time that the innovating firm will meet its greatest test. Heightened consumer interest in and awareness of the competing products may expand the market faster and further to the advantage of several, if not all, manufacturers producing the type of product concerned.

But profitability will reach a peak before sales do because, after a certain point, increases in sales become progressively harder to achieve and the marginal costs of obtaining each successive increase, e.g. heavier advertising and selling costs, product modifications, lower prices, extension of distribution to lower-quality smaller-turnover outlets, become greater.

The Competitive or Consolidation Phase

It is during the oncoming phase, *the competitive or consolidation phase*, that the real troubles start. Poor or uncompetitive products are squeezed out. Differences between competing products become insignificant from the consumer's point of view and no manufacturer is able to achieve a technological breakthrough that would give consumers a strong enough reason for buying his product instead of some other manufacturer's. New forms of advertising and promotion are tried out to improve the worsening sales and profit trends.

Larger advertising campaigns are mounted to gain the consumer's attention. It is at this stage that the worst forms and excesses of advertising and promotion take place, due to the sheer volume of advertising noise, the proliferation of dubious superlatives unsupportable on the basis of product merits, and the employment of promotional devices and 'gimmicks' unrelated to the inherent properties or uses of the product. A product's life can frequently be lengthened by such measures although usually only at greater cost and, therefore, lower unit profit. A manufacturer will attempt to consolidate his position at a worthwhile level of sales and profitability for as long as competitive conditions allow.

The Declining or Revitalisation Phase

Eventually, the product enters the *declining or revitalisation phase* where the manufacturer is faced with the inevitable task of choosing between accepting a long-term decline in sales and profitability until it ceases to be economic to market the product at all, or finding some new way of prolonging the life of the product on a profitable basis such as a novel advertising approach, a more convenient form of packaging, new selling methods, a lower price, a better service, etc. Quite a few companies manage successfully to extend the profitable life of products by rejuvenating or re-invigorating them in this way.

The Significance of the Product Life Cycle Concept

The significance for product planning of the product life cycle concept lies in two directions. First, it places management in the position of having to ask itself some very fundamental questions about its existing business and future plans. What stages have the company's various products reached in their life cycles? Which products are in decline? Can they be revitalised and given a new lease of life, or should they be deliberately 'milked' for maximum profits? In what areas is the company developing new products to ensure continued growth and to replace declining products? What product ideas should be currently investigated with a view to their being introduced a year from now, two years from now? On the basis of the answers given to these and like questions product planning decisions must be made and action taken which clearly affect the future growth and profitability of the company's operations.

Product planning activity continues throughout the life of a product and will vary as the product goes through the different phases of its life cycle. The various elements of the product planning function—market research, product research and development, packaging policy, pricing policy, advertising and sales promotion planning, consumer promotions (sampling schemes, couponing, reduced-price offers, competitions, etc.)—all have to be adjusted and given changes of emphasis during the different phases of a product's life cycle.

At certain stages, some elements will assume greater importance and be given higher priority than others, e.g. sampling or couponing a new product through the housewife's letterbox, increasing the weight of advertising, changing the content of the advertising, adding a new size, flavour, style or colour to the product line, lowering the price, changing the packaging. At any stage in a product's life the right mix or balance of marketing ingredients must be determined to meet the particular circumstances in which the product finds itself in the market.

Second, the life cycle concept highlights the necessity of systematic new product planning and development. Every manufacturer is continually faced with three main problem areas affecting product development. What to do with his existing products in relation to their existing and potential markets? What to do about new products in these same markets? What to do about new products to meet the needs of new and developing markets? These are the tasks of product planning.

Ideally, a manufacturer should have some kind of time-table setting out the various product development priorities related to the long-term objectives of the company. On the basis of the decisions made as to the priority of various product projects, research and development time and facilities must be allocated, tentative profit plans prepared and preliminary marketing (test or national) plans drawn up. In other words, the total company marketing effort and its associated costs must be set against a total company product programme covering each of the three areas outlined above.

(c) THE IMPORTANCE OF NEW PRODUCTS

The description 'new product' applies to any major changes of significance to the consumer or user in the form, content or packaging of the product. It can be a completely new type of product that has not been on the market before, e.g. three-course frozen TV dinners, accelerated freeze dried (AFD) foods, smokeless fuels, portable television sets, oral contraceptives or the rotary piston engine. It can be the addition of a new ingredient, e.g. whitening agents in industrial and domestic cleaners, fluoride in toothpaste, special additives in petrol, silicones in waxes and polishes, new heat-resistant materials in oven-ware, plastic reinforced steel; or it can be a change in packaging, e.g. aerosols, canned beer and soft drinks, boil-in-the-bag foods, pre-packaged coal, etc. The main criterion, however, is that the new product must be sufficiently different from the existing alternatives to constitute a basis for genuine consumer preference. A change in the materials or ingredients used by a manufacturer in making a product, unless made known to the potential user and used as a selling point, would not qualify for inclusion under the above definition.

Three main reasons are advanced for introducing new products.

1. To insure against the inevitable obsolescence of existing products, as a result of competition or attrition. A decline in the profitability of an existing product can only be reversed in the long run by bringing in a successful new product to replace it. In other words, a flow of new products is necessary to protect the existing assets in the business.
2. To expand more rapidly than is possible with a single line of products and to spread business risks over a broader product base, and reduce the likely impact of competition in any one product area. However, entry into new product fields carries its dangers as well as its rewards, particularly where a new product venture does not fit into the company's established marketing operations, distribution channels or requires new technical skills and manufacturing know-how.

3. To increase the overall profitability of the business, expressed as the return on capital employed, more quickly and more continuously through the maintenance and widening of differential advantages over competition, the more profitable use of by-products, the fuller utilisation of production and selling capacity and the consequent spreading of certain overhead costs, or the reduction of seasonal and cyclical fluctuations in output and sales.

Evidence is available indicating that the development and successful marketing of new products is perhaps the most important single factor in long-term company growth and profitability. Lord Heyworth, Chairman of Unilever Limited, went on record in one of his annual statements to shareholders that in 1957 approximately 20% of his organisation's sales of detergents, 25% of sales of toilet preparations and 22% of sales of food products were accounted for by products not on the market six years previously. Figures for later years are not available but it may not be unreasonable to surmise that in 1963 probably something in the region of one-third of total sales and possibly more in terms of net profit contribution of these three categories were accounted for by products introduced since 1951. The Association of the British Pharmaceutical Industry has gone on record as saying that seven out of ten of today's prescriptions could not have been written in 1938 because the products did not then exist.

A study undertaken by the Economist Intelligence in 1958 produced the comparison of sales of certain food and toiletry products between 1951 and 1957 seen in Chart 16.

These estimates related only to entirely new products. With the sole exception of shaving preparations, they did not include major packaging changes in existing products such as aerosols. An entirely new and rapidly developing section of a well-established packaging and container industry has come into existence as a result of the invention of the aerosol. Estimated production of aerosols in 1964 was some 90 million compared with 13 million in 1957, two million in 1953 and only 500,000 in 1950. 1964 total aerosol production broke down into the following product uses:

Table 3. Estimated Production of Aerosols in 1964 (millions of units)

Hair Sprays	30
Insecticides	14
Air-fresheners	14
Polishes, Waxes, etc.	11
Pharmaceutical and Veterinary	6
Starch	4
Perfume and Colognes	3
Shaving Cream and Toiletries	2
Miscellaneous	6

Source: I.C.I. estimates published by *The Grocer*. January 23rd, 1965.

CHART 16. PERCENTAGE OF 1957 TOTAL SALES OF CERTAIN PRODUCT CLASS SALES ACCOUNTED FOR BY PRODUCTS INTRODUCED SINCE 1951

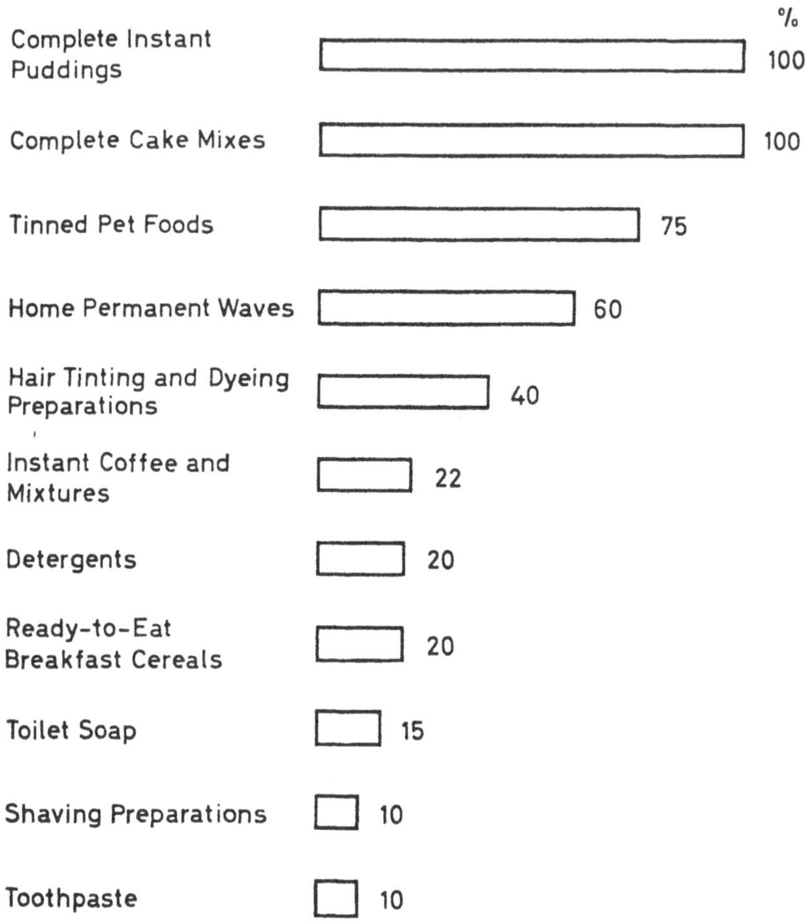

In the United States a McGraw-Hill study among manufacturers, reported in a leading marketing journal,[1] provided the following estimates of sales in 1963 likely to be accounted for by products that did not exist four years earlier as shown in Chart 17.

The Risks of Product Innovation

Product innovation, important as it is for long-term company growth, is an extremely risky business. A great many new product ideas never see the

[1] *Printer's Ink.* 1st February 1963. p. 27.

CHART 17. PERCENTAGE OF 1963 TOTAL SALES IN EACH PRODUCT CLASS ACCOUNTED FOR BY PRODUCTS INTRODUCED SINCE 1959

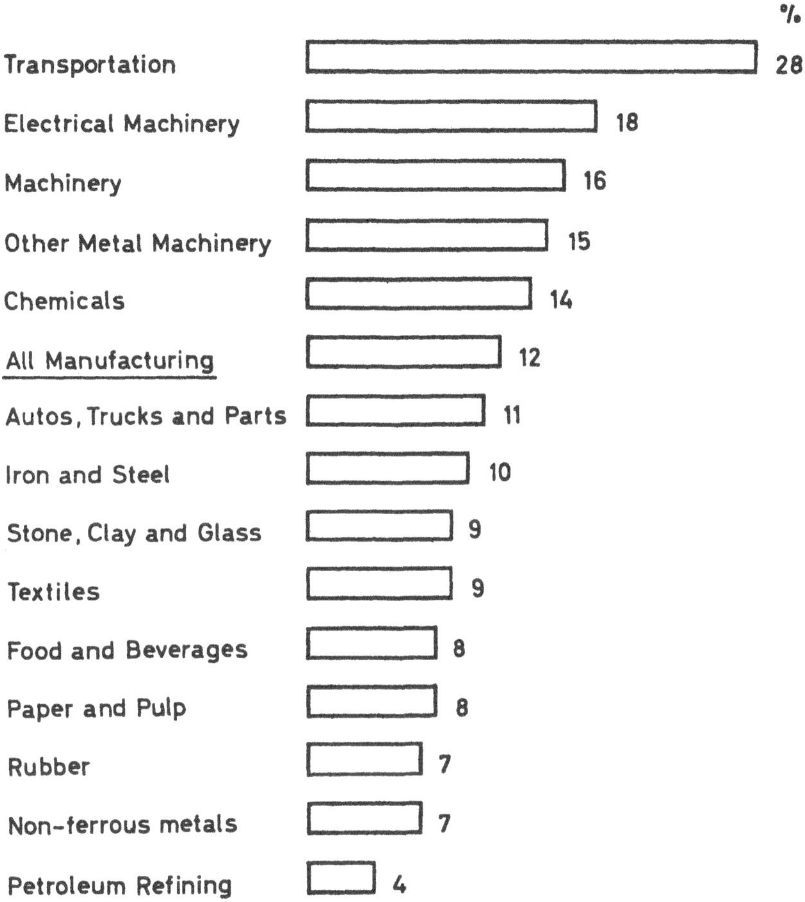

light of day but are filed away in company laboratories. Estimates of the failure rate of new products vary between 50% and 90% according to the product field in question. One reasonably firm estimate which does emerge is the failure rate for grocery products in the United States as measured by the A. C. Nielsen Company, a leading independent marketing research organisation. In the American grocery business, it is claimed, eight out of every nine new products turn out to be commercial failures, i.e. are either not test marketed and are later judged to be commercial failures or never get beyond the test market stage. This is an 88% failure rate. According to the A. C. Nielsen Company, 'The net of Nielsen's world-wide experience in measuring test marketing results in recent years is that in 54% of the cases the client decided, on the basis of test showings, to launch the product'.[1] In other words, even when a manufacturer goes to the trouble and expense of trying out his new product under 'live' test marketing conditions, there is still only a fifty-fifty chance that the product will go on to be successful. But at least these are better odds than those facing the manufacturer who does not believe in the efficacy of test marketing.

How, therefore, can the risk of product innovation be reduced to a more acceptable level? First, manufacturers can reduce the risk by systematic product planning involving all the well-tried steps of product testing, market research, and test marketing and by asking all the right questions while the new product is still in the planning stage. In this way they can ensure that action is based on knowledge of the facts rather than guesswork, provided the former can be obtained in a reasonable time and at reasonable cost. Second, they can reduce the risk by analysing and following established patterns of success based on their own past product and marketing experience and on the experiences of others in their own or related fields where these are discernible.

The Evaluation of New Products

A variety of new product check lists or evaluation techniques have been drawn up for individual industry or company use. Inevitably, they cover a lot of common ground although, obviously, some questions are considerably more relevant to some companies and products than others. The chief value of such techniques lies in the discipline it imposes on management thinking in relation to new product development. It ensures that all relevant criteria are given due consideration and that product policy consciously takes account of the inherent strengths and weaknesses that make one company different from another company.

The new product evaluation chart opposite rates the product on a simple semantic scale—'Above Average', 'Average' and 'Below Average'—for a number of factors grouped according to certain key criteria.[2] The ratings are illustrative only since the relative importance of the different factors used in the chart will vary from industry to industry and from company to company. The relative weight assigned to each of the rating factors must be considered in relation to their assumed importance to the company.

Established Patterns of Success

On the basis of the successes which certain companies have achieved with new products it is possible to make a few tentative generalisations. These fall into three groups—those generalisations that can be made about the company itself, those that can be made about the product conditions which appear to be favourable to successful new product introductions, and those

[1] *The Nielsen Researcher.* Oxford edition. A. C. Nielsen Company January/February 1963. p. 4.

[2] Ibid.

CHART 18. RATINGS FOR EVALUATING NEW PRODUCTS

Criterion	Rating		
	Above Average	Average	Below Average
MARKET CRITERIA:			
Degree of Need	Product will meet need not being filled at present or represents a significant improvement on existing products.	Product offers improvements in minor features only, that should appeal to a reasonably large number of users.	Product barely distinguishable from and does not meet a need better than existing products.
Degree of Growth Potential	A national homogeneous market which should grow substantially among a wide variety of customers. Good overseas potential.	Market more or less static or only a moderate expansion to be looked for and this, perhaps, only regionally or among a restricted range of customers. Overseas potential may also be small.	Market declining or likely to decline. A small specialised market among very restricted and diminishing number of users. Declining or no overseas potential.
Degree of Competitiveness	Absence of strong well-entrenched competition. Low average ratio of advertising to sales. Low rate of product innovation. Competition not in favourable position to counteract quickly against the new product.	Fairly well-entrenched competition but requiring moderate investment for only a moderate return. Not an unduly high rate of product innovation.	Market domination by small number of equally powerful competitors. Very high selling costs and advertising to sales ratios. Prohibitive cost of matching competitive innovation. Competitors able to counteract quickly and effectively against company's new or established products.
Degree of Stability	General economic conditions affect market only very slightly or not at all. Not subject to seasonal fluctuations. (If a seasonal product, sales peak will not coincide with that of other products, and thus add to the selling problems.) Product can expect to be in constant demand. Above average rate of profit can be expected over a period of years.	Sales moderately sensitive to general economic fluctuations and subject to minor seasonal variations. Product will be in demand long enough to recover investment and make a reasonable profit over a period of years.	Sales very sensitive to or severely affected by economic changes. Effects felt before general decline or upturn. Very large season movements in sales possibly involving appreciable lay-offs and stock losses. Investment may or may not be recovered and profit returns highly speculative.

CHART 18—*contd.*

Criterion	Rating		
	Above Average	Average	Below Average
PRODUCT CRITERIA:			
Technical Characteristics	Product has unique properties markedly superior to competition and fully protected by patents.	Product has unique and superior properties but patents either not air-tight or may be circumvented. If product features are not patentable at least they cannot easily be duplicated.	Product features cannot be patented and can be readily copied by major competitors.
Packaging	Consumer and/or trade packaging is unique, superior to competition and patented. Manufacturer may have exclusive contract with supplier.	Packaging is superior but not patentable. Duplication involves expensive machinery, processing, and technical know-how.	Packaging features cannot be patented and can easily be copied by any other manufacturer or supplier.
Pricing	Product offers better or equal quality at lower unit price. If priced above major competition then quality differential wide enough to discourage competitors from following suit.	Product priced the same as major competition but of higher quality.	Product more highly priced than major competition for the same quality.
MARKETING CRITERIA:			
Product Line Fit	Adds to incomplete product line. Should help sales of present products.	Can be made to fit present product line if required. No effect on sales of existing products.	Does not fit in well with or belong at all in present product line. May take sales away from existing products.
Distribution	Can be marketed entirely through existing distribution channels. Can be handled satisfactorily by existing sales force.	Can be distributed mainly or only partially through present channels. May require some slight reorganisation of the sales force and re-adjustment of sales territories.	Must be distributed entirely through different channels. In all probability will require major changes in sales force organisation and development, or may have to be handled by an entirely new sales force. A different type of salesman and special training may be necessary to sell the new product.

Criterion	Rating		
	Above Average	Average	Below Average
MARKETING CRITERIA —*cont.*			
Promotion	Product's unique features lend themselves to strong advertising, promotion and display, particularly of the kind that the company excels in.	Product features no more than equal to those of competitive products. But company expertise in advertising and promotion may be superior.	Product may have some or no promotable features. Company advertising and promotion may be markedly inferior to major competitors.
PRODUCTION CRITERIA:			
Plant Facilities and Personnel	Can be manufactured entirely with present plant and equipment. Will use up idle capacity or fit in well with present commitments. No additional personnel required.	Can be manufactured entirely or with mainly present facilities but some additional equipment may be necessary. Additional personnel and some retraining of existing personnel may be needed.	A considerable amount of additional equipment or completely new facilities will be required together with the necessary personnel. A personnel training programme will almost certainly be needed.
Raw Material Resources	Makes use of existing raw materials (or by-products). Company can continue to purchase its raw materials from its present supplier.	Makes considerable use of existing raw materials (or by-products) but may involve purchasing additional materials from existing or new suppliers.	Makes little or no use of any existing raw materials (or suppliers). Major purchases of raw materials will have to be made.
Know-How	Product enables maximum advantage to be taken of company's basic technical skills and product knowledge. It also provides an unusual opportunity to develop those skills and knowledge further.	Present skills and knowledge will be sufficient to produce new products. Some new expertise and personnel may be needed.	The product will make very little use of or be right outside the company's present range of skills and knowledge.

that can be made about the market conditions for new products under consideration.

First, as regards the company itself, success seems to be more likely if (a) the company has a background of engineering, marketing and research knowledge, skill and experience in the product fields concerned; (b) top management gives adequate attention and priority to the new product programme; (c) the company has experience in the planning and management of test markets and in the analysis and interpretation of the results of test markets; (d) there is an opportunity to use existing facilities, resources and personnel in order to keep down the level of costs.

Second, as regards the product conditions favourable to successful new product introductions, these would appear to include (a) the necessity for having a new product which offers a difference which is of significance to, demonstrable to and preferred by a large enough group of customers (this is by far and away the most important source of a company's competitive differential advantage); (b) the necessity for providing an opportunity to create a difference in advertising and promotion (it is often possible to build into a technically undifferentiated product a genuine customer benefit which will serve to distinguish it from the competition and provide a basis for customer preference, e.g. a better or more convenient form of packaging, a better way of distributing and making the product available at a time and place more convenient to the customer); (c) the necessity for making a product that will meet a real need either not being filled at present or better than any competing products and that will sell in sufficient volume and provide a sufficient margin to pay for the promotional support needed to create sales.

Third, a new product, generally speaking, has a better chance of succeeding if (a) the market is an expanding one, and is broadly based across a large number of potential customers; (b) if the market is going through a period of change; (c) if there is a lack of strongly entrenched competition in the mind of the customer and therefore an opportunity to create a strong brand identity for the new product; (d) if the competition is unlikely to be able to take serious counteraction quickly against the new product or the initiating company's established products; (e) if the market is relatively stable in the sense of being free from violent ups and downs of a general economic or seasonal nature.

A company can develop or acquire new products *either* out of its own skills, knowledge and resources *or* by the skills and knowledge of others through patent and know-how agreements, licensing arrangements to market other companies' products, or by outright acquisition or merger. In the latter case, the object of a take-over or merger is unlikely to be motivated solely or even largely by the desire to acquire new products.

Company acquisition is, in general, much more likely to be dictated by the need for (i) consolidation—the reduction of existing or potential competition by buying out a particularly troublesome competitor or 'fishing' for some of the more up-and-coming firms in the market; (ii) integration

—the direct control of sources of raw materials, processes, suppliers or outlets for the company's operations; (iii) economy—the lowering of production, marketing, management or overhead costs and the more efficient use of centralised specialist services; (iv) finance—to achieve the fuller utilisation of under-employed reserves, or to acquire greater liquid resources to finance future expansion; (v) management skill—the more profitable use of good surplus management through the build-up of companies bought on favourable terms when in difficult circumstances, or the buying-in of good outside management to strengthen the business. The search for new products, therefore, emerges as probably the least important single reason for company acquisition or merger, and certainly the more expensive way of going about it since the purchase of some fairly costly and possibly superfluous and unwanted assets will usually have to form part of any deal.

(d) THE FUNDAMENTALS OF TEST MARKETING

Experience indicates that the chances of a new product being successful are significantly greater if it is first put into a controlled test market where it is exposed to realistic competitive conditions. Evidence collected over many years by the A. C. Nielsen marketing research organisation shows that at least nine out of every ten products launched on the national market *on the basis of results in test markets* turn out to be commercially successful.

The purpose of test marketing is to provide more than an indication of probable success or failure. It should aim at identifying the specific factors which seem most likely to contribute to the success of the product and at finding out what combination of factors works best, what does not work and what can be made to work better. There is no mystique about test marketing. The difference between good and bad test marketing procedure lies in the planning and management of the test market and in the analysis and interpretation of the results.

The fundamentals of good test marketing practice can be demonstrated in the answers to five basic questions—What can be tested? How big should a test market be? How many things can be tested at any one time? How long should a test market be kept going? What are the most common pitfalls in test marketing? These questions, and the answers which follow, have been adapted from the findings of a report prepared by the A. C. Nielsen Company[1] based on its research and analysis of test market operations over many years and covering a broad spectrum of consumer products.

What can be tested?

With regard to new or improved products, controlled test marketing enables the manufacturer (1) to find out at relatively low cost whether

[1] *20 Steps to Successful Test Marketing*. A. C. Nielsen Company. Oxford. 1960.

customers will purchase and re-purchase the product under real competitive conditions in the market-place—before being committed on a much broader scale at much higher cost; (2) to test out and evaluate the various components of the marketing plan, i.e. the introductory sell-in; the most profitable amount of advertising; the most effective kind of advertising, e.g. media, themes; the most effective consumer promotions and in-store display; the most profitable size/price combination; (3) to make national projections of sales volume, marketing costs and profits.

In addition to measuring the performance of new products, and changes in existing products, test markets can be used to gauge the effect of changes in marketing strategies for existing products, viz. consumer advertising (weight and frequency, media selection, effectiveness of advertising copy or TV commercial), promotions (sampling, couponing, straight price-offers, premiums, related items), price (to consumer, to the trade, special trade deals), and packaging (shape or appearance of package or case, contents in ounces, tablets, number, etc., and multiple units).

How big should a Test Market be?

The size of the area used for test purposes depends primarily on five factors. First, the size of shop and/or population samples needed to support national projections. This, in turn, depends on (1) how widespread the purchase and usage of the product in question is likely to be; (2) the expected volume level and share of market at which the product will be judged to be a provisional success; (3) the expected level of effective distribution for the product; (4) if the product is completely new, what existing product most closely matches the new product for purposes of comparison; (5) whether it is proposed to compare the relative effectiveness of alternative versions of the same element, e.g. weight of advertising, media mix, or creative approach.

The second factor is the type of advertising, promotion and display to be used. For instance, a test involving television advertising should cover the area served by the station used. A test of a special in-store promotion or display might be confined to one section of an area.

The third factor is the inflexibility or costliness of the test operation. Any production or supply limitations on the product, the packaging or display material might favour as small a test market as practicable.

The fourth factor is the degree of risk involved. Any major change in product formulation and presentation or in trading policy may carry substantial risks of loss as well as gain. The greater the risk of loss, the stronger the argument for confining the test operation to a few towns or a small area followed by a broadening of the area if the results warrant it. There has been a tendency to move away from town tests and to use larger area tests because the latter offer greater flexibility from the standpoint of media availability, particularly where television advertising is likely to feature importantly in the marketing of the product. Additionally, other things being equal, the larger the shop or population samples the greater the degree of accuracy attainable and the greater the confidence that can be placed in the results and the national projections made from them. They also serve as a broader base for a subsequent region-by-region or national marketing programme.

Finally, the larger the test area is the less likely and the more difficult and costly it will be for competition to foul. A competitor can muddy the waters in a town test very quickly, easily and cheaply. He will usually be less ready to commit large amounts of money and effort for this purpose, although there will always be exceptions.

How many things can be tested at any one time?

The number of elements or variables which can be incorporated in a test are limited only by time and cost considerations. This is because only one element or variable should be tested at a time, and a minimum of two test areas is required for each variable tested. Thus, if the only variable being tested is the *weight* of advertising expenditure, then the new planned level of advertising must be applied in one area and the results compared against those obtained by the normal level of advertising running in a control area. The characteristics of the control area must match those of the test area in all major respects, in order to establish what would have happened in the absence of any change in the level of expenditure. Experience indicates, with new products particularly, that it is always advisable to test alternative weights of advertising in different areas so that the results can be compared and the 'best' alternative selected, i.e. testing one level of expenditure gives no guidance on whether it is the 'right' level or whether or not a different level of expenditure might have produced a better and more profitable result.

When only the weight of advertising or any other single variable is to be tested, everything else should be held as near constant as is feasible. Different creative approaches, different media combinations, the use of alternative types of consumer promotions (such as sampling or couponing) should be tested in other areas.

How long should a Test Market be kept going?

In a very real sense, a test market never stops being one. It continues to be a 'pathfinder' market in advance of the national market. The results being achieved in the area should continue to be carefully watched through the years and if any changes occur, upwards or downwards, then these should be quickly and methodically investigated. Such changes will either be temporary aberrations of no particular significance for the national market pattern, or they may portend more deep-seated causes, making for similar changes in other areas or, in time, even nationally.

In relation to the specific purposes for which a particular test market is planned, it should be kept going for just as long as it takes to get a result on which a clear-cut decision can be taken to proceed with or abandon the attempt to market the product on a larger scale. All the investment of time and money and the most meticulous attention to detail can count for nothing by a premature decision. Initial customer response to a new product does not form an adequate basis for deciding the product's future. A good initial response will indicate that the marketing plan has achieved the first step of making the product available and of getting customers to try it. So far as the majority of consumer goods is concerned time must be allowed for the customer to come back into the market again, and re-purchase at least once, particularly if the first purchase was made on an introductory special offer basis.

The time required to judge new product success, after completion of the test market, can vary from under six months to over three years depending on the particular product. Moreover, the frequency distribution over the time range is normal, i.e. in about half the cases the time required is over two years and in the other half of the cases, less than two years. But in only one out of every five cases is it likely to be possible to judge a product's success in under one year.

What are the common pitfalls in Test Marketing?

Among the more frequent planning and organisational failures made in test marketing are the following:

1. Failure to decide what is to be tested—each test should aim to find an answer to one major question, for example, the most effective weight of advertising, a new creative approach, a new price structure or simply product acceptance. The more elements which a manufacturer tries to test at the same time in a single test area the more difficult it becomes to identify the *real* causes of success or failure.
2. Failure to base the test market plan on an overall national marketing plan which is both realistic and affordable—the sales target in the test area should be proportionate to the expected national target, and the marketing mix (or alternative mixes if more than one test area is being used) should duplicate as closely as possible that which is proposed for the national launch.
3. Failure to make comparative tests—no single test permits the comparative evaluation and choice of the best plan from among a number of possible alternatives.
4. Failure to establish benchmarks in the test area—before any test begins, it is necessary to establish individual and total sales and/or market penetration of competitive brands (and, where necessary, customer attitudes and preferences) so that subsequent changes can then be compared and evaluated against this base.
5. Failure to select representative test areas—the areas selected must be as representative as possible of the country as a whole in terms of geographic location, trade and customer characteristics, media facilities of the type to be used later, etc., in order that the test will serve as a 'projection model' for future national operations.

6. Failure to adhere to the test market plan—this applies particularly to changes in advertising weight or content, the media used and pricing; 'changing horses' in mid-market can lead to confusion when it comes to analysing the test results (the need to test the effect of changes in the plan in response to strong competitive counter-measures can be allowed for by choosing another test town within the larger test area for this specific purpose at the outset, in order that results of both the original plan and the changed plan can be compared).
7. Failure to consider and get objective and reliable data on all factors influencing sales results in the test area—such as the calibre of salesmen used, seasonal influences, weather conditions, economic conditions, levels of shop distribution, stock levels and stock cover, out-of-stock ratios, competitors' activities, etc.
8. Failure to stay in the test market long enough to get a clear-cut stop-or-go decision—slower-moving products require longer test periods than fast-selling products and the temptation to jump the gun and take a final decision should be resisted by the manufacturer until he can be reasonably sure that the sales pattern has stabilised and the results have been properly analysed.
9. Reading into test market results more than is supportable by the objective facts—an apparent initial success in test market can all too rapidly turn into a comparative failure as the test market 'matures' due to an over-optimistic reading of the situation, based on considerations other than those directly related to the test market findings or due to the failure to recognise danger signals from the test.

To date the technique of test marketing has largely been applied in the consumer goods field. Market experimentation as distinct from product testing is a good deal more difficult in industrial marketing. Among the chief reasons for its limited application over the broad range of industrial products are the high cost of tooling-up for a new product, the much higher unit value of the product, the greater need for secrecy with respect to new products and processes, the fact that the market for an industrial product is likely to be much more widely dispersed than for a consumer product and less accessible in terms of advertising media, and the fact that customers may be reluctant to experiment with a new product, service, process or distribution pattern which could interfere with normal production.

Much of the technical information needed from an industrial test market operation can be obtained by other means such as controlled pilot plant, simulation tests, and customer application studies. Most of the investment in connection with a wide range of industrial goods will already have been undertaken before a product is actually available for test marketing purposes. The introduction of a new generation of jet aircraft or computers can cost in excess of £100 million before it reaches the marketable stage. However, this does not mean to say that the technique of test marketing has no application to industrial products. But it will have to be adapted to take account of the special problems and needs of industrial manufacturers and their customers and be the subject of a great deal of further experimentation.

(e) ORGANISING FOR PRODUCT PLANNING AND DEVELOPMENT

Product planning and development is an integral part of marketing. Good sales and advertising policies will not compensate for weaknesses in earlier product planning procedures, i.e. product screening and evaluation, product testing, market research and test marketing. Potential friction between manufacturing and marketing, between technical research and development and product planning, can stultify the best efforts of both and result in unsatisfactory compromise.

Product planning involves the co-ordination of a number of linked activities—technical research and development, marketing research, sales and distribution and promotion. Maximum effectiveness more often depends upon the sum of the parts rather than on the separate optimisation of the individual components. The separation of marketing responsibilities into tight specialist departments invites the danger that each department will regard its own activity as being the most important and having first call on available resources.

This rigid compartmentalisation has led in the past to the familiar situation where sales department has been handed a product by the technical research people, probably produced in great secrecy on the basis of specifications which satisfied the engineers and developed for the convenience of the manufacturer rather than of the customer. In these circumstances, marketing people and, probably, the customer for whom the product is intended only get into the act at the tail end of manufacturing. From the marketing perspective this is the reverse of what should be done. Any new product idea must first be checked with the potential customer to determine whether there is a real need or latent want for the product, how it might be used, and within what sort of price range it might sell. If the idea is favourably received then it must be translated into a customer 'proposition'. The job of product planning, initially, is to prepare a *customer specification* for the product for the guidance of the engineering department, and thence to see that the prototype is tested, modified as necessary and brought to the marketable stage.

Logical as all this may sound it has to be admitted that still relatively few companies use product planning in this way and even fewer place product planning directly under marketing management. The reason is not hard to find. The British Institute of Management was recently forced to admit in one of its surveys[1] that a trend towards the adoption of the

[1] *A Survey of the Functions of Marketing, Product and Brand Managers*. British Institute of Management. Information Survey No. 93. London. September. 1961.

marketing perspective in British business was barely perceptible and that relatively few companies were organised to implement the marketing concept. Unfamiliarity with the concept among British business men was reflected in the pitifully low response to the questionnaire sent out on this particular survey which, in fact, offered a totally insufficient statistical basis for valid generalisations of any kind whatsoever.

It seems clear, therefore, that product planning, as described, is not carried out by the great majority of companies in this country. Yet it clearly makes sense to place product planning decisions in the hands of those executives responsible for the total company marketing effort. For it is they who must decide when it is more important to spend money on changing the product instead of putting more behind its distribution and advertising or lowering its price. It is the marketing executive who must decide when the time is right to bring in new products at the expense of, or in addition to, existing products.

The product planning function can be organised in a number of different ways according to company size, needs and policies. Four examples are given of its organisation in companies of widely differing character. They have one common feature, however, in that the responsibility for product planning is placed directly under marketing management.

CHART 19. ORGANISING THE PRODUCT PLANNING FUNCTION

Medium-sized pharmaceutical manufacturer supplying both ethical and proprietary products to doctors and chemists

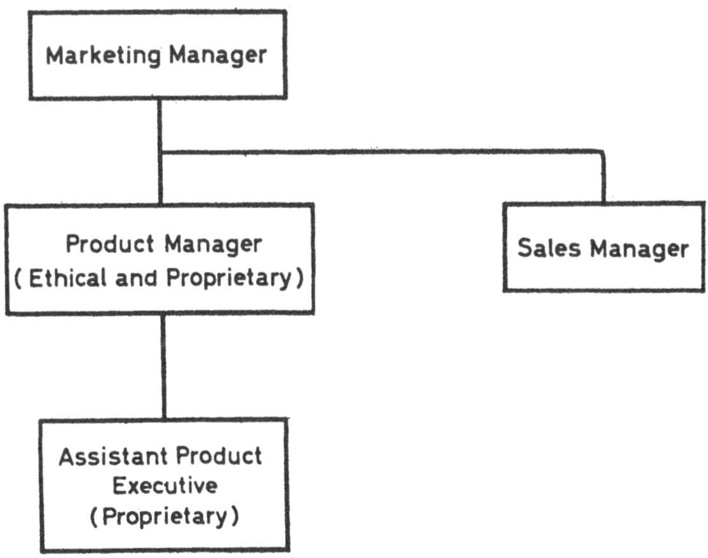

The Product Manager is responsible to the Marketing Manager for the entire product planning operation on existing and new products. He has one assistant to handle assignments on proprietary products selling through chemists only. The latter is a recent appointment due to the firm's expansion into the proprietary field. The company's previous experience is almost entirely in the marketing of ethical preparations to doctors and hospitals. All marketing research is placed with outside organisations. The Product Manager also acts as Advertising Manager and is responsible for the placement of the company's advertising through an advertising agency. The Sales Manager has a small specialised and highly qualified team of medical representatives calling on doctors and hospital staff. He is also responsible for a small but growing chemist sales force to meet the planned expansion of sales in this type of outlet.

CHART 20. ORGANISING THE PRODUCT PLANNING FUNCTION

Large multi-product food manufacturer distributing mainly through grocers

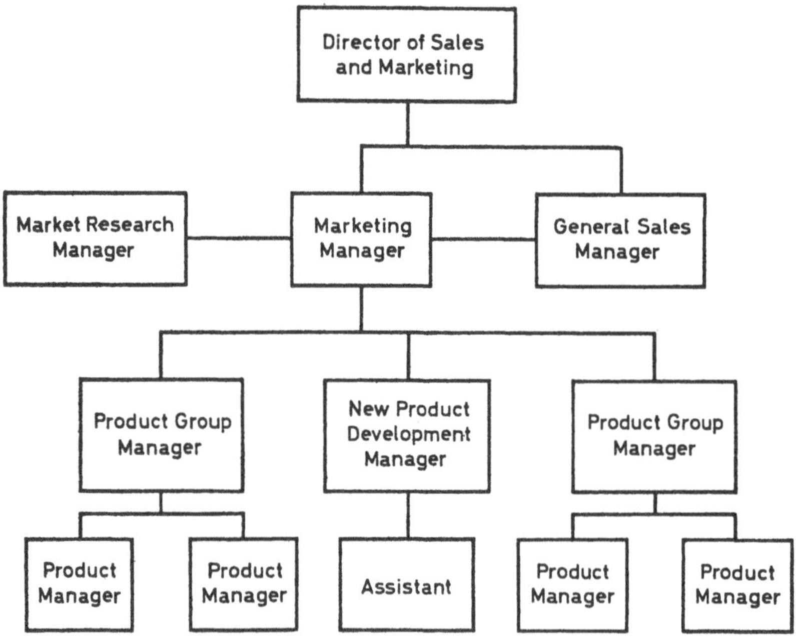

In this company, the Marketing Manager is directly responsible to a Director of Sales and Marketing. The Marketing Manager has under him two Product Group Managers, a New Product Development Manager and a Market Research Manager.

Each Product Group Manager is responsible for the day-to-day product and marketing planning on an existing group of brands and products (there are a number of related products sold under the same brand names). In this case, although all the company's brands and products are distributed through the same retail trade channels, there are two distinct types of product involved requiring different distribution, sales and promotion treatment. The New Product Development Manager, as his title implies, is concerned only with research and development on new products not previously sold by the company up to the national marketing stage. At this point, the 'going' product is handed over to the Product Group Manager who is responsible for all further marketing, research and development on it thereafter. Product reformulations, pricing and packaging changes of an existing 'going' brand do not come under the New Product Development Manager.

The company does not employ an Advertising Manager as such, all advertising for individual products being the responsibility of the Product Group Manager in conjunction with the firm's advertising agencies. In fact, the company employs separate advertising agencies for each of its four major brands and new product advertising is assigned to one or other of them according to circumstances, e.g. an agency may already be handling the advertising for an established product that competes directly with a new product.

CHART 21. ORGANISING THE PRODUCT PLANNING FUNCTION

Large consumer durable manufacturer whose products are mainly sold through departmen stores and shops specialising in the sales of this class of commodity

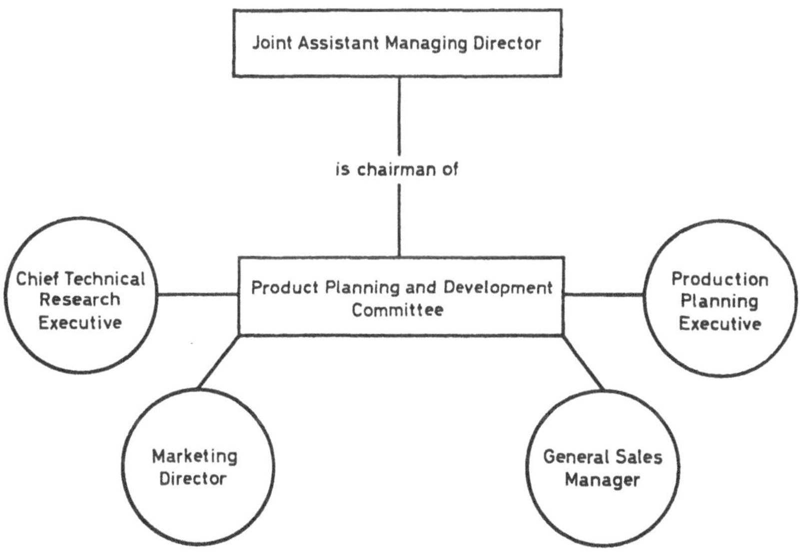

In this company a certain number, but not all, of the elements of product planning are carried out by a committee which meets at least monthly, or as the need arises, under the chairmanship of one of the two joint assistant managing directors. Permanent members appointed to the committee are the Marketing Director, General Sales Manager, a Senior Production Planning Executive and the Chief Technical Research Executive. Others who may be called in on an *ad hoc* basis include the Financial Controller, a Sales Analyst, the Service Manager, and the head of the Design Department. The committee is not concerned with day-to-day product or marketing planning and administration, which is carried out by Design and Marketing Department personnel. Its main function is to review the company's products with the object of (1) eliminating unprofitable lines, sizes and designs, (2) initiating research and development projects on possible new products or alterations to existing products, (3) giving approval to selected new or existing product development plans and programmes, (4) authorising expenditures on agreed projects and plans.

CHART 22. ORGANISING THE PRODUCT PLANNING FUNCTION

Medium-sized manufacturer of moulded and extruded plastics for a limited range of industrial uses

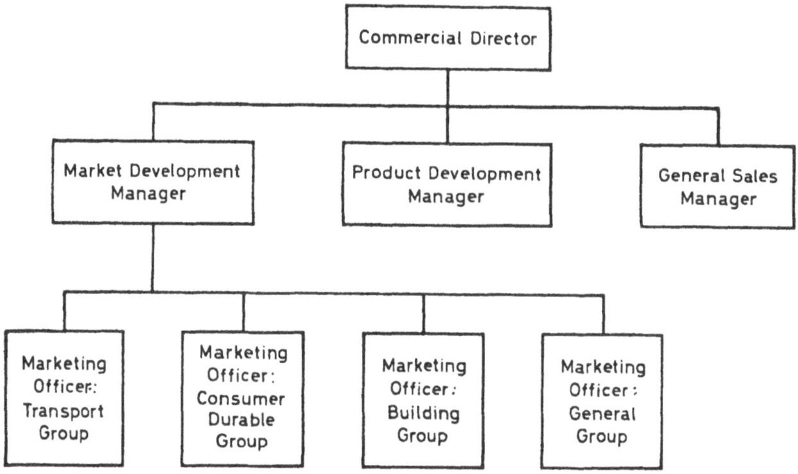

The Commercial Director of this company is for all practical purposes in sole charge of the total marketing effort. He has reporting to him a Market Development Manager, a Product Development Manager and a General Sales Manager. The Market Development Department consists of four marketing development officers, each of whom is responsible for a major group of products which contribute about the same proportion of total company turnover. These are the Transport Group, the Consumer Durable Group, the Building Group and the General Group which includes the electrical and general engineering industries principally. Each marketing officer is responsible for the study of market uses and potential applications of the company's products and their exploitation in terms of product sales publicity and advertising.

The Product Development Department which is staffed by qualified engineers is structured to correspond to the same industry breakdown. Each product development executive is responsible for advising on and progressing the technical research needed on any product assigned to him, for liaison between Market Development Department and the Engineering Division and for advising both on existing or new applications. The General Sales Manager controls an industrial sales force covering all the markets in which the company is currently engaged.

While final responsibility for the total product planning and development function must rest with company management, certain specific product planning and development activities can be delegated to outside specialists. The main external sources of such practical help and advice are advertising agencies, market research organisations, product and package design consultants and independent marketing consultants.

Apart from considerations of cost and the availability of internal personnel and facilities the chief argument made for the use of the outside specialist organisations is the breadth of experience, objectivity and the application of a high degree of professional skill which they can often bring to the problem. They are better able to afford the employment of highly paid and qualified experts than is the average manufacturer who may not be in a position to make full and continuous use of such services. Companies which have their own full-time product planning staff may experience bottlenecks or especially difficult, out-of-the-usual-run problems with sufficient frequency which make it advantageous to call on the help and guidance of outside experts.

5

Managing the Sales and Distribution Function

(a) THE IMPORTANCE OF THE SELLING COMPONENT OF MARKETING

STOCKS of a commodity piled high in a factory warehouse are about as useful to the customer or user as milk down on the farm is to a householder living in the middle of London or Manchester. Goods, to be of value, have to be distributed to places where they are needed and can be used at the right time and in the right quantities. This is the function of the sales and distribution organisation. Everything that is done by a manufacturer, right up until the moment a product is sold to his customers, represents a cost. The only way in which he can get his money back plus something extra to compensate for all the trouble he has gone to is to sell it.

The importance of the selling and distribution function is in no way diminished as a result of the adoption of the marketing perspective by business managements. On the contrary, the marketing perspective enhances the status and role of the selling function in three ways.

First, it places greater emphasis on marketing requirements as opposed to production needs. The major concern of the business becomes one of marketing products that it knows stand a very good chance of being sold profitably rather than trying to sell a certain volume of products which it happens to make. This may sound simple and obvious but for the sales organisation, as well as for the company as a whole, the difference in approach can be the difference between success or failure.

Second, selling as part of marketing becomes more effective as a result of closer integration with advertising, research and product planning. Instead of the sales organisation operating quite separately from the marketing research, advertising, and product planning departments and contributing little to these functions or to day-to-day marketing management, it becomes intimately involved as a member of a marketing team under a chief marketing executive.

Third, the character of the selling job changes. The marketing perspective involves a fundamental shift in emphasis away from the needs and convenience of the manufacturer or seller and towards the needs and convenience of the buyer. This means tailoring the company's sales force and distribution methods to the requirements of the customer and concentrating on ways of helping him with his problems.

The consumer goods salesman ceases merely to sell *to* the trade; he must sell *through* the trade by advising on all manner of stock, display and merchandising problems. Instead of being an order-taker and deliverer of goods, he must offer technical advice and service to his distributors on how their merchandise (other goods as well as the company's own) should be displayed, how much space should be allocated, how the latest promotion should be featured, and how display material should be used. He will, where necessary and permissible, physically erect the displays himself. He must demonstrate the profitability to the retailer or wholesaler of handling his company's products and advise him on how they could be made more profitable. He will talk about profit per linear foot of display shelving or per square foot of floor space for his company's products compared with competing products. He will talk about stockturns, i.e. the number of times a year the average stock of a product is sold. The sales force through closer integration with marketing research, product planning and advertising will have access to a great deal more information about its customers than hitherto and will be armed with selling aids, special buying inducements, sales presentation folders, specimens of the advertising, etc.

Similarly the industrial goods salesman must sell through his own immediate customers to *their* customers and must understand the problems they face in relation to their end-use markets. Too many salesmen of industrial and consumer goods—and their managements—suffer from selling myopia and never see beyond their immediate customers. This is perhaps even less excusable in the case of industrial selling since most of the goods sold depend upon a derived demand for other things which make use of or incorporate the products or services of the industrial goods manufacturer. Hence, the customers' customers are of critical importance to the industrial goods manufacturer. He may not be concerned with linear or square footage of retail display space and store traffic flows but if he is a supplier to the consumer durables industry or the building industry, he may be very much concerned with what is happening in housing, and what the housewife is buying for her kitchen this year or whether her husband is contemplating buying a car instead and so on.

But while the marketing perspective enhances the role of selling in a company it does involve some re-structing of the sales organisation and of sales management. This may, on occasions, result in some loss of status and authority in respect of individuals. The sales manager, unless he is promoted to general marketing management, will lose some of his former autonomy and have far less, if any, direct control over such matters as advertising, market research, pricing, packaging, new product development, credit policy, etc. The transference of these responsibilities to other 'experts' does mean confining sales management to a more limited theatre of operation, namely the direct supervision and motivation of the field sales force, internal sales administration, the implementation of sales plans, the control of distribution activity (including warehousing and transport), customer service and the recruitment, training and remuneration of sales personnel.

However, it will have much greater planning responsibility as opposed to operational responsibility, since it will assist marketing management to develop marketing and sales objectives, policies and plans. It will participate in the formulation of these plans and policies and will work in harness with the other marketing forces—research, advertising, product planning—to achieve the agreed objectives.

A team approach and a continuing team responsibility are implicit in the adoption of the marketing perspective. And although some diminution of operational responsibility may be called for on the part of sales management, planning participation and responsibility are considerably broadened. In addition, sales management is, in a large number of cases, still the best source of potential marketing management. This does not mean, of course, that the present sales manager is always the most logical candidate for the position of marketing manager. He may be the most logical choice, but he must also be the man best fitted for the job.

(b) THE CHANNELS OF DISTRIBUTION

The function of distribution is to move goods from the producer to the final consumer or user. It applies both to industrial and consumer goods or services, to titanium oxide as a raw material in paint manufacture as well as the actual tin of paint bought by the do-it-yourself home decorator. There are a number of ways open to any producer to get his product into the hands of the final user, some of which are competitive or substitutable for one another, some of which are complementary to one another. The following chart shows the principal alternative channels of distribution open to a producer:

CHART 23. CHANNELS OF DISTRIBUTION

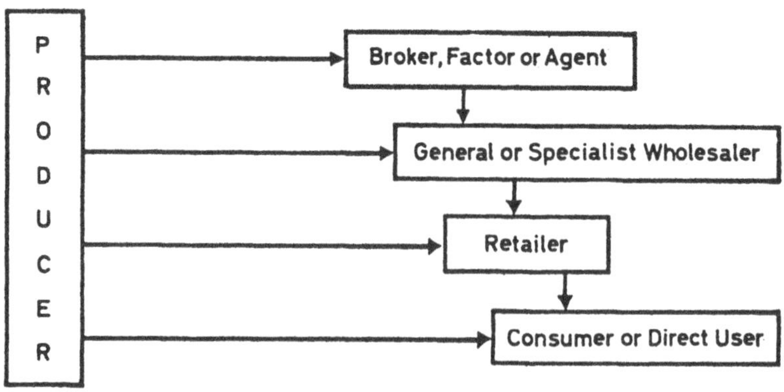

The five alternative routes which a producer can take are: (1) producer direct to consumer or final user; (2) producer direct to retailer to consumer; (3) producer direct to wholesaler to retailer to consumer; (4) producer to broker, factor or agent to wholesaler to retailer to consumer; (5) producer to broker, factor or agent to retailer to consumer.

Most industrial goods, excluding basic raw materials, are sold direct to the industrial user or to a factor or agent standing between the producer and the industrial user. A consumer goods producer can distribute direct to the consumer either through the post (mail-order) or through door-to-door salesmen (e.g. certain domestic appliances, cosmetics, plastic kitchen utensils, brushes and household cleaning materials). A producer can distribute exclusively or selectively through independent retailers, variety chain stores (Woolworths, British Home Stores, etc.), department stores, or mail-order houses. Some producers sell direct to consumers through their own retail outlets, e.g. petrol companies owning their own sites, brewers owning their own public houses, men's clothing manufacturers, shoe manufacturers, some domestic appliance manufacturers, home decorating material suppliers, sewing machines and carpets.

A few companies own their own wholesale merchant organisation handling competing brands and classes of merchandise, e.g. certain food, confectionery and tobacco manufacturers. At least one major food manufacturer, Associated British Foods, not only operates its own wholesale organisation but also owns a voluntary purchasing group for the smaller retailers, its own cash-and-carry wholesale warehouses for the very smallest retailers and a chain of supermarkets.

Combinations of channels are sometimes used. In America, for example, the General Electric Company has embarked on a policy of distributing samples only of their domestic appliances for display in retail outlets but delivering directly to the consumer in response to enquiries installing and servicing the equipment and financing the sale. In the opposite direction, Marks and Spencer, the retail and wholesale Co-operative Societies, and Boots the chemists are outstanding examples of retail organisations which have gone in for manufacture of a wide range of merchandise either directly through their own fully owned factories or by concluding exclusive product manufacturing arrangements with a number of independent producers.

Two further points emerge from the chart. First, it is necessary to distinguish between the functions performed by a broker, factor, agent and wholesaler respectively. In contrast to the wholesaler, the other 'middlemen' do not take title to the goods in which they trade. They sell on behalf of manufacturers either on a percentage of the value of the goods they sell or on a fixed commission per unit of sale. Specifically, a broker or commission agent takes neither title to nor possession of the goods he sells. He does not buy or sell on his own account. He is primarily a negotiator between the seller and potential buyers. The majority of brokers tend to specialise in specific types of goods such as tea or sugar since the greatest strength of the broker is his detailed knowledge of market conditions, of buying and selling opportunities and his range of contacts. A broker will provide a ready-made salesforce and is only paid for the sales he makes.

The distinguishing characteristics of a factor is that he takes possession of the goods in which he deals, although he does not buy them and take title. He maintains premises and has facilities for receiving, handling, warehousing and selling the goods in question. Generally speaking, he works on a straight commission basis. An agent may be either a manufacturer's agent appointed to sell part of the output of a producer (price and terms of sale being fixed by the producer) and to represent the producer on a continuous basis in a restricted area, or a selling agent appointed to sell the whole output of a manufacturer anywhere he likes and on terms of sale which allow some room for negotiation. The general wholesale merchant takes title to and possession of the goods and earns his profit by selling to retailers at a higher price than that at which he buys from the manufacturer. The wholesale margin tends to fluctuate within fairly narrow limits for each class of goods dealt in.

It is difficult to generalise about the circumstances in which a manufacturer would find it advantageous to appoint a broker, factor or agent but the most important factors entering into such a decision would include (1) the degree to which the manufacturer wishes to retain or divest himself of the problems and risks involved in selling and distributing the product, (2) the inability to make maximum and continuous use of a company sales force, (3) the degree of knowledge and experience which the manufacturer has of the market for his product and of the selling and distribution techniques used in the field, (4) the degree of difficulty in gaining adequate distribution for the product due to the manufacturer being small and relatively unknown, (5) the relative efficiency and costs of using 'middlemen' who are not handling competing products and can be relied upon to do a good selling job for the product.

The second point that emerges from the chart is the variation in the length of the different channels of distributions. It clearly takes longer for a product to pass through the hands of a broker or wholesaler, retailer and hence to the final user than it does to go direct from the manufacturer's warehouse direct to the user. Except for certain kinds of industrial goods, however, the real comparison is between the manufacturer-direct-to-user channel and the retailer-direct-to-user channel. Provided adequate stock is always on hand at the retail outlet it is probably quicker and easier, in most cases, for the consumer or user to buy from the retailer. Where a product is purchased to order, on the other hand, direct delivery from the manufacturer to user is the quicker route.

The Selection of Distribution Channels

The selection of the best channels of distribution for a company's products will depend upon a balance of factors and the relative importance which the management of the company attaches to each of the factors in any particular set of circumstances. There is no one 'best' channel of distribution for all manufacturers of a single class of products. Even if there were, today's 'best' channel might be different from yesterday's and tomorrow's might be different again. This is because conditions change. Customer requirements are constantly changing; technological developments enable more efficient methods of storing, handling and selling goods to be used. Distribution channels which were once considered to be satisfactory but were superseded by 'better' channels may again come back in the same or some new form. For example, direct door-to-door selling, which declined after the last war, is on the increase again and is being extended to a number of new product fields. Or again, the modern gleaming supermarket and the more rough-and-ready discount store are nothing more than technological developments of the old open or covered market still to be found in many urban and rural areas. J. Lyons and Company decided in 1963 to reverse its policy of delivering its food products to approximately 80,000 of its retail customers directly through an army of van salesmen and use instead the services of some 1,000 wholesalers. Seven years earlier it had stopped using the wholesale merchant completely and went over to direct delivery!

Developments in the grocery trade itself are forcing many manufacturers to reappraise their distribution channel policies. Supermarkets, voluntary wholesaler-retailer groups, cash-and-carry wholesale merchants, and the concentration of buying power in fewer and fewer hands are causing an increasing number of manufacturers to change their distribution and selling policies.[1] Already in the food field it is common practice to use more than one trade channel. For example, a manufacturer may sell direct to some of the larger independent retailers and multiple groups, but use wholesalers to reach the large number of small and medium-sized independents which it would be uneconomic to deal with direct. The same manufacturer's products may be sold direct to the consumer through mobile vans and/or milk-roundsmen.

For a large number of manufacturers, especially in the consumer goods fields, the effective choice of distribution channels is not between one channel or another but between one combination of channels and other alternative combinations. By and large, under the marketing concept, the determining factor in this choice will be the requirements and convenience of the ultimate consumer or user of the product. The function of distribution is to make the product *conspicuously* available at the time and place of greatest convenience to the user. Given this general criterion, there are several other important considerations which a manufacturer must weigh in the balance before deciding which particular distribution pattern suits him best. These considerations fall into four groups: (1) those that concern the company itself, (2) those that concern the product, (3) those that concern the customer or user market and (4) those that concern the relative

[1] For a detailed study of distribution channels and developments see *The Changing Pattern of Distribution.* N. Stacey and A. Wilson. Business Publications Ltdi-a in assoc., tion with B. T. Batsford Ltd. 1958.

effectiveness of the different trade channels. None of these groups of considerations can be viewed in isolation. They are, to a very large extent, interdependent and inter-acting.

Company Characteristics include its overall objectives and policies, organisation, financial position, size and competitive standing in the market. A company's overall policy may be to concentrate on production and research and to minimise or avoid altogether the risks of selling and distribution. Its organisation will reflect such a policy and physical selling and distribution by the company will be kept to a minimum. Lack of finance may preclude, initially at least, the incurring of the costs of marketing.

Generally speaking, the fewer the number of 'middlemen' between the producer and the user, the greater the costs that must be incurred by the producer who must hold valuable stocks of the product and warehouse, handle and sell them at some later stage in the chain of distribution. The larger the company and the greater its dominance over competitors, the more likely it is to retain and increase its direct control over the marketing of its products. Especially is this the case with companies manufacturing a wide range of products broadly served by the same channels of distribution. An additional consideration is the channels of distribution used by competitors in the same line of business.

Product Characteristics include the type of product (e.g. bulk commodities or raw materials, consumer goods, capital goods), the degree of technical service called for to install and maintain it, the unit-value and terms of sale of the product, its seasonality, and the need to control quality or availability. So far as technical service is concerned, the more complicated the product is to demonstrate, install and maintain the more advantageous it will normally be to deal directly with the ultimate purchaser or user and to keep the number of intermediaries between the manufacturer and the user to an absolute minimum. This is true of a very wide range of industrial goods.

For products with a high unit value and high distributors' margins the advantage is also likely to lie in having fewer intermediaries between the manufacturer and the final user due to a lower ratio of selling cost to unit sales value and to the desire of the manufacturer to retain at least part of the distributor's margin. A highly seasonal product, such as canned fruit, presents problems of holding heavy stocks in anticipation of consumer and trade buying and of keeping the company sales force profitably occupied throughout the year. In such circumstances, and particularly in the absence of complementary products, the interest of the manufacturer may be better served by getting a broker or wholesale merchant to finance the holding of stocks and the sale of the product. Some products require rigid quality and price control, extremely careful handling and, in the case of prescribed drugs, sale under restricted conditions. In such cases, the use of specialist wholesalers and retailers is a paramount consideration in the selection of distribution channels.

Market Characteristics take in the size of the market, the potential sales volume, the location and degree of concentration of customers or users, user buying habits, the need for exclusive or special representation, etc. For a tea manufacturer, complete distribution coverage is desirable within the area he seeks to serve since the product is used by virtually everyone week in and week out. Manufacturers of soft drinks, chocolate and sugar confectionery and cigarettes seek maximum coverage because of the high impulse factor in sales and the need to make the product accessible wherever and whenever the consumer wants to buy. Indeed, all of these items can now be purchased from automatic vending machines at any time of the day or night.

Ethical drugs and surgical appliances are specialised demands and can only be sold by a registered qualified distributor. Complete coverage of all possible outlets is neither desirable nor necessary. The manufacturer of machine tools or heavy electrical equipment has a relatively restricted number of potential buyers with whom close contact must be maintained during the specification, installation and servicing stages. For most capital goods, close and direct customer contact is the predominant consideration. Some manufacturers desire special or exclusive representation either at the commission agent, wholesaler or retailer level. Fashion wear, cosmetics, perfumes, motor vehicles, domestic heating appliances and fuels are among the more common examples.

Trade Channel Characteristics include the relative amount and quality of service provided by the different channels together with their comparative costs, the degree of exclusive representation given, the extent of coverage achieved and the importance of this coverage to the manufacturer, the individual or collective bargaining strength of the various distributors, and the ways in which these distributors can be most efficiently and economically served by the manufacturer.

Inefficiencies in production have been subject to critical examination over many years. The need for higher productivity is constantly being stressed by the government and business leaders. Comparatively little organised effort has been devoted, as yet, to the elimination of inefficiency in distribution and to raising 'distributivity' or productivity in distribution. The area of physical distribution is likely to come in for more searching analysis than hitherto as more and more companies realise the economies to be found there.

In some companies, selling and distribution costs account for as much as 40% of total costs and include not only field selling, transport and central and regional warehousing expenses, but also order-processing, order-handling, packing, insurance, stock deterioration and obsolescence charges. All of these costs depend ultimately on distribution-channel policy. The average size of customers' orders and deliveries, the timing and location of such deliveries, the ways in which the product must be packaged and shipped to customers can each contribute materially to the total costs of distribution.

From the manufacturer's standpoint, it is the total cost of distribution which is the really significant figure and not the individual costs of the separate activities. On the one hand, a cost reduction in one activity—such as warehousing—may add to the cost of some preceding or follow-on activity such as transport—with the net result that the total cost of distribution is increased. On the other hand, it is quite feasible for a higher cost incurred in one area, by reducing costs in other related areas, to result in a net saving on the total distribution operation.

Similarly, when a manufacturer comes to select the most effective distribution channel or combination of channels for his product it does not necessarily follow that the best choice is that which provides maximum sales volume or minimum cost short-term. Such quantitative criteria can be misleading and, in the long run, expensive. The quality of the distribution effort is of at least equal importance and this is very often unquantifiable and unmeasurable. A gradual but sustained distribution effort built up on mutual confidence between buyer and seller and on the basis of a continuing and reliable standard of service is more likely to pay in the long run than is a quick, cheap and probably misdirected distribution effort which cannot be sustained and in which the selected distributor later loses interest.

It should be borne in mind that distribution is only one element in the total marketing process and it does not necessarily follow that in the case of any particular manufacturer a high cost of distribution is a bad thing or a sign of inefficiency. There may be a number of good reasons why the cost of distribution is high and should remain so. A high ratio of distribution to total costs may merely be a reflection of very efficient low-cost production. Nevertheless, distribution costs should be kept under close review and analysed in order to determine whether they ought to be or could be lower (or higher) or whether better results could be achieved at the same level of costs.

(c) THE ELEMENTS OF SALES PLANNING AND CONTROL

The primary responsibility of sales management is the planning and control of the physical selling effort to achieve company sales and profit targets. To achieve these targets it directs and controls field selling activity, selects and organises the channels of distribution in line with company distribution policy, defines and communicates the sales tasks to be carried out and organises the means for their accomplishment within the limits of the expense budget set by marketing management. It is also responsible for establishing procedures for field sales reporting and statistical sales analysis, setting up standards of performance for all sales personnel, analysing and evaluating the results achieved against planned accomplishment and for recommending any changes of plan designed to correct indicated deficiences or to otherwise improve results.

The basic elements of sales planning and control are: (1) the preparation of general business and market forecasts, (2) the preparation of the company sales forecast, (3) the preparation of the sales budget, (4) the establishment of sales quotas, (5) the selection of distribution channels, (6) the preparation and implementation of selling and merchandising plans, (7) sales communications, (8) sales reporting, (9) statistical sales control, (10) the review of manpower performance (including the selection, training and development of field sales and management personnel).

In addition to these operational responsibilities, sales management has a number of other responsibilities in the areas of marketing planning, co-ordination and integration. It takes part in the formulation of overall marketing objectives and specific marketing plans. It advises marketing management on any aspect of planning affecting or affected by the field selling and distribution effort, both long- and short-term. It makes itself accessible to executives engaged in marketing research, product planning, advertising and sales promotion. It integrates itself with and makes use of the work of other executives such as marketing research, product planning, advertising and sales promotion specialists. The means of accomplishing a working integration of the selling and distribution function with the other marketing functions is the establishment of the proper organisational framework within which the position, functions, responsibility, and authority of each management executive and his relationships to other executives is set out comprehensively and unambiguously.

Preparing General Business and Market Forecasts

Business forecasting involves a series of projections proceeding from the general to the particular. The most general forecast is of the economic climate with particular reference to conditions in those sectors of the economy which bear directly on a company's business, e.g. industrial, durable or consumer goods. The next stage is a forecast of anticipated total industry volume. This is followed by a company market forecast which takes specific account of those sections of the industry in which the company operates or intends to operate. Although a manufacturer produces solid fuel domestic boilers only, he must estimate what share of market is likely to go to competitive heating systems, e.g. gas, oil and electricity, in order to arrive at a forecast for solid fuel installations. If he produces all types of central heating equipment then the company market and industry forecast will be identical.

The importance of preparing general business or economic forecasts will depend on the individual company and the nature of its business. The sales of individual companies will be influenced to a greater or lesser degree by the general level of economic activity, industrial goods more so than consumer goods. The general business outlook should enter into every company's forecasting procedure at some stage since few companies are completely immune from outside influences. But the degree of detail and accuracy required in such forecasting is a matter which only the individual company can determine. Industry and market forecasts are certainly necessary but it has to be borne in mind that much industry and market data either does not exist or is not accessible to the individual company in usable form. The intelligent forecasting of company sales can only be based, however tentatively, on the industry or market potential.

Economic, industry and market forecasts can cover varying periods of time. There are no ideal time periods for forecasting purposes which are applicable to all companies or even to companies competing in the same industry or market. It is usual to distinguish between short-range, medium-range and long-range forecasts. A short-range forecast may be for three months to a year ahead, a medium-range forecast from one to five years ahead, a long-range forecast from five to twenty-five years ahead. Medium-range and, particularly, long-range forecasting are especially useful for industrial and consumer durable goods producers who must plan capacity requirements a long way ahead and for whom reliable estimates of economic growth and market growth potentials are of greater importance even than current conditions. In a sense, long-term forecasting charts the general direction in which the economy, an industry or a market or individual company is moving. Short-term forecasting aids day-to-day planning for the near future. Medium-term forecasting acts as a check-point indicating whether or not progress is being maintained along the long-term trend line or whether the long-range forecast needs revising. However, forecasts of whatever length are no more than working assumptions about future expectations and as such are only as good as the assumptions on which they are based. Frequent revision is not necessarily an indication of poor forecasting technique so much as a reflection of the need to take greater care in formulating assumptions and to work out their detailed implications. Forecasting can be a painful process, and greater skill will only come with practice and the critical review of past attempts. Company management must not be too impatient with the forecasters for there is no occupation more hazardous than that which attempts to project the business of the firm into a rapidly moving and rapidly changing future.

Typically, the responsibility for general business, industry and market forecasting usually rests with the company economist (if there happens to be one), the commercial research department or the marketing research department.

Preparing the Company Sales Forecast

The company sales forecast has been described as 'a market forecast, plus a sales goal in the expected market, based on carrying out successfully a sales plan for achieving a desirable and feasible degree of penetration into that market'.[1]

In other words, the manufacturer, having taken account of those sectors of the industry or market with which he is not in active direct competition, and having assessed the potential for his particular product in relation to

[1] B. E. Estes. 'What Management Expects of Forecasting.' Special Report No. 16. *Sales Forecasting: Uses, Techniques and Trends.* (American Management Association Inc. New York. 1956.) p. 13.

competitors' plans, so far as they are known, and customers' plans (particularly important in industrial marketing), must then decide on a specific sales target to aim for expressed in terms of unit volume or selling value and representing a certain percentage share of the total market.

Many companies are faced with the problem of having to prepare sales forecasts with only scant knowledge of the size of the industry or market or of the trends within it. This is certainly true for a wide range of industrial markets and for some consumer goods markets as well. Similarly, a completely new product for which no recognised market already exists presents additional problems for the sales forecaster. The word 'forecast' implies a precision which is lacking in a great many markets and where the manufacturer finds himself in the position of having to make his projection on the basis of the company's own past performance, competitors' expected performance, his customers' expected plans, and the scale of his own planned marketing effort.

Sales forecasting is normally the responsibility of sales and/or marketing management. In many companies the detailed work of preparing the forecast is done by the marketing research department, which is then reviewed and approved, with modifications perhaps, by the sales manager and chief marketing executive. The most important considerations are that the sales forecast should emanate from one source only, be it the sales manager, the marketing director or the market research manager, and that it should be reviewed and agreed by the heads of departments affected by it.

There are still strong differences of opinion on the degree to which the field selling organisation should participate in the preparation of sales forecasts. It is said that information provided by the salesman which will be useful in preparing the sales forecast is one thing but the final responsibility for actually making the forecast is quite another. Where detailed and specialised knowledge of customer or user-industries' plans are of critical importance, as with most industrial goods, then clearly the salesman must supply the necessary information on such plans and even participate in the forecasting process.

But, as a general rule, the final responsibility for preparing sales forecasts must rest with management because the salesmen themselves are frequently not temperamentally or technically equipped to objectively analyse sales data and make forecasts; they are also interested parties in the sales goals or quotas which must be achieved and may err on the side of over-optimism or pessimism, or may not be aware of other key factors influencing sales, i.e. economic, business and industry factors, as well as internal company factors.

A sales forecast serves a number of different purposes. First, it is the basis of the company's selling operations in the coming months and over the year. The sales budget and individual salesman's quotas are derived from it. Advertising and other promotional expenditures are planned on the basis of the forecast. The total forecast can be broken down into individual forecasts for each product, sales territory, type of customer or channel of distribution. Each sub-forecast can be broken down further—daily, weekly, monthly, quarterly and so on.

Second, a short-range sales forecast, looking several months ahead, is of great use for production scheduling and stock control. This avoids the unnecessary accumulation of stock and the tying-up of working capital in unwanted stocks of raw materials, semi-finished goods, finished goods and spare parts. Production schedules and stock levels should be related to expected sales rather than to actual sales. How far ahead the sales forecast will need to look will depend upon the length of the production cycle and the speed with which the company's suppliers can deliver the necessary materials and parts.

Third, an annual sales forecast covering the company's financial or marketing year is necessary for budgeting and profit-planning.

Fourth, the long-range company sales forecast is necessary for planning future requirements in terms of plant capacity, raw materials, manpower, service facilities, financial resources, research and development activity. Such a forecast may look five, ten or twenty years ahead depending on the nature of the company's business, its products, the age and economic life of its present plant and equipment. Manufacturers and suppliers of natural raw materials may need to look even further ahead taking into account the relative cost and accessibility of existing mineral and other resources, probable developments of competing or substitute resources, and the likely growth of demand by user-industries.

Finally, a realistic sales forecast can be of great importance in setting prices. Industrial producers supplying basic raw and semi-processed materials, such as chemicals, are very often able to adjust their prices 'dynamically' on the basis of the sales outlook.

Sales forecasting is essentially a tool of management, a planning and control instrument. The sales forecast and the budgets derived from it together delineate the company sales and profit goals, but these goals can only be achieved through the allocation of men, money, materials and time to the different tasks. A great deal, therefore, hangs on the sales forecast. How much time and effort should be devoted to forecasting activity will depend principally upon the degree of accuracy called for which, in turn, ultimately depends upon the effect on company profit of an error of any given size. The greater the reduction in profit arising from a minor shortfall in the forecast, the more time and effort it will be worth putting into the forecasting effort. The relative degree of accuracy attainable in practice is dependent upon the skill of the forecaster in formulating realistic assumptions and applying the correct statistical procedures and upon the availability of accurate data relevant to making the forecast. As regards the latter requirement, most industrial goods producers are at a disadvantage compared with consumer goods producers due to the comparative lack of accurate and sufficiently comprehensive information and to the greater inherent instability of industrial markets.

There is the same need to make adequate provision for the methodical review of sales forecasts as in the case of general business and market forecasts. The revision of a forecast once it has been made and found to be in error should not be looked upon as a failure on the part of the forecaster. The very fact that the factors underlying the initial forecast have changed—and the assumptions on which a forecast is based should *always* be explicitly stated—would be reason enough for having a forecast in the first place. The factors making for the change may be peculiar to the company or apply to the entire industry; or they may, in fact, be new factors affecting sales for the first time. These are important things for a company to know for it will then be better able to take account of the changed circumstances, adjust its policies accordingly and produce better forecasts.

Preparing the Company Sales Budget

The company sales budget is more than just a sales forecast. In quite simple terms, it relates what the company expects or plans to sell to the estimated cost of selling it and the likely profit to be made if things turn out as expected. It brings together two forecasts—of sales volume and of selling expenses—to produce a third forecast of profit on sales. Generally, there will be a consolidated sales budget made up of a number of individual budgets for each product or group of products.

For example, a food manufacturer, in addition to having a consolidated sales budget, may have separate budgets for canned goods, frozen goods, sausages and pies. The canned goods sales budgets may be in turn broken down into itemised product budgets as follows: canned peas, canned beans, canned spaghetti, canned peaches, canned pineapple. And similarly for frozen foods and sausages and pies. In each case, there may also be a separate catering trade sales budget where the company operates a catering sales force in addition to a retail selling force. The company sales budget is therefore a composite built up from individual product budgets, expressed both in units and value, and based on estimated sales by geographical territories, by class of customer or type of distribution channel, by month or by week during the coming year. Its purposes are to put into practical effect the declared sales policies of the company in terms of the specific sales goals to be achieved within fixed expenditure limits and the delivery of a predetermined rate of profit on sales. Responsibility for preparing, administering and controlling the sales budget lies with sales management under the direction of the chief marketing executive.

Typically, the annual sales budget for a given product will set out the sales volume forecast, the gross sales revenue, the total cost of goods, total selling expenses (i.e. sales force expenses, transport, warehousing, trade margins and discounts), the gross margin before advertising and promotion, general and administrative expenses and net profit.

Many companies prepare sales and profit forecasts for several years ahead, particularly when new products are being launched. In today's highly competitive markets, a new product may not produce a profit for a

Table 4. The Product Sales Budget

Sales Volume Forecast (Units or cases)	300,000
	£
Gross Sales Revenue	600,000
Total Cost of Goods	300,000
Total Selling Expenses	125,000
Gross Margin	175,000
Advertising and Promotion	100,000
General and Administrative Overhead	10,000
Net Profit before Tax	65,000

company in its early years and, therefore, estimated sales revenues and outgoings are projected in order to determine the point at which the product can be expected to break even and the length of the pay-out period. For a particular product moving from a loss-making situation towards a profit-making situation, the break-even point may be said to have been reached when, at a certain level of turnover, the total sales income and total costs associated with that level of turnover are more or less in balance. The pay-out period is the elapsed time required for cumulative sales revenue to equal the cumulative expenditures incurred for research and development, manufacturing, selling expenses, advertising and promotion, general and administrative expenses and overhead. In the following example, the break-even point is reached about the middle of Year 3 and the pay-out period is four years.

Table 5. Four-Year Sales and Profit Forecast

	Year 1	*Year 2*	*Year 3*	*Year 4*
	£'000	£'000	£'000	£'000
Gross Sales Revenue	240	300	375	425
Gross Margin	70	100	110	125
Advertising and Promotion	100	100	100	80
G. and A. Overhead	5	5	5	5
Net Profit (+) or Loss (−) before Tax	−35	−5	+5	+40
Cumulative Profit or Loss before Tax	−40	−45	−40	nil

It should be noted that the cumulative net loss at the end of the first year is £40,000 although the actual loss attritutable to the year's trading (the Gross Margin *less* advertising and promotional expenses and overhead) is only £35,000. The difference is due to the carrying-over of a £5000 loss incurred in the previous year in respect of certain non-recurring development and test market costs. It should also be noted that the ratio of Gross Margin to Gross Sales Revenue shows a significant rise in Year 2 due to a forecasted fall in the average cost of goods arising out of a particularly favourable forward purchase of the basic raw material used to make the product. In subsequent years, higher raw material and selling costs are expected to reduce the Gross Margin more or less to its former level.

The Establishment of Sales Quotas

In much the same way that a company plans to achieve a certain quota or share of the total market for its product in competition with other firms, so a sales quota is a quantitative sales task to be accomplished to a specified degree within a specified period of time by a salesman or group of salesmen. The setting of sales quotas is not simply a matter of dividing the company sales target by the number of salesmen which the company has. Each quota has to be tailored to the sales potential of the individual salesman, the area within which he works, the class of customers or type of distribution channel he has to deal with, the degree of local competition encountered, and local economic and business conditions. Individual quota-setting not only should be fair and equitable but should be seen to be fair and equitable, not in the sense that all salesmen have the same quota, but that each quota is related to individual potential and is capable of attainment. If quotas are set too low they will be too easily attained, and some loss of incentive and cost control will ensue. If set too high, quotas will cause discouragement and some ill-feeling, since a proportion of a salesman's earnings is frequently linked directly to the attainment of his sales quotas.

The objectives of setting sales quotas are to give effect to and implement the sales budget which aims at achieving a certain volume of sales at a given cost; to provide a means of planning and controlling the selling effort in line with budget and profit plans; to establish standards of performance for salesmen and provide incentive to achieve these standards; to provide a basis for the promotion and remuneration of salesmen.

Realistic sales quotas can be set to take account of one or any combination of the following factors:

Type and level of salesman	*e.g. Field supervisor, area manager, or salesman.*
Type of Distribution Channel/ Class of customer	*e.g. Wholesaler, multiple retailer, independent retailer, agent, factor, user-industry.*
Geographical	*e.g. Sales region, division or territory.*
Product	*e.g. Single product, line or range of products.*
Kind of activity	*e.g. New customer calls, number of demonstrations, new orders, repeat orders, building displays, special activities.*
Unit of measurement	*e.g. Volume (tons, gallons, yards, value).*
Basis of measurement	*e.g. Number of units of achievement, value of units of achievement, percentage over average or standard achievement, points value per unit of achievement.*

Time period	*e.g. Daily, weekly, monthly or annual.*
Basis of remuneration	*e.g. A fixed or variable sum of money paid according to an agreed basis of measurement (points earned, percentage achievement over quota, number or value of units sold over quota).*

Sales management is mainly responsible for the setting of all sales quotas and is wholly responsible for their attainment. If other departments, such as marketing research, are involved in setting quotas then it must be under the direction and supervision of the sales department, and subject to the latter's approval, rejection or modification. The ultimate success of any quota system will be determined, on the one hand, by sales management's ability to set realistic quotas in the sense of being attainable within the limitations of authorised budget expenditures and, on the other hand, by the speed with which actual results can be compared with targeted results, and appropriate action taken.

It all too frequently happens that sales management tries to hedge its bets by running two sales forecasts alongside one another, one of which is used for financial budgeting and control purposes and the other, usually less inhibited, for the purpose of setting sales quotas. The general tendency, however, is to have a single sales forecast and sales budget covering the entire company selling operation.

The prompt analysis of sales reports and regular comparison of cumulative actual results against forecast results, in the form of a 'rolling' sales budget, can do much to eliminate crises and hasty, ill-considered action in the face of shortfalls. If the planned-for sales do not materialise, there is often great pressure on sales management to increase the quotas for later periods and to provide special added incentives to the sales force to achieve and, if possible, exceed them. Such a policy will only succeed if the original quotas were set at a realistic and equitable level in the first place. Even if some part or the whole of a subsequent 'deficit' is to be made up, it may only be possible by increasing selling costs over and above what the budget allows for. In other words, although the original sales volume target can be achieved, the profit target cannot.

The setting of realistic performance targets in terms of units to be sold, buyer contacts to be made, demonstrations to be given, displays to be set up, etc. is a key element in sales planning to ensure that each individual salesman's effort is co-ordinated with that of his colleagues to achieve a defined company marketing task. A salesman left to work out his own targets will tend to allocate his time and effort in a way which will maximise his individual earnings in the short term. This will be the case particularly when a significant part of his earnings is made up of commission on the sales he makes. In such circumstances his efforts could be at variance with the aims of sales management. As a consequence, more companies are moving away from the fixed commission rate system linked directly to turnover and adopting instead a system based on a minimum basic salary and bonus incentive payments linked to the performance of specific sales tasks that cannot be directly related to turnover. Group bonus schemes are also being used increasingly to encourage the development of group sales activity and teamwork and to ensure the accomplishment of group tasks.

Selecting Distribution Channels

A manufacturer will seek to select that channel or restricted combination of channels open to him which provides the maximum sales volume at minimum cost in the long-term. In making his selection he will be guided by the size and accessibility of his consumer or user market, the periodicity of customer purchase and of stock-replacement by the distribution channel, the cost of transport, storage and stock maintenance, the traditional or prevailing level of distributors' margins, competitors' distribution policies, and the degree of technical knowledge needed to sell the product to the final user.

Thus, products which have a large consumer market, which are purchased with a relatively high degree of frequency and involve a minimum of technical knowledge in selling to the final user, can be sold through retailers dealing in the particular class of goods concerned, or from automatic vending machines, or direct to the customer door-to-door or through mail order. Manufacturers of such products, as a general rule, will choose the shortest available route between factory and user, since the purpose of distribution is to place the product with a minimum of delay where it stands the greatest ch ance of being bought. Hence cosmetics and toiletries are sold not only through grocers and chemists but also door-to-door. Cigarettes, books and magazines and sugar and chocolate confectionery are sold through a multiplicity of different types of retail outlets to meet the convenience of the consumer. Consumer durables such as washing machines, refrigerators and other appliances are sold door-to-door as well as through specialist retail outlets and department stores.

The pressure on firms to shorten the distribution route between factory and user, which reaches its ultimate form when a manufacturer's salesman confronts the prospective user face to face on his or her doorstep or in the home, usually stems from the need to reduce the costs of distribution through the elimination of wasteful movements and transfers of goods at intermediate points between the factory and the customer, and the desire to exert greater direct control over the market for the product. Such efforts are easier when large conglomerations of consumers are readily accessible in terms of their physical location, and the degree to which they can be influenced directly by the manufacturer to buy his product. Other things being equal, it will be easier for a manufacturer to reduce the distribution gap between himself and his potential market if he can readily identify that market and reach it economically with his sales and advertising messages. It is then up to the manufacturer through personal selling and advertising to persuade potential customers that it is more convenient, less time-consuming, cheaper or, what amounts to the same thing, better value to buy his product in this way rather than an alternative product in some other way.

Direct contact between a consumer goods manufacturer and his retail customers enables the former to gauge his distribution levels more accurately, to keep stock levels at a maximum and to apply additional stock pressure when necessary. It enables him to obtain more effective and more continuous point-of-sale display for his product and quicker distribution of new or improved products.

However, it would not be worth while, from the profit point of view, for a producer of canned foods, say, to supply every grocer in the country direct. The cost of making up some orders, of shipping them, and of obtaining payment would be unprofitable in relation to their size This arises because a relatively small proportion of the grocers in Great Britain account for a very large percentage of the total value of sales. The A. C. Nielsen Company has estimated that in 1964 less than 20% of all the retail grocery outlets in the country, representing some 28,500 shops, accounted for 51% of total grocery sterling turnover.

CHART 24. LONG-TERM TRENDS IN SHARES OF GROCERY TURNOVER

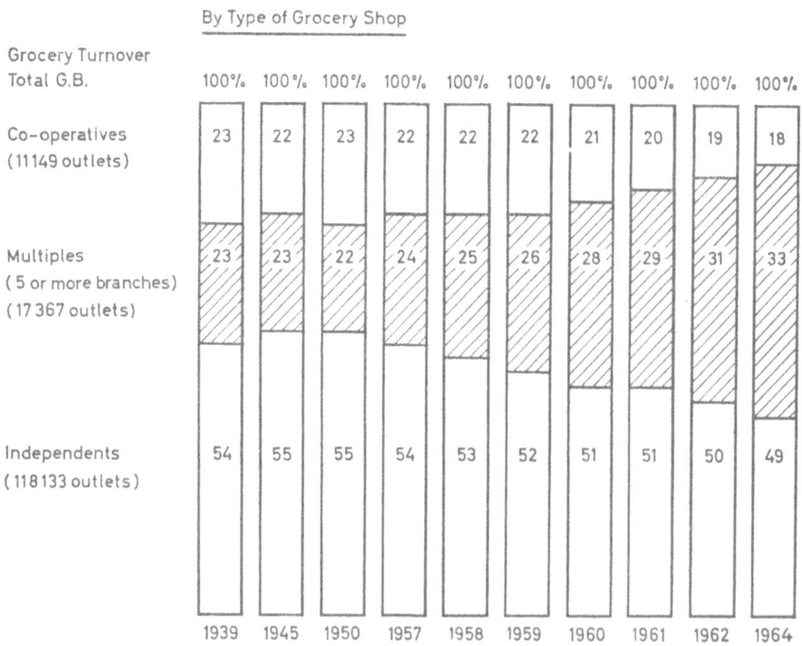

Source: Jeffrey's ***Retail Trading Prior to 1950***
Neilsen Food Index and Board of Trade.

It is estimated[1] that in 1964 about 76% of total grocery business in Great Britain could be reached through less than 1,600 trade buying points servicing some 75,000 shops or a little under half of all grocers. These 75,000 shops comprised members of multiple groups (with five or more branch shops), retail co-operative societies and independent grocers affiliated to voluntary wholesaler-retailer groups and chains and retail buying groups.

Most manufacturers operating in the grocery and chemist fields organise their distribution on a selective basis. This simply means 'fishing where the fish are' by maintaining direct contact with those shops which account for the bulk of the trade in their particular product classes and employing wholesalers to cover the remainder. Theoretically, a sales force of forty senior sales negotiators could call on the key central buying points and independent wholesalers on average once every four weeks, assuming an average of five calls per working day per salesman. A supporting merchandising force of 100 display representatives could cover about 24,000 shops (one out of every three key outlets) every six weeks assuming an average of eight merchandising calls per day per representative.

Implementation of Selling and Merchandising Plans

The great majority of manufacturers organise their selling activities on a regular sales journey cycle basis. A sales journey cycle is the period of time needed to complete all the sales calls on the company's customers at least once. For most fast-moving consumer products the typical journey cycle averages between four and six weeks. The actual length of the cycle will depend on the product itself (perishable items may require weekly and sometimes daily sales and delivery calls) and on the type of retail outlet (more frequent calls being made on the larger and more important customers with a faster turnover and less frequent calls on the smaller and medium turnover outlets).

The following pattern is not uncommon in the grocery field:

Multiples and Co-operative Head offices	—once every two weeks
Voluntary Groups and Chains	—once every two weeks
Large and Medium Independents	—once every four weeks
Small Independents	—once every 6–8 weeks
Independent Wholesalers	—once every 2–4 weeks

The time element plays a critical part in all marketing problems, changes in one factor having repercussions on other factors either instantaneously or after some lag of time. Such time lags can be of fundamental importance. Consider, for example, the effect of time lags on sales resulting from the interplay of distribution, advertising and in-store promotion and display. Theoretically, variations in sales results are possible according to the time relationships between these three factors alone. Potential sales can

[1] *The Nielsen Researcher*. Oxford edition. A. C. Nielsen Company. March–April 1965.

be lost as a result of premature advertising unsupported by adequate retail distribution and display activity; or due to the product being in stock but not widely known about as a result of delayed advertising; or due to too little stock being sold in relation to the level of demand created by a particularly heavy advertising campaign.

To ensure the effective co-ordination and integration of the total marketing effort, sales force briefings, sales quotas, distribution targets, sales promotion and advertising plans must be geared to the journey cycle.

The following is an illustration of a typical selling-in plan for a new packaged food product introduced for the first time, let us say, early in 1965. It is assumed that the company operates a six-week sales journey cycle.

Table 6. Typical Selling-In Schedule

Regional Sales Managers' Briefing	19th December 1964
National Sales Conference	2nd January 1965
Selling-in Begins	4th January 1965
Wholesale Bonus Begins	4th January 1965
Multiple and Co-operative Bonus Begins	18th January 1965
Advertising Breaks	22nd January 1965
Wholesale Bonus Ends	30th January 1965
Special Display Drive Begins	8th February 1965
Multiple and Co-operative Bonus Ends	13th February 1965
End of 1st Sales Journey Cycle	13th February 1965
1st Burst of Advertising Ends	1st March 1965
End of 2nd Sales Journey Cycle	27th March 1965

On Saturday, 19th December 1964, marketing and sales management executives met with the six regional field sales managers in the sales office of the Midland Sales Manager and presented the company's plans for the launching of the new product. Regional targets were discussed, advertising plans presented, specimens of the display material to be supplied were shown, and trade bonus terms explained.

At a national sales conference held in London the total marketing plan was presented to the company's 120 sales representatives. The new product was unveiled, consumer product research findings were shown in chart form, advertising and sales promotional plans presented on film, and trade bonus terms and distribution targets announced. The conference then broke up into a series of smaller regional meetings at which the Regional Sales Manager presented to his own group of salesmen complete details of the selling-in plan, the time schedule, individual salesmen's quotas and distribution targets. Minimum distribution targets were set at 75% of all multiple and co-operatives, 40% of all large and medium independents and 50% of all wholesalers during the first sales journey cycle. Details were given of a special display drive to be concentrated in the shops during the period 8th February–27th March, and supported by trade bonuses and a continuous period of heavy TV and press advertising from 25th January to 1st March. Display material included a cardboard dump display floor bin, a special sell-out counter display unit containing six packs and a recipe leaflet dispenser. During the four-week period 4th–30th January a stocking bonus of 1*s*. 6*d*. a case and a movement bonus of another 1*s*. 6*d*. per case of product moved out to the retailer over the period was paid to all wholesalers. A bonus of 3*s*. per case was paid on all orders placed by multiple and co-operatives during the four weeks 18th January–13th February.

Merchandising is the sum total of effort to move goods at the point of sale through the exploitation of the product, its packaging, pricing, display material, and any related special consumer buying incentives. Merchandising, in this sense, only takes place at the actual point of sale. A manufacturer can suggest ideas for merchandising and can supply materials in support of merchandising activity but the *sole* responsibility for merchandising rests with the distributive outlet. To merchandise means literally 'to expose goods for sale' using whatever devices seem most likely to induce a sale. The most basic form of merchandising is, of course, display of the product itself. Branding and advertising and, more recently, self-service retailing have each had a tremendous impact on merchandising technique in relation to consumer goods.

The development of this technique has made the greatest demands on product presentation and packaging design. In particular, with the growing importance of self-service retailing and, consequently, of the display factor, the package has had to take over a major part of the selling task previously undertaken by the retailer. Hence, modern packaging has been described, with some justice, as 'the silent salesman'. The burden of communicating to the potential buyer what the product is and does, why it is better than some other competing or substitute product, how much it costs and why it represents better value for the money spent and so on, has come to rest more and more on the package itself.

The planned selling effort of the sales force armed with product information, selling aids, display materials, trade incentives and any special promotions, is the basic selling-in process. Its object is to move the product towards the final user. The aim of consumer advertising and consumer promotions is to move consumers towards the goods available. The function of merchandising is to bring the two together—customers and products—in a buying situation that provides the maximum opportunity to make a final sale.

Merchandising, therefore, is essentially a selling-out process, and is specific to each distributive outlet. Every other activity—personal selling, advertising, trade and consumer promotions—carried out by the manufacturer and distributor is designed to bring about the confrontation of well-displayed products and potential customers favourably pre-disposed towards the products through advertising and special buying inducements of one sort or another. In the chain of responses that leads to the final sale of a product, the last and most vital link is point-of-sale merchandising.

So far as the great majority of consumer goods is concerned, the public buys only what it can see. Customers do not make a bee-line for a particular manufacturer's brand of product nor are they usually thinking nice things about his product either before or after they enter a shop. In today's self-service store or supermarket, out-of-sight means out-of-mind. Only when the product is *conspicuously* available is the advertising seen for it likely to begin to take effect. If the product is part of a prominent display sited at a key traffic point in the shop, if it is linked to a special promotion or 'selling event', and carries an offer or suggests a new idea for use, then the chances of making a sale are considerably greater than for a competing product which is not plainly visible and carries no special inducement to buy.

Consumer goods merchandising uses a variety of special attention-getting devices or events, e.g. National Dairy Week, Ritz Crackers and Nescafé related-item promotion at a special reduced price, a free plastic rose with every packet of Daz detergent, a '2-for-the-price-of-1' banded soup offer, a 'Dream House' or 'Summer Cruise' competition for a breakfast cereal, etc. All these activities are designed to add that extra interest or difference that will attract attention, provide consumer appeal and stimulate buying action. Most of the larger multiple organisations and wholesaler-retailer voluntary groups plan their promotional and merchandising activities months ahead so that a manufacturer is likely to find that he no longer has the same freedom to pick and choose his own time for running a promotion. Hence the need for forward promotional planning by the manufacturer if he is to obtain regular display and merchandising for his products.

The manufacturer will obviously initiate and continue to be a major source of merchandising and promotional ideas, materials and services through his own sales organisation. He will seek to strengthen his links with his retail customers by giving technical advice on general store merchandising policy including such things as shop-layout and fitments, and the allocation of stockroom, shelf and display space. However, the big retail organisations and voluntary wholesaler-retailer groups and chains have themselves become increasingly merchandising-minded and plan and organise the merchandising activities for all their members on a continuous basis as well as providing financial and technical assistance. Many of them devise their own consumer promotions and integrate them with manufacturers' promotions. Backed by a massive concentration of buying power, they are very often in a position to negotiate exclusive promotions and terms with individual manufacturers.

Scientific stock control, better shop-space management, i.e. allocating shelf and display space on the basis of product sales performance and profit contribution, are adding considerable strength and bargaining power to the large distributor *vis-à-vis* the manufacturer. Much retailer-inspired merchandising has as its main objective the attraction of more customers into the particular outlet rather than a short-term lift in the sales of a particular manufacturer's brand. The latter may be of assistance to the retailer in achieving the longer-term objective of increasing average store-traffic but many other methods are open to him.

The development of self-service retailing and cash-and-carry wholesaling are, fundamentally, applications of a basic merchandising technique. Self-service retailing makes it easier for the customer to identify, select and buy the items of his choice. It makes it easier for the display- and promotion-minded retailer to increase his turnover and profitability through a reduction in wage costs relative to his total costs and through the promotion and display of both manufacturers' brands and specially packed own-label brands carrying higher profit margins.

The use of 'loss leaders' i.e. well-known brands of products in general consumption, such as sugar, which are marked down below cost to attract passing shoppers, the provision of credit facilities, dividends on purchases, and trading stamps are a few examples of some of the methods used.

The sales force of any consumer goods manufacturer has two major responsibilities. First, it must obtain and maintain a required level of retail distribution for the full line of products. The A. C. Nielsen Company has carried out research[1] showing that two out of three consumers of food products in grocers buy a substitute brand when the brand they want is not in stock. The other third try somewhere else or defer buying. Among non-food products in grocers a slightly lower proportion [60%] will accept a substitute brand. Clearly, therefore, it is the sales force's first task to see that the products of the company are available wherever they are most likely to be bought by consumers. Thus, the penalties a manufacturer incurs if his product is even temporarily out-of-stock can be serious not only for the manufacturer but also for the retailer himself. More than this, the manufacturer and retailer must also ensure that a representative range of sizes is held in stock since the same research study indicates that only about two out of every three consumers not finding the size they want buy another size of the *same* brand. Over a third buy the same size of another brand, go elsewhere or do not buy at all.

What these figures do not reveal, however, is what happens when a particular manufacturer's brand is in stock but not on display or is poorly displayed and promoted in relation to competitors' showings. In other words, even a respectable in-stock distribution is not enough by itself.

The second major responsibility of the sales force, therefore, is to achieve 'on-display' distribution. This is the task of merchandising whether it be manufacturer-inspired or retailer-inspired or, as it should be, the results of a joint effort by both manufacturer and retailer. A number of factors are combining to make new demands on the manufacturer's traditional selling skills and resources. The main ones are the emergence of new forms of distributive organisation and retailing methods, the growing concentration of trade purchasing power in fewer hands and the trend towards top-level directorial negotiation between manufacturers and multiple- and group-buying head offices. By means of the application of

[1] 'The High Cost of Brand Absenteeism.' *The Nielsen Researcher*. Oxford edition. A. C. Nielsen Company. May–June 1963.

automatic data processing at central buying office and warehouse levels, the increasing sophistication of distributors in the arts of group merchandising and promotion planning, and the application of scientific methods to warehouse and shop-space management, the large-scale distributor is showing every sign of redressing the balance of negotiating advantage which has hitherto tended to be with the larger manufacturers.

These developments do not mean any diminution in the importance of the manufacturer's selling function but rather a transition from the traditional type of order-taking sales force to a two-tier structure consisting of high-level sales negotiators and teams of merchandising representatives to back them up and follow through. The former talk products and promotions with multiple head office and group buyers and negotiate orders and promotional arrangements. The effective selling time spent face to face with the buyer or buying committee must be put to the most profitable use through planned sales presentations by top-level sales transactors with full on-the-spot authority to negotiate large-scale deals.

Once the order has been placed and the promotional arrangements authorised, the merchandising teams move into action. At the retail level, it is their job to check stock levels and the condition of stocks, to explain to individual shop managers the details of the current or planned promotional schemes agreed with Head Office, to evaluate shop display opportunities and develop display differentiation for the company's products by suggesting how displays should be laid out and where they should be sited. In other words, it is their essential task to help the retailer in every way possible to move off the shelves and out of the shop what has been previously sold-in by the manufacturer.

The modern merchandising representative must, therefore, understand retail shop management and operating problems, must be trained to interpret the company's sales and promotional plans and policies in terms of the retailers' own problems and interests, and must talk to the progressive retailer in terms he understands—about product throughput and related-item promotions linking the company's own product with complementary products, about profits per square foot of floor-space or per linear foot of shelf-space, about rates of stockturn and stock rotation.

The demands imposed on manufacturers to meet present-day marketing requirements call for creative ingenuity and planning skill of a high order, not only with respect to sales promotion and merchandising schemes but also to the manner in which they are presented and communicated down through the chain of distribution to the final consumer. The growing number of such schemes with which the average trade buyer is confronted daily not only taxes his abilities, and perhaps his patience as well, but also places an enormous strain on the manufacturer's own planning abilities and communication skills. Breaking through the competitive 'noise barrier' and putting selling and promotional ideas across to the minds of salesmen, wholesalers and retailers with enthusiasm and conviction is the task of good *sales communications*.

Sales Communications

Everyone at some time or another has played the party game in which a message is whispered down a line of people from one to the next. The original message hardly ever reaches its final destination in recognisable form. A similar sort of thing can happen in selling. Sales messages can fade as they pass from man to man and from distribution channel to distribution channel. Loss of urgency and impact, omission of important detail, distortion, memory lapse, misinterpretation can be the consequences of unplanned sales communication.

Sales communication is the communication of any information, verbal or visual, which is intended to motivate and secure the active support and co-operation of anyone connected in any way with the distribution and sale of a company's products or services. It is concerned with the presentation of sales arguments by company personnel to and through those whom the company wishes to stock and sell its products. It covers all types of sales presentations (to groups of people within the company itself, to distributors and other interested groups outside it), sales briefings and conferences, sales letters and bulletins, sales training manuals, advertising specifically aimed at distributors, trade and distributor catalogues and other forms of dealer literature, salesmen's portfolios and sample cases, direct mail to distributors and trade exhibition material. The purpose of planned sales communication is to project a consistent and strong selling story to and through the company sales organisation and the trade.

Sales communication is an integral part of the overall marketing plan. It sets out what has to be said, to whom, when and by whom. It must relate to and reinforce the basic selling objectives laid out in the marketing plan. It must be oriented towards the seller, take account of the seller's problems and talk the seller's language. This applies whether it is a management presentation to the sales force, a sales demonstration to distributors, or a direct mail shot to retailers. Any weakening in the strength of the sales message at any single point down the line is a communication loss which the manufacturer pays for as surely as he pays for inefficiency in production or advertising.

Company marketing and selling plans must be 'pre-sold' to everyone inside the organisation concerned with their implementation. If sales personnel are to put a maximum effort behind these plans and work loyally and enthusiastically as members of a team, then they must be convinced of the soundness of the plans, that the targets they have been set are realistic and attainable, and that they are going to get all the help they need in the way of sales aids, advertising and sales promotion material.

National and regional sales conferences are the formal occasions for presenting the company's plans to all members of the sales organisation. Such occasions provide the opportunity to mount a carefully rehearsed and stage-managed presentation to the sales force. The business of organising and staging a sales conference is now a highly skilled and specialised art calling on the services of professional sales conference planners with an arsenal of dramatic techniques and attention-getting devices at their command. Some sales conferences make use of professional actors, singers, female models and well-known public personalities. It would be quite wrong to suppose that they are introduced purely for their entertainment value. On the contrary, the serious intent of the occasion is never lost sight of and the skilful use of professionals can do much to get the main points of the conference programme over to a receptive audience. Company executives are often assiduously coached and rehearsed for their parts in the proceedings by the conference producer. Theatrical productions, films, tape recordings, panels of speakers, brains trusts, and a wide variety of visual aids are frequently used for sales conference purposes.

Quite apart from these big annual get-togethers in some large hotel ballroom or banqueting room, there must be facilities and procedures for communicating selling plans, tasks and instructions on a more or less continuous all-year-round basis. Regular communication between senior marketing and sales management and regional sales managers and supervisors by personal visits to and from Head Office, by telephone or in writing, is of great importance if the latter are to be clear in their own minds as to company plans and policies. Opportunities to discuss and exchange views are essential to the development of sound workable plans and their effective implementation in the field.

Many companies regard their regional sales managers and field supervisors as the main channel of communication with the sales representatives and, therefore, directly responsible for briefing the men under their control. In these circumstances, communication between the General Sales Manager and the representatives is kept to an absolute minimum unless, of course, the sales force is fairly small. Regional sales managers should be in regular contact with their field supervisors either by letter, telephone or visits. Both should know of each other's movements and those of the representatives in their charge so that they can be contacted at any time.

Local sales meetings of representatives will normally be the responsibility of the regional sales manager or field supervisor. At these meetings, plans will be outlined, tasks assigned, and instructions given in detail to the representatives. It is at this point that the efficiency of the sales communication process will receive its first major test and the outcome will depend on the thoroughness of the earlier presentations and briefings given to regional managers and supervisors by higher management. A communication failure or loss at this stage can be absolutely critical, for the loss in communication effectiveness down through the chain of distribution is a compound process. At each succeeding level of distribution the sales message will be still further diluted either through lack of proper selling aids, omission of important detail, inadequate preparation, bad presentation technique or lack of conviction and enthusiasm.

That this is not an overstatement of the problem is evidenced by the fact that independent estimates of the wastage of sales promotion and merchandising equipment and materials in the grocery field range from

65% to 80%. One firm of marketing consultants has reported[1] that a survey of 1,500 salesmen in the food and off-licence fields revealed that 1,300 were not aware of their company's advertising and promotion policies; out of 800 who had been provided with the conventional folder of advertisement pulls, only thirty-six had them in their cars at the time the survey was carried out and only a handful actually used them as part of their sales presentation.

Hence it is vital that regional sales managers and field supervisors should receive adequate practical training in communication with particular regard to verbal and visual presentation techniques, the organising and chairing of meetings, the writing-up of the minutes of meetings and the preparation of written reports. Just as important is the proper training of sales representatives in proven selling techniques, i.e. methods of presentation and selling psychology, ways of handling and influencing customers and overcoming their resistances. The fast-moving, fast-talking, dynamic nature of selling and the geographical spread of the sales organisation throughout the country makes communication much more difficult than in the factory. All the more imperative, therefore, that sales management should take steps to plan and improve the quality of its sales communications.

Sales Reporting

Sales managers, sales supervisors and salesmen, to carry out their work effectively, must do a certain amount of report writing and while it may only be a fractional part of their responsibilities, it is an important part. The primary job of the sales organisation is to achieve the company's required sales volume and the achievement of this task should not be jeopardised by overloading sales personnel with demands for unnecessary or complex reports. Therefore, sales management will want to keep paperwork to the absolute minimum necessary and the actual reporting system as simple and straightforward as possible.

The sales organisation is both a provider and user of information. The field salesman is a basic source of information of vital importance to company planning and control. This information must be communicated upward to management and the latter, in turn, must supply the salesman with information that will enable him to do a better and more intelligent selling job.

The kind of information requested and supplied by management depends upon the position of the supplier or recipient in the organisation. Generally speaking, the minimum detail necessary for making planning and control decisions is required by top marketing management. Whereas top management is more concerned with the broad picture, middle and junior management executives are necessarily involved in the detailed administration of day-to-day operations. Moving down through the organisation the

[1] Sales Audits International Ltd. January 1964.

amount of necessary detail tends to increase as operational responsibilities become more detailed. There is at the same time, however, a compensating reduction in the scope of information required by the individual executive.

Marketing management requires selective, summarised information on cumulative performance to date against planned performance—that is, sales results, selling and other marketing costs, distribution achievement, market trends, etc. It will also want early warning of significant deviations from plan, competitive data on new or improved products, new packaging, new advertising, new special promotional activities and test market developments. The sales manager will want to know how the sales force is performing by products, by regions and by class of trade or outlet-type in relation to quotas and budgets; he will want information to help him keep a running check on the cost of getting sales. The field supervisor will want more detailed information than his sales manager on the performance of the individual salesman under his control—information telling him how well the salesman's territory is being covered, how many calls are being made each day, how many new sales prospects have been contacted, whether the representative is working a planned route, whether the representative is using a planned sales presentation and making use of the visual aids supplied by the company, and whether he is obtaining the necessary quantity and quality of point-of-sale displays. The supervisor will also want to check on the progress of new men recently introduced into the territory to see whether they need help and further training.

The individual salesman is the source of all sales data up the line. The raw data are subjected to varying degrees of summarisation as they pass to the field sales supervisor to sales manager to marketing manager. However, in summarising the data any deviation from plan must be accompanied by an explanation of the actual or probable cause. Information must be presented in sufficient detail to enable the responsible manager on the spot to take a sound decision.

For example, if sales in a certain territory are well down on quota it may be because a new competitive product has been introduced into a test market, or a new competitive advertising campaign or special consumer offer is being run; or because the territory is being worked by a new and still fairly green trainee salesman who replaced the company's elder and senior salesman recently deceased. Alternatively, a report that selling expenses in a certain area of the country have gone down by 10% over a period may not be so commendable if one of the five representatives working the territory has been ill in hospital for several months and sales during the same period have fallen by 20%.

In short, any report must provide the relevant information and an interpretation of the facts on which management can make a judgment and take action. In more and more companies, sales reporting goes beyond the mere forwarding-on of expected information on pre-printed report forms. Even at the sales representative level, the principle of reporting by exception is being applied so as to focus management's attention on the more urgent problems arising out of the unanticipated occurrence or unforeseen development.

Reporting, like all forms of communication, is a two-way process. Not only must information be reported up the line to management but, equally important, information must be reported down the line from management so that managers and executives are kept in the picture as fully as their position and responsibilities require, know the reactions of supervisors to their own reports and efforts, and know what is expected of them.

Everyone needs to be motivated to do a better job and the feedback of information, suggestions and instructions is a vitally important part of the process. The Sales Manager wants to hear from top management whether the sales results he is providing are in line with the company's overall financial targets and cost budgets and what, if any, are the areas of sales operation causing the most concern. The regional sales manager or field sales supervisor wants to hear from the Sales Manager how his performance compares with the quotas set for him and with the performance of other regional managers and supervisors. The sales representative wants to know where he stands in the regional and national sales league table, how his results measure up against his quota and against what he achieved the previous year, how much commission or bonus payment he has earned, how his sales group is doing compared with groups in other parts of the country. He also wants tangible evidence that all the hours he spends on paperwork, usually at home, are appreciated, that the information he is asked to supply is of real value and is being used, that suggestions are being acted upon and requests followed up.

There are literally thousands of different sales reporting forms in current use. Mainly they consist of variations of a few dozen basic report forms tailored to the particular requirements of the individual company. There is no ideal sales reporting system and no collection of ideal report forms applicable to all companies. Differences in company structures, products, marketing policies, distribution methods and sales organisations have to be taken into account in framing the sales reporting procedures and report forms most suited to the particular circumstances. The most important thing is that whatever reporting system is devised should meet the information needs of the business at every point in the organisation where someone has to take a decision and should provide that degree of detail which is necessary for taking a sound decision.

The following, in brief outline, are typical examples of some of the basic report requirements commonly used to transmit sales data up the line to management from the field.

Journey Plan Sheet—This sets out day-by-day for a week, or in some cases for as long as a month, the area or towns that the salesman intends to work. It may also include details of the actual calls he plans to make or for which appointments have been made and the addresses at which he can be contacted. This is sent in to his regional supervisor a week or more in advance of the itinerary. In this way the salesman is encouraged to plan his sales journey ahead of time and in a logical travel sequence.

A recent survey by a firm of management consultants,[1] based on an investigation of twenty-four sales forces, indicated that a typical salesman in the consumer goods field spends only 16% of his working day actually selling his company's product, that is, in the presence of buyers. 50% of his time is spent calling on buyers, 39% in travelling, and 11% on lunch, etc. Of the 50% spent calling on buyers, two-fifths were spent waiting for the interview, one-third in social talk and filling orders and less than one-third in effective selling. Taking an average cost to the company of keeping a salesman on the road to be £2,435 per annum (the average figure quoted in the survey for 710 salesmen), then the cost per working day, on a 220 working-day basis, was approximately £11 per salesman and, on the basis of nine calls per day, a little under 25/– per call.

Hence the need to reduce travelling time and increase the effective selling time by planning sales journeys and calling cycles. The more effective time-management of the sales organisation is probably the most pressing sales management problem since it is an immediate means of reducing the cost of selling and of bettering sales results.

It is not enough for sales management to know where the salesman plans to be. It also wants to have the particulars of every call he makes. The daily call report was devised for this purpose.

The Daily Call Report—The tests of the effective use of a salesman's time, and more especially of the time he spends in front of prospective buyers, are (1) the itemised list of calls he makes during the day by the class of customer or type of outlet, (b) the number of orders he takes as a percentage of calls made, (c) the average size of order taken, (d) the number of new customer accounts opened, (e) the number of customer accounts lost or not re-ordering. All of this is entered on the salesman's Daily Call Report sent in to Head Office and/or the regional supervisor at the end of each day's work. Other information may be provided such as number of product samples left with the buyers, quantity of point-of-sale display material left, physical displays erected at the time of call, specific customer complaints, car mileage and special information on competitive activity.

Call reports can cover single visits or a complete day's work. Some companies require both, the first report giving full details of each visit, the second giving a statistical summary of all the day's visits to buyers. With industrial goods, in particular, call reports of each visit may require elaborate detail giving names of all the people interviewed, specification requirements, and instructions to sales, engineering or service departments at Head Office.

[1] Sales Audits Ltd. A survey on *The Effectiveness of Sales Forces*. London 1963.

Customer Record Card—This is a permanent record of the business done with each customer for every journey cycle. It will normally show the name and address of the customer, his classification and grade, the name of the salesman, his territory and area. Order details are entered against the list of products at each call. Any changes in ownership, management, trade classification and status are recorded. The card provides the salesman with a continuous summary of the customer's order record which should be consulted before each call. It shows both the salesman and his management whether the company is doing more or less business with each customer over any given period. These cards are normally sent in to Head Office after each call for statistical control purposes.

Weekly Activity Summary Report—This is a statistical summary of the week's work by each salesman and will usually show for each day of the week and in total the number of calls made, the ratio of orders to calls, type of order, average size of order by volume and value, number of new customer accounts opened, number of customer accounts lost or not re-ordering and details of display activity as above. The report goes to the regional supervisor and/or Head Office.

Vehicle Record—This is submitted weekly or fortnightly by each representative and provides a daily record of opening and closing mileage, business and personal mileage and petrol consumed.

Expense Claim Form—This is submitted weekly or fortnightly by each representative and gives details of all expenses incurred in the course of his work. Daily allowances, hotel expenses, entertainment, car expenses (oil, maintenance, washing and petrol charges where a credit-card system is not in use) and miscellaneous charges are entered on the form. Some companies do not operate an expense-by-claim system. Instead a fixed expenses allowance is allocated per man but usually he is required to render an account of how it has been disbursed.

Other forms used by the representative, depending on individual company practice, include variants of Customer Complaint and Investigation Report, Customer Service Report, New Customer Report, Customer Closure Report, Competitive Activity Report, etc.

Generally speaking, the larger the company the greater the number of reporting levels is likely to be. Again, the greater the technical complexity of the company's products, the fewer levels there are likely to be. For example, in a large consumer goods company, where the sales reporting procedure may be from salesman to regional or district supervisor to area or branch manager to general sales manager, the executive at each level will be concerned with collating and summarising the reports of subordinates. Thus, the regional supervisor will summarise the call reports of the representatives in his region and the results achieved against quota. He will report on business prospects, local trading conditions, contacts with important or special customers, field accompaniment with his representatives or on any product or marketing problem in which his management is currently particularly interested.

These reports are normally presented weekly or monthly. The area or branch manager will then summarise their contents and the area reports, in turn, will be collated and analysed by executives in the office of the general sales manager so that a national picture can be built up. Reports from the field selling organisation may not give the complete sales picture. To the orders coming in from salesmen must be added any postal or telephone orders. For many companies customers' orders received directly at Head Office account for a significant part of the turnover.

Many large customers prefer to have their requirements dealt with at source and their buyers may be in frequent telephone contact with the headquarters' sales office. Selling by telephone either between salesmen's calls or, as with some of the smaller outlets, in place of the salesmen's calls, is tending to become more important in the consumer goods field particularly with perishable commodities requiring frequent delivery to and close stock control in the sales outlet, e.g. ice-cream, frozen foods and fresh meats.

Much of the information obtained at the various supervisory levels, however, is not of a statistical nature. A considerable amount of the regional or district supervisor's time is spent on accompanying their subordinates for training and assessment purposes. One of management's prime concerns and responsibilities is the training and evaluation of sales personnel.

Statistical Sales Control

Different people within the company need sales information for different purposes. Not all of the incoming reports or the whole of the contents of each individual report are relevant to the various people and departments who will receive them. The needs of the sales department, the production department, the financial department, the market research department and the advertising and sales promotion department are all different.

The sales department needs information to evaluate actual against planned performance, to see how results compare against quotas and how actual costs compare with budgets, and to control the overall distribution and selling effort. The production department needs sales and stock information in order to schedule manufacturing programmes. The financial department needs data for cost-control purposes. The advertising and sales promotion department is responsible for controlling the advertising and display effort and for seeing that adequate materials are available and being used. The market research department wants detailed information to help it with its market analyses and forecasts, and its assessment of competitors' activities. In contrast to the typically decentralised sales organisation there is, therefore, a need for centralised statistical control.

The purpose of statistical control is to provide adequate warning of any significant deviations from selling plans and budgets so that additional pressure can be applied where needed or plans and budgets revised to take account of any new factors arising. A plethora of graphed and tabulated sales reports and analyses can be produced with the aid of modern techniques and equipment. The selection of the information to be presented is all-important and is determined by the needs of the user. Top management requires, with the minimum amount of detail, information on the total operating results of the company—sales revenue, costs, profits or losses. Only major deviations from plan need be brought to its attention, detailed control being the responsibility of the managers of the operating divisions.

Review of Manpower Performance

In addition to studying itinerary sheets, daily call reports, expense claim forms and the like in the normal way, sales management must know how well each man is performing his job, whether or not he is being properly supervised and motivated and is receiving and responding to training. New sales representatives must be recruited, selected and trained up to the required standard of competence. The performance of sales representatives and supervisors must be kept under constant review for purposes of promotion to positions of greater responsibility within the organisation.

So far as recruitment of salesmen is concerned, most companies advertise for applicants internally and externally and the initial screening of candidates will usually be carried out by the field sales supervisor or area manager or both together. Short-listed candidates will then be interviewed by the General Sales Manager with the supervisor or area manager usually present, and a final selection made. It is customary to use rating forms in the selection procedure by which candidates are allotted marks or graded for personal appearance, physical characteristics, voice, poise, ease of expression, self-confidence, intelligence, ambition and experience. In some large companies, field sales management do not get involved in either recruitment or selection, this being the job of the Sales Manager and/or Personnel Manager. However, at some stage, field management should be allowed some say in the final selection to ensure that the chosen candidate is acceptable to his immediate superior.

Once recruited the new salesman will normally go through a period of company indoctrination and on-the-job training under the direction of his field supervisor or a sales training executive. The latter will accompany the representative and demonstrate how he should tackle his job. The representative will then work on his own and subsequently will be revisited by his supervisor on as many occasions as are felt to be necessary. After each field accompaniment the field supervisor submits a report to his area manager and/or General Sales Manager using a special pre-printed Training Report form. These are used to assess the representative's strong and weak points, and provide a continuing check on his development and improvement in terms of (a) his specific selling abilities, i.e. journey planning, sales preparation, selling approach, sales presentation, product knowledge, use of selling aids, closing the sale and getting the order, standard of sales reporting, expense control, etc., and (b) his personal attributes, i.e. enthusiasm, conviction, tenacity, adaptability, initiative, punctuality, organising ability, general appearance and state of equipment and materials.

The evaluation of salesmen is a continuing major responsibility of the field supervisor (i) to determine the suitability of the new salesman after initial training and the need for further training, (ii) to compare actual against required performance and against the performance of other salesmen, (iii) to determine suitability for promotion. Such assessments may be required annually, or half-yearly. An initial assessment is normally carried out three months after a representative's appointment to a territory.

The performance of field supervisors and district managers must also be evaluated by higher management. This is done by analysing records of achievement and by personal field visits by area managers or the General Sales Manager. Objective criteria by which the performance of supervisory tasks can be judged include the following:

Territory Development in terms of increased sales volume (or well-maintained sales volume in the face of a total market decline), reduced costs or greater profitability of sales, number of new customer accounts opened and held, improved quality of distribution, build-up of optimum stock-levels, more and better product displays, better use of sales promotion and display material.

Manpower Development in terms of the representatives' performance and morale, team spirit, lower staff turnover, more efficient use of personnel on more productive calls, better journey planning, improved standards of reporting, number of promotions in the field, strengthening of company goodwill with customers.

Higher management must also add its own personal assessment of the individual supervisor's capabilities, personal qualities, ambitions, and capacity for executive development with training. The task of evaluating personnel and assessing their suitability for promotion to jobs of a different character, wider scope and greater responsibility is, in general, still a relatively unscientific business. Better methods will undoubtedly be developed but it seems unlikely that batteries of interviews, aptitude tests and suchlike will ever completely eliminate the element of personal opinion and judgment in such decisions.

(d) THE SALES ORGANISATION

Purpose and Form of Organisation

The purpose of the sales organisation is to implement sales plans so as to achieve the company's sales objectives and sales budgets.

The adoption of the marketing perspective in business affects the way in which company sales objectives and selling plans are arrived at and usually involves changes in the way in which the selling function is organised and carried out. Traditionally, business operations have been separated into manufacturing (production) and sales (presentation). Product decisions have been made either by top management or the manufacturing division on the basis of judgment and, by and large, without the aid of market research. In this form of organisation, which is still fairly widespread, the sales manager has the unenviable job of selling whatever products are manufactured and he must only hope that what he is instructed to sell is what the customer wants to buy. Product design and production orders under such circumstances often have little relationship to actual market demand. Advertising, merchandising and sales promotion are either relatively undeveloped or poorly co-ordinated with sales.

The shift in emphasis in many companies away from production and towards the presentation aspect reflects the greater importance that management attaches to the unified control of all presentation activities as well as the need for consulting the customer or user when drawing up product plans. Product design is in this way directly related to the customer's product or service requirements and production orders based on careful market assessment. In this form of organisation the sales manager has the happier task of selling products to his customers for whom the former have been designed, tested, manufactured and promoted.

Under the unified control of the chief marketing executive, sales are co-ordinated with market research, product planning, advertising, and sales promotion so as to produce the optimum profitable volume of sales as opposed to the absolute maximum volume of sales. The sales manager is still responsible, as in the past, for getting the orders and for directing and controlling field selling operations. But whereas previously this was probably the limit of his responsibilities, the sales manager, under the marketing concept, takes part in product planning, packaging, pricing and promotional policy decisions as a member of the marketing management team. As such he is an initiator or planner as well as an implementor and it is part of his job to interpret and communicate company marketing philosophy and policy to and through the sales organisation. He must see to it that selling activities are integrated with the other marketing functions, particularly advertising and sales promotion. He must give more attention to the findings of marketing research, to sales communications and to manpower motivation.

A number of basic organisational forms do exist but, in practice, many variations and combinations of these patterns are found. The important considerations are that the particular form of organisation chosen should follow sound organisational principles and should be adapted to the company's special marketing needs.

Basic Principles of Organisation

For most of the time the activities of the field sales organisation are unobservable to management. Because the greater part of the average salesman's time is spent out of the office, on his own and without day-to-day supervision, a higher degree of self-discipline and organisational discipline is called for. Organisational discipline requires the application of certain basic principles. The first is the principle of *delegation* derived from the easily observable fact that the more complex human activity becomes the greater the need for specialisation. Responsibility, in the sense of being obligated or committed to the performance of a prescribed task or activity, and authority, in the sense of having the power to do certain things or to command others to do certain specified things, must both be delegated to subordinates.

Responsibility, in a business sense, generally means being accountable to someone for the performance of an assigned task or activity and this involves the prospect of reward and recognition or penalty and censure according to how well or how badly it is carried out. But no executive can be held accountable for the discharge of responsibilities assigned to him unless he is also given the necessary authority to carry them out. Thus, the salesman is responsible to his supervisor or sales manager for obtaining orders for the company's products subject to certain limitations of authority, e.g. he may not vary prices or other conditions of sale. The sales manager is responsible to the chief marketing executive for the performance of the sales force but has authority to direct, recruit, select, train, admonish or dismiss sales representatives.

A second basic principle of organisation is the *classification of activities*. Different people are responsible for carrying out different activities or duties. This means that those activities for which each individual or type of executive is to be responsible must be grouped together to provide a job description. A job description or specification should include a list of the activities or duties to be performed, the location and status of the individual to whom the executive will be responsible or accountable, and the specific authority delegated to the executive to enable him to carry out his assigned responsibilities. The grouping of activities under various job descriptions must be mutually exclusive so that only one individual is responsible for carrying them out. The groups of activities for which the salesman, the field sales supervisor, the branch or area sales manager and general sales manager are reponsible are quite different in each case.

There is little unanimity in business either in the matter of executive titles or of job specifications. The designation 'Manager' can be deceptive. What really matters is the matrix of functions, activities, responsibilities and authority that lies behind the title. Branch Manager, Area Sales Manager, Regional Supervisor, Field Sales Supervisor and District Manager can be different titles for the same job carried out in different companies or they can stand for quite different jobs and areas of responsibility.

A British Institute of Management Study Group[1] on the subject reported as follows: 'The title conferred should depend partly on the established practice in the trade, but mainly on the role of the executive concerned. Thus, "Branch Manager" is acceptable if he in fact manages a

[1] *The Field Sales Supervisor*. British Institute of Management. Marketing Series 4 London 1959. p. 1.

branch and "Area Manager" if he controls an area. When the greater part of his time is spent with salesmen on their territories then there is merit in the prefix "Field" to his title. Apart from these points, it does not appear to matter much whether "Supervisor" or "Manager" is used.' However, the title of manager or supervisor can only be conferred on someone who has one or more subordinates reporting to him, over whom he exercises some authority and to whom he can delegate responsibility. An executive with no powers of delegation is not a manager, regardless of his title.

A third principle is concerned with the *span of executive control* by which is meant the natural limitations imposed on the number of separate functions, activities or individuals which any one executive can effectively co-ordinate and control. There is no ideal number of subordinates who should report to one superior and no ideal number of functions that one executive can co-ordinate and control. It will depend on the nature of the functions to be co-ordinated and on the capabilities of the person doing the co-ordination. Generally speaking, the higher the level of co-ordination and control the fewer the functions or executives that can be effectively controlled since top management does not have the time, nor is it its job, to control day-to-day operations.

Moving down through middle and junior management the number of subordinates whose activities can be effectively co-ordinated by any one superior will increase. This is so not merely because there are more subordinate executives than there are managers (and the ratio tends to widen as one moves down through the organisation) but also because the activities of subordinates tend to be similar and more routine in character. Thus salesmen's activities are broadly similar and the span of control of a sales supervisor may range on average from five to fifteen sales representatives, depending on the number and nature of the activities, customers and products involved.

The sales manager, on the other hand, because of his diverse duties and responsibilities, i.e. overall control of field selling, sales office administration, warehousing and transport, sales records and statistics, merchandising, sales promotion, etc., will normally have fewer people reporting to him. All that can be said is that where the span of management co-ordination and control takes in more than six different functions or subordinates then the company should make provision for the periodic and systematic review of the organisation structure to determine whether or not any changes may be called for. Such a review is particularly necessary when a company is developing and growing rapidly.

A fourth principle of organisation concerns the distinction between *operational and functional authority*. The operational or line executive is the man with the authority to tell subordinates 'do this, here and now'; the functional or staff executive only advises the operational executive to whose staff he is attached, on methods, procedures and policies. The staff man's authority over any executive or department other than his own is always functional.

Thus, while the Market Research Department may have responsibility for preparing sales forecasts and area sales quotas, it has no authority to tell Area Sales Managers, over the head of the General Sales Manager, that these are the targets to be met. Similarly, the Sales Analysis Department does not have authority to tell a Branch Sales Manager that certain named customers are unprofitable to the company and must be dropped forthwith. In many companies the Product Manager or Brand Manager, who is responsible for the overall marketing planning of the product(s) assigned to him, does not have any executive authority over the sales force unless, of course, he combines the functions of Product Manager and Sales Manager. The Market Research Department, the Sales Analysis Department and the Product Manager must work through the responsible operational executive. In each of the above cases, this would be the General Sales Manager.

Types of Sales Organisation

The form of organisation in existence will reflect the type and range of products or services that have to be sold, the number and location of the customers most likely to buy them, the distribution channels and methods in use or contemplated (direct sales, sales through wholesalers and retailers, sales through brokers, etc.) and the size of the firm.

The great majority of companies adopt one or some combination of the following four basic types of sales organisation:

1. Organisation by Function
2. Organisation by Region
3. Organisation by Product Groups
4. Organisation by Customer Groups or End-Use Markets.

The examples which follow have been simplified in order to emphasise the chief characteristics of each type of organisation.

Organisation by Function

This type of sales organisation tends to be most common among small and medium-sized companies selling a single product or limited range of homogeneous products through similar distribution channels. It groups together all similar sales activities into functional groups or departments which report, in this case, to the Sales Director.

The company shown in chart 25 is a medium-sized manufacturer of domestic insulation materials distributed through builders' merchants and retail hardware outlets. The Sales Director co-ordinates home and export sales, advertising and sales promotion. The Home Sales Manager is responsible for the field selling function through three Area Sales Managers and twenty-five Sales Representatives, for the sales office administration

CHART 25. FUNCTIONAL SALES ORGANISATION

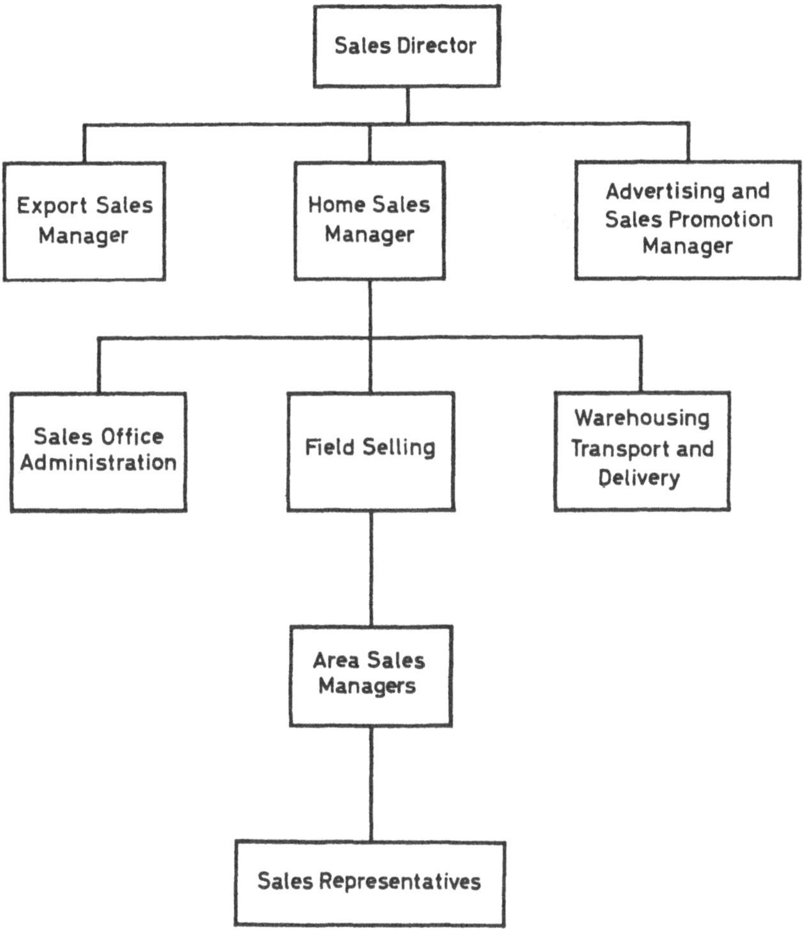

function (including order-processing and sales analysis) through a Sales Office Supervisor, and for warehousing, transport and delivery through a Warehouse and Transport Supervisor. There is only one central warehouse adjoining the factory and the company mainly contracts its deliveries to public and private hauliers.

A functional sales organisation of this sort runs into serious difficulties however if the range of products is extended, particularly if they are very dissimilar products requiring different selling methods and distribution channels, or if they are aimed at different markets. Such a situation might well arise if the company decided to enter the industrial insulation field or into the contract building trade.

Organisation by Region

This type of sales organisation is probably one of the most common in use particularly among companies with a limited number of relatively homogeneous products in widespread distribution through a large number of outlets. The nature of the product, methods of distribution, the degree of dispersal and the location of valuable fixed assets, are also major considerations. For example, national bakeries, brewing organisations, petroleum

CHART 26. REGIONAL SALES ORGANISATION

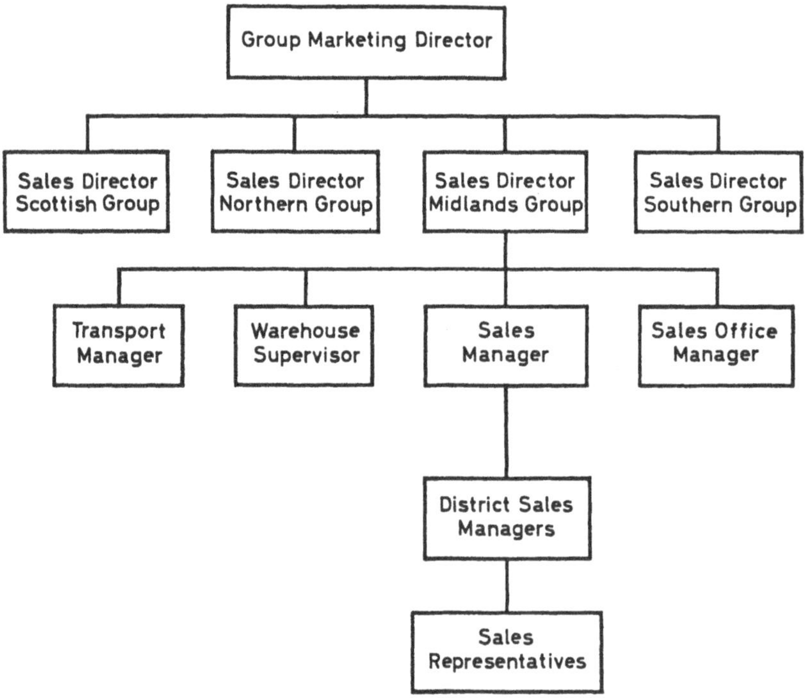

companies are strongly regionalised, areas being served by the local bakery, brewery or storage depot. The supply of certain industrial goods which can be made in any one of several manufacturing locations, as well as most public utilities and services (gas, coal, electricity, transport, etc.), are organised on a regional basis because of the convenience of serving particular areas.

Chart 26 shows the regional structure of a large brewery group with four sales divisions—Scotland, Northern England, Midlands and Wales and Southern England—each under its own Sales Director. Although most of the company's products are local brands, limited to one or, in some cases, two contiguous divisional areas, certain products are sold on a national basis by all four divisions. This structure was dictated by the widely scattered operations and local area concentrations brought together under one overall management by a series of acquisitions and mergers over a period of several years.

The convenience of serving particular areas through local chains of public houses, the considerable amounts of capital tied up in premises and brewery capacity, the strength of local brand loyalties and sectional differences in consumers' tastes and preferences were other factors which have influenced the choice of this type of sales organisation. Functional services such as advertising, marketing research, product planning and development, formerly dealt with on an autonomous regional basis, are now centralised at Head Office along with accounting, legal and property development services and are available to the groups as required.

Organisation by Product Groups

Some companies have separate sales forces for different groups of products, selling to different customer groups or markets through different distribution channels, and possibly requiring specialised selling techniques in each case. Multi-product consumer goods manufacturers, particularly, have developed the concept whereby overall product and marketing planning responsibility for a specific product or group of products is assigned to a Product or Brand Manager who develops the marketing strategy, sales forecasts and budgets, packaging and pricing policies, advertising and sales promotion policies. If the company is a very large one with a considerable turnover in each type or group of products, there may be a different sales manager and separate sales force for each. In some

CHART 27. SALES ORGANISATION BY PRODUCT GROUPS

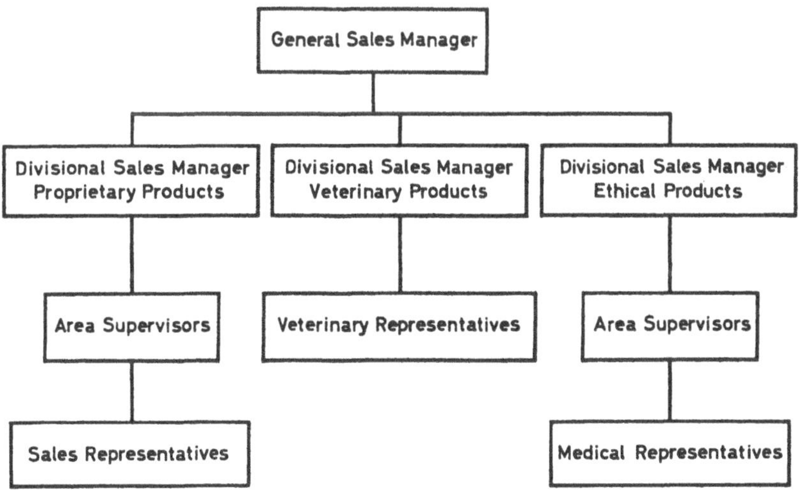

companies the Product Manager is more or less the 'managing director' of a product division and is responsible for the sales and profitability of the products in his care.

Chart 27 shows a large multi-division pharmaceutical manufacturer marketing a wide range of ethical, proprietary and veterinary products through separate sales forces to different types of customers. Two of the divisions—Veterinary and Ethical—require specialised knowledge and qualifications of quite a different order from those needed by the Proprietary salesman.

Within the Ethical Division a team of medically qualified representatives call on hospitals, clinics and doctors under the supervision of three area supervisors who report to the Divisional Sales Manager. The Veterinary Division comprises a smaller team of qualified veterinary representatives calling on veterinary surgeons, animal hospitals and other specialist institutions. They report directly to their own Divisional Sales Manager. The Proprietary Division is much the largest of the three divisions and is responsible for the sales of a wide range of proprietary remedies through chemists, and where permissible, grocers. A significant share of the sales made by this division came from products which can only be sold in outlets where a registered pharmacist is permanently in attendance, that is, predominantly in chemists'. Forty-five salesmen make, on average, some 18,000 calls every eight weeks. There are four area sales supervisors responsible to the Divisional Sales Manager.

Organisation by Customer Groups or End-Use Markets

Some companies sell to several types of customers or markets with very specific and differing marketing requirements. The more specialised or technical the customers or markets served, the greater the need for a specialist sales manager and sales force who understand their particular product and service needs. A great many industrial goods manufacturers are organised in this way because of the diversity and technical complexity of their end-use markets. However, even in mass consumer goods marketing certain types of customers call for different selling techniques. A growing number of packaged food products manufacturers have different salesmen calling on different classes of buyer.

Chart 28 shows a large cereal-based food products manufacturer selling branded consumer packaged foods through retailers and wholesalers, bulk packaged foods to catering establishments and institutional suppliers, and bulk raw materials to other industrial users.

Under the General Sales Manager there is a Catering Sales Manager in charge of a small force selling direct to restaurants, hotels, cafés and to institutional users (hospitals, factories, canteens, schools, prisons, Naafi, etc.); an Industrial Sales Manager selling to a variety of secondary users for further processing and incorporation in other products (he and the men under him must know every manufacturer who is a potential user of the company's bulk materials, the estimated capacity of each manufacturer, who influences the buying decision and so on); a National Sales Supervisor responsible for negotiating sales to head office of multiples, co-operatives, voluntary groups and chains, and for organising special promotions through their branch shops; and finally, a National Sales Supervisor responsible for sales to independent wholesalers and retailers unaffiliated to any voluntary buying group. These latter are called on direct and any orders taken are passed to nominated wholesalers.

The reason for this division of sales is that the scale and methods of

CHART 28. SALES ORGANISATION BY CUSTOMER GROUPS

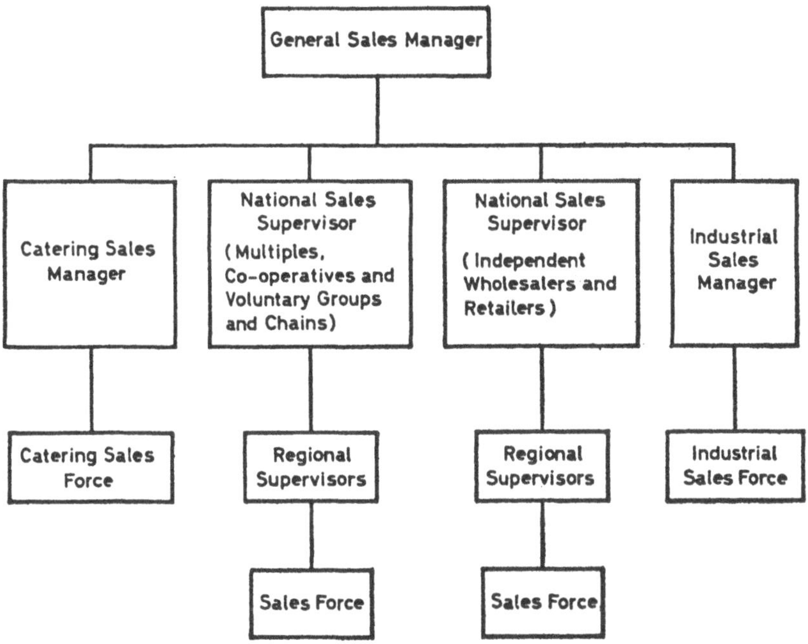

buying, merchandising and in-store promotion are basically similar for multiple, co-operative and voluntary group outlets and different from those normally employed by the independent wholesaler and smaller retail outlet. Special quantity terms, price deals, promotional arrangements and allowances are more easily negotiated with the former on account of their concentrated buying power, aggressive salesmanship and planned promotional activity.

At the same time, the value of the tens of thousands of smaller outlets who still account for a sizeable but diminishing share of food sales must not be minimised. But this type of sales organisation does reflect the fact that they may have to be treated differently if the company selling effort is to maximise marketing opportunities.

CHART 29. SALES ORGANISATION BY END-USE MARKETS

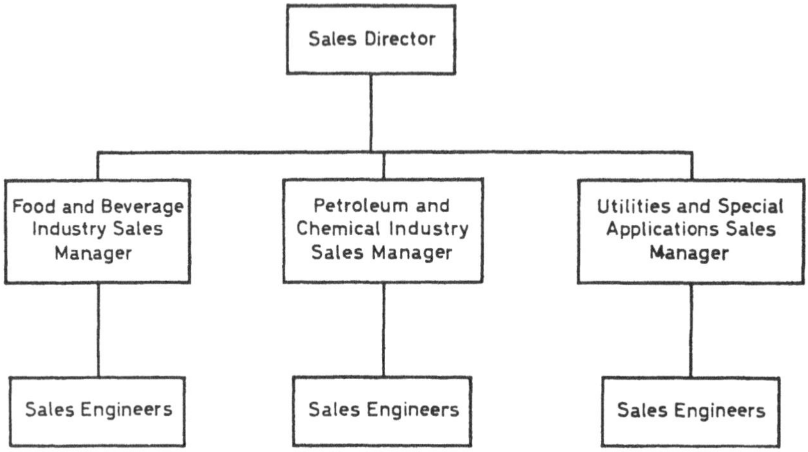

This is a manufacturer of metal and plastic tubes and vessels for bulk handling and process control of industrial liquids. The sales organisation consists of three divisions or industry-groups, each requiring its own body of specialised technical knowledge and skills and salesmen with engineering or some comparable qualifications. One team of 'sales-engineers' handles applications in the food and beverages fields, a second specialises in petroleum and chemical applications, and a third is concerned with utilities (gas and water) and with special or unusual applications. Firms organised along these lines tend to look outward to the industries they are already serving to see what other products or applications they can sell to them.

Compound Organisation

Many combinations of the four basic types of organisation are possible. Some are the outcome of simply trying to superimpose one or more structures on top of each other. This frequently happens in fast-growing companies. Others represent a deliberately planned attempt to adjust to changing demands on the organisation as a result of natural expansion, product or market diversification, amalgamation, new customer requirements and so forth. A common combination is by customers or end-use markets and by region. For example, a food manufacturer with a basic regional sales structure may have a specialist national sales division handling sales to institutions, hotels, industrial caterers and government and military organisations.

A soft-drinks manufacturer has the following regional-functional-customer group organisation.

CHART 30. COMPOUND SALES ORGANISATION

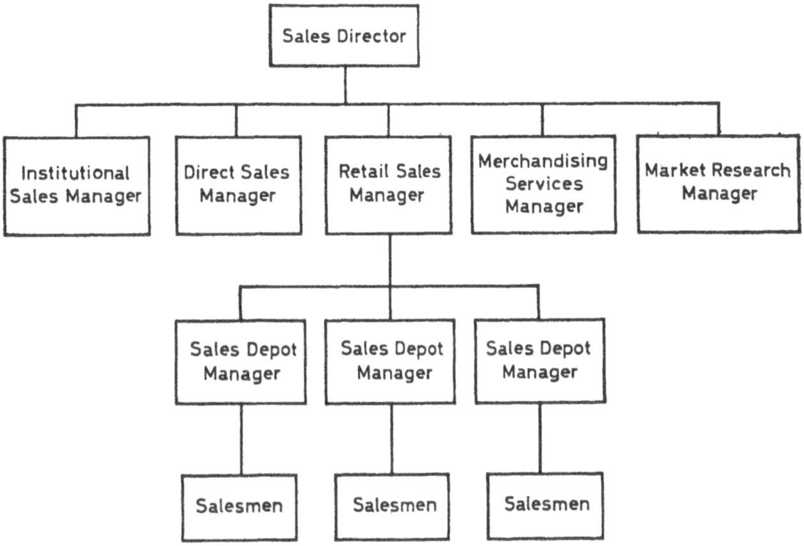

Note in this example that there is a direct sales force selling the company's products to housewives door-to-door through a fleet of vans based on each of the three main depots in London, Birmingham and Newcastle. Sales to retail outlets are made by the company's own delivery vehicles based on the same depots, whose managers report directly to the Retail Sales Manager.

6

Managing the Advertising and Promotion Function

(a) THE NATURE AND PURPOSE OF ADVERTISING

COMMERCIAL advertising, in its modern sense, is the persuasive force that makes use of mass communication media and is aimed at changing customer attitudes or patterns of behaviour towards a product or service in a direction favourable to the advertiser. The theoretical distinction between informative (constructive) and persuasive (combative or competitive) advertising is spurious since the purpose of all advertising is to persuade the person addressed to do something that the advertiser wants him or her to do.

The provision of information is, to a greater or lesser degree, itself persuasive. A restaurant menu is strictly informative but is designed to persuade people to eat certain selected dishes. An omnibus time-table is designed to persuade people to travel by bus. As Harris and Seldon[1] have observed, '. . . descriptive information about a product is not necessary for an advertisement to have its desired effect. Information may be helpful in advertising a new product. Even then a description may not be as revealing to the consumer as a trial; and an advertisement directing attention to the *existence* of the new product and inviting the public to buy a trial supply, or perhaps accept a free sample for trial, may be rendering a desirable service even though it contains no word about the product's composition or performance. There must be, of course, information that the product or service (or employment) is available but for an established product information may be superfluous. The essential function of advertising is then to *remind* the consumer of the product's existence.' The need for the latter stems from the fact that 'every day there are new products or services to try, new incentives to spend money differently' and 'consumers do not have perfect memories nor are they a static body'. Furthermore, 'there are continually new potential recruits to be drawn from the newly employed, married or retired, those changing home, and generally from people constantly acquiring fresh interests and needs'.

In other words, people's needs and desires are constantly changing as they pass through the different stages of their life cycles. Advertising must

[1] Ralph Harris and Arthur Seldon. *Advertising and the Public*. The Institute of Economic Affairs. André Deutsch. 1962. p. 74.

continue to remind them of the products available to meet their changing needs, persuade them that certain products can do this better than others, and reinforce or confirm that the products they have used in the past are still the best. Thus advertising may be considered as an effective means of reducing marketing risks by giving a greater measure of control over changes in demand, by cushioning the disruptive effects of change and facilitating the process of change.

It is fairly commonplace to hear the purpose of advertising defined as 'making a sale' or 'to increase sales'. In certain cases this may be true as, for example, mail order advertising, personnel recruitment or company share issues. In general, however, the sale of a product or service is the outcome of a combination of factors or forces in which the relative importance of the contribution to the sales result of any single factor, such as advertising, cannot be isolated.

Advertising is only one component within the marketing mix that leads to a sale; the others are product features, product availability, price, packaging, sales promotion, merchandising and point-of-purchase display. Additionally, any single marketing operation has to contend with competing operations, changes in consumer tastes and preferences, changes in economic conditions, etc. In other words, although advertising contributes in some way and in some degree to the final sale of a product or service, this is not usually determinable except in those very exceptional circumstances where it is the only variable factor in the situation.

The immediate purpose of advertising is not to physically bring buyer and seller together but to communicate *sales-motivating* information, ideas and suggestions to particular target prospects or customers, so as to increase the likelihood of a sale. In other words it can accelerate the demand process by creating potential customers for a product much more quickly than would be possible without advertising. This is of great importance in the introduction of new products where it is necessary to gain an early foothold in competitive markets and, if possible, establish a substantial lead over major competition. The pace of technological innovation and change is such in many product-markets that unless a manufacturer can expect to build a profitable level of sales reasonably quickly many fewer, newer and better products would see the light of day.

A reputable company must look well beyond the next immediate sale. In the longer-term, a company's future growth and profitability is bound up in its present sales and advertising policies just as its present situation is the cumulative outcome of past policies. In the same way that products and plant are the results of past capital investment decisions, so its present customers and markets are the result of past marketing and advertising decisions. No business can continue and grow on the basis that today's sale is all that matters or that its only concern is with the advertising campaign which is currently running.

The effects of advertising are not confined to the period in which it appears. As an 'investment' in customers it is difficult to measure the extent to which advertising is responsible for building goodwill for a range of products or a business among distributors and consumers. The creation of business goodwill is by no means solely a function of advertising. However, ill-judged or misleading advertising can do irreparable damage to the fund of customer goodwill built up over the years for a product or a company. At the same time, well-devised advertising can, in the long run, do little to sustain a product which is competitively inferior or does not match the claims made for it.

The Link Between Mass Production and Mass Consumption

Advertising is mass salesmanship direct to the customer or general public. Mass production is predicated on mass consumption. Neither is possible without the other and, in a highly competitive economy, advertising is the link between the two. The great majority of firms employ the services of advertising agents in the creation and placement of advertisements.

As the following chart[1] shows, the advertising agency stands between the manufacturer and the media owners. In the preparation of advertisements the agency employs the specialist services of many different types of research and supply organisations, although these may also be retained directly by the advertiser himself if he so wishes. A firm will usually have its own advertising department or personnel responsible for the overall control of advertising policy and expenditure through its appointed agency.

CHART 31. THE STRUCTURE OF THE ADVERTISING INDUSTRY

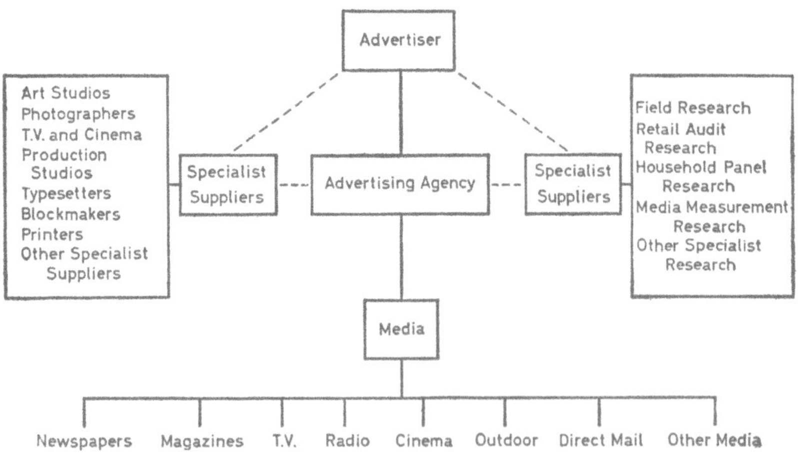

The advertising agency, in turn, places the advertisements it prepares for its clients in the particular media selected for a campaign. For this

[1] Brian F. MacCabe. 'An Essential Link in a Competitive Economy.' *Financial Times* Survey of Advertising. 4th May 1964. p. 11.

purpose it has a number of expert media planners and buyers who are in close and continuing contact with the advertisement departments of all the media. The agency negotiates all space and time buying with the media owners concerned and draws its income from the commissions earned on all space and time bought on behalf of its clients.

Advertising Communication as a Two-way Process

Advertising, as a means of communication, is a two-way process. In the words of one leading authority on advertising research,[1] 'The person addressed by the advertiser is not a passive blank open to any message directed at him. He is a bundle of interests, attitudes, values and ties; he is guided by images of himself and his neighbours; he moves through a variety of roles even within a few hours. His attention and favour will be enlisted only when the advertiser engages him psychologically. To achieve this the successful communicator must himself accept various limitations on what he says.' Mark Abrams then lists four basic requirements for effective communication:

(i) The effect sought by the advertiser (e.g. the purchase of a particular product or service) should itself be a path to achieving some general material or psychological goal the recipient already has.
(ii) The effect sought by the advertiser should directly promote the well being of the particular group to which the recipient belongs, e.g. his family, his work-mates, his neighbours.
(iii) The message communicated should report recognised facts, i.e. facts recognised as true by the recipient, relevant to his needs and interests and congruent with his own experiences, past and present.
(iv) The path of action required of the recipient should be specifically set out for him.

The communication process can be visually expressed as shown in Chart 32.[2]

The elements of communication on the left of the chart, which are not listed in any particular order of importance, are:

(i) *Specificness*—in terms of precision and clarity of thought and expression; precise in terms of the target at which the communication is directed.
(ii) *Authority*—in relation to both the source and content of the communication.
(iii) *Impact*—in terms of the immediate attention it gets due to a distinctiveness, individuality or urgency of expression which forcibly impinges itself in a memorable way upon the person addressed.

[1] Mark Abrams. 'Contacting Whom?' *Investors' Chronicle* Survey. October 1962.

[2] This chart is adapted from *Defining Advertising Goals for Measured Advertising Results*. Association of National Advertisers. Ed. Russell H. Colley. New York 1961. p. 55.

CHART 32. THE COMMUNICATION PROCESS

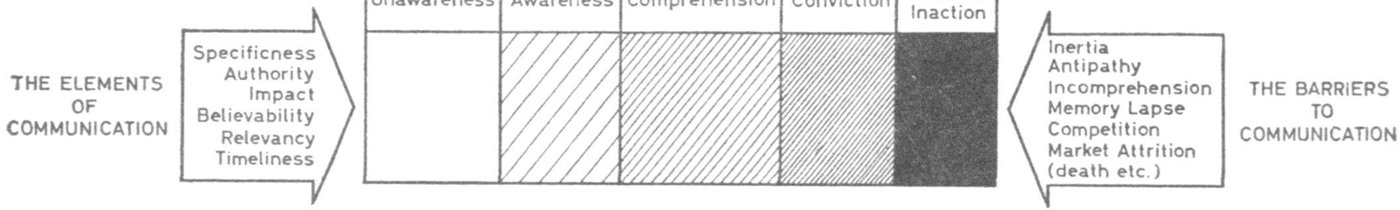

(iv) *Believability*—in terms of what is acceptable to the person being addressed in the light of his own knowledge, past and present experience.
(v) *Relevancy*—in relation to the requirements of the particular situation and the recognised needs of the recipient.
(vi) *Timeliness*—in the sense of being apposite or opportune from the standpoint of the recipient.

It is possible to identify five phases or states through which the person addressed is likely to have to pass before responding to an advertising communication:

(i) *Unawareness* of the existence of a product or service or of a known want or need; consumers may fail to want something because they do not appreciate its importance or convenience (e.g. educational services, banking services) or because they under-estimate its probability of occurrence (e.g. life, fire and burglary insurance).
(ii) *Awareness* of a particular product or service, problem or need; awareness involves knowledge of the availability of specific products to meet known generalised wants, e.g. evening lectures or correspondence courses by particular recognised educational institutions, the various services offered by different banks, and the different types of insurance cover offered by particular insurance companies.
(iii) *Comprehension* as to what the product or service is and will do i.e. specific product or service features.
(iv) *Conviction* as to the specific value, benefits or usefulness of the product or service in relation to the person's particular situation or need; conviction can be based on reason or emotion.
(v) *Action* (*or inaction*)—at which point the person takes a positive step towards the purchase of the product or service, e.g. arranges for a demonstration, calls at a shop or showroom; alternatively the person decides to take no further action. Consumer action or inaction results from the degree to which he is convinced that the product or service will meet a recognised need in the way and to the extent anticipated.

An advertiser may do an excellent job of making consumers aware of his product and of getting them to comprehend its features and promised benefits, but fail to develop a strong enough conviction to spur them to action. For, in addition to the advertiser's own skill in developing awareness and comprehension, he must also contend with opposing forces—competitors' activities, consumers' forgetfulness, and the distraction caused by the many other demands on the customers' time and attention.

The main barriers to communication shown on the right-hand side of the chart—the countervailing forces that tend to neutralise or reduce the effectiveness of advertising communication—are:

(i) *Inertia* due to the indifference, slackness or laziness of the people at whom the communication is aimed.

(ii) *Antipathy* based on a rejection of the communication in relation to any or all of its basic elements, i.e. it may be regarded as being unbelievable, irrelevant or inappropriate.
(iii) *Incomprehension* arising from inherent defects in the communication itself, i.e. its ambiguity, lack of precision both as regards what it is trying to convey and the specific target at whom it is aimed.
(iv) *Competition* from other communications of varying degrees of impact and effectiveness.
(v) *Memory lapse* due to forgetfulness or distortion caused by competing communications and the demands made upon the recipient from many other different directions.
(vi) *Market attrition* due to the movement of customers out of the market as a result of death, emigration, changes in the family life cycle, and sociological changes in behaviour patterns, etc.

To communicate effectively with customers, the advertiser must see his problems as customer problems that he hopes to solve. This means diagnosing the problems of customers through market research, developing products or services that will facilitate their solution and persuading customers through advertising that their problems can be solved by using the particular manufacturer's products or services. The advertiser must present his proposed solutions, i.e. products or services, to those people he can identify as having the greatest need or desire for what he makes and sells, in language and using appeals which he considers will best convey what he is making and selling and which will provide a basis of preference for his product.

(b) THE COST OF ADVERTISING

Trends in Advertising Expenditure

Advertising expenditure in Great Britain increased from £309 million in 1956 to £479 million in 1962, a rise of some 55%.[1] Estimates published by the Institute of Practitioners in Advertising[2] from data produced by the Advertising Association are as follows:

Table 7. Advertising Expenditure in Great Britain 1956–62

	£m.	*% net national income*
1956	309	1·8
1957	339	1·9
1958	373	2·0
1959	402	2·1
1960	453	2·2
1961	470	2·1
1962	479	2·1

[1] Latest estimates by the Advertising Association put total advertising expenditure for 1963 at £501 million.

[2] John Treasure. *Advertising Expenditure in 1962: a reappraisal.* Occasional Paper No. 14. Institute of Practitioners in Advertising. October 1963. For the purpose of this section the author has drawn extensively on this publication.

Real national income (net national income at constant prices) over the period 1956–62 rose by 11%. Adjusting for price changes and advertising's increasing share of net national income, the real increase in advertising expenditure in volume terms was nearer 29%. Estimates prepared by the Institute of Practitioners in Advertising suggest that the indicated increase may be on the low side.

The trends in expenditure on the major advertising space media since 1956, unadjusted for price changes, provide the following comparisons:

Table 8. Expenditures on Major Advertising Space Media 1956–62[1]
(1956 = 100)

	1956	*1960*	*1962*
National daily and London evening newspapers	100	158	160
Provisional newspapers	100	119	130
Magazines and periodicals	100	122	123
Trade and technical journals	100	145	145
TOTAL PRESS	100	140	144
TELEVISION	100	678	733[2]
CINEMA[3]	100	91	91
OUTDOOR (posters, transport signs, etc.)	100	108	120

Over a five-year period 1956–60 television showed the greatest growth by a very wide margin—nearly a seven-fold increase. National daily and London evening press showed the next fastest rate of growth followed by trade and technical journals and magazines and periodicals. Cinema advertising registered a decline from which it has not yet recovered.

Although all media, except cinema, registered expenditure increases since 1960, when the rising cost of space and time are taken into account, such changes as there have been would appear marginal except, possibly, in the case of provincial newspapers which has shown a real increase. What is apparent is that the great increase in advertising expenditure on television has been on top of other media spending, although it is impossible to say whether a similar increase in total advertising expenditure would have taken place in the absence of television and, in such circumstances, which of the other main media would have benefited or suffered the most.

The Component Costs

There is some confusion as to what the figure of total advertising expenditure includes. Whereas it might be thought that the figure of £479 million represents expenditure on press and television advertisements, in fact it covers a much broader range of media and types of advertising. For example, it includes £35 million worth of classified advertising (for jobs, houses, goods and services and personal transactions) and £106 million spent on sales promotion activities (catalogues, leaflets, window and interior display, exhibitions, free samples and gift schemes). In other words,

[1] Advertising Association estimates.
[2] Includes Television tax.
[3] Excluding non-theatrical film productions.

by no means all of the expenditure included in the grand total relates to 'advertising' in the normally accepted sense or even to advertising of goods and services by manufacturing organisations directly to consumers.

The breakdown of the 1962 advertising expenditure by type of media, including production costs, has been estimated as follows:

Table 9. Advertising Expenditure in 1962 by Type of Media

	£ million	Percentage
PRESS:		
(a) Space:		
National and London evening newspapers	76·0	15·9
Provincial newspapers	54·5	11·4
Magazines and periodicals	39·5	8·2
Trade and technical journals	32·0	6·7
Other publications	2·5	0·5
Production costs	15·5	3·2
Total press	220·0	45·9
TELEVISION:		
Time charges	69·4	14·5
Tax	7·6	1·6
Production costs	5·5	1·1
Total television	82·5	17·2
Poster and transport	16·2	3·4
Outdoor signs	14·5	3·0
Cinema	5·1	1·1
Catalogues, leaflets, calendars, etc.	41·0	8·6
Window and interior display	32·0	6·7
Exhibitions	17·0	3·5
Free samples and gift schemes	16·0	3·3
Miscellaneous (inc. radio)	8·2	1·7
Administration	26·5	5·6
Total	479·0	100·0

Source: The Advertising Association.

If a number of items included in the above table are re-allocated it is possible to arrive at a more realistic estimate of the actual amount spent on advertisements directed at consumers of goods and services (Table 10).

Allowing for the fact that under 'display advertising', i.e. advertising directed at the private consumer, there are certain items of expenditure—such as advertising for political parties, the Armed Services, Road Safety, charities and other non-commercial enterprises [totalling perhaps £10–£15 million] which should really not come under this heading—and allowing also for the fact that some £10 million or so of classified advertising should be included under consumer advertising expenditure, it can be estimated that the amount actually spent on 'consumer advertising' of goods and services was of the order of £290 million in 1962. Of this £290 million of consumer advertising expenditure it is further estimated that about 20% (some £65 million) was accounted for by retail, financial and

Table 10. Advertising Expenditure in 1962 by Type of Advertising

	£ million	*Percentage*
1. DISPLAY ADVERTISING:		
National and London evening newspapers	63	
Provincial newspapers	34	
Magazines and periodicals	38	
Other publications	3	
Production costs	15	
Total press	153	
Television	83	
Posters and transport	16	
Outdoor signs	15	
Cinema	5	
Miscellaneous and administration	18	
	290	60·5
2. CLASSIFIED ADVERTISING:		
Personal	15	
Business (jobs, houses, etc.)	10	
Goods and services	10	
	35	7·5
3. TRADE AND TECHNICAL ADVERTISING:	32	6·5
4. SALES PROMOTION ACTIVITIES:		
Catalogues, leaflets, etc.	41	
Window and interior display	32	
Exhibitions	17	
Free samples and gift schemes	16	
	106	22·0
5. MISCELLANEOUS AND ADMINISTRATION: (Other than for display advertising)	16	3·5
Total	479	100·0

Source: The Advertising Association.

other organisations, leaving £225 million to be accounted for by manufacturers. Furthermore, of the total expenditure on sales promotion activities, over a quarter went on promotions directed at distributors.[1]

[1] Consumer Sales Promotion Activities	*£m.*	
By manufacturers	56	
By retailers and others	20	
	—	
		76
Trade Sales Promotion Activities		30
		—
Total		106

Independent estimates of total billings of advertising agencies in 1962, at £285 million, would tend to confirm that the estimates derived from the foregoing tables are reasonably accurate since, by and large, agency billings are composed mainly of expenditure on 'consumer advertising'. The fact that some non-commercial expenditures are incurred by some advertising agencies is countered by the fact that some consumer advertising expenditure by both manufacturers and retailers is placed direct with the media proprietors.

The breakdown of the total advertising expenditure of £479 million in 1962 into its component parts can now be attempted graphically.

CHART 33. BREAKDOWN OF ADVERTISING EXPENDITURE IN GREAT BRITAIN IN 1962

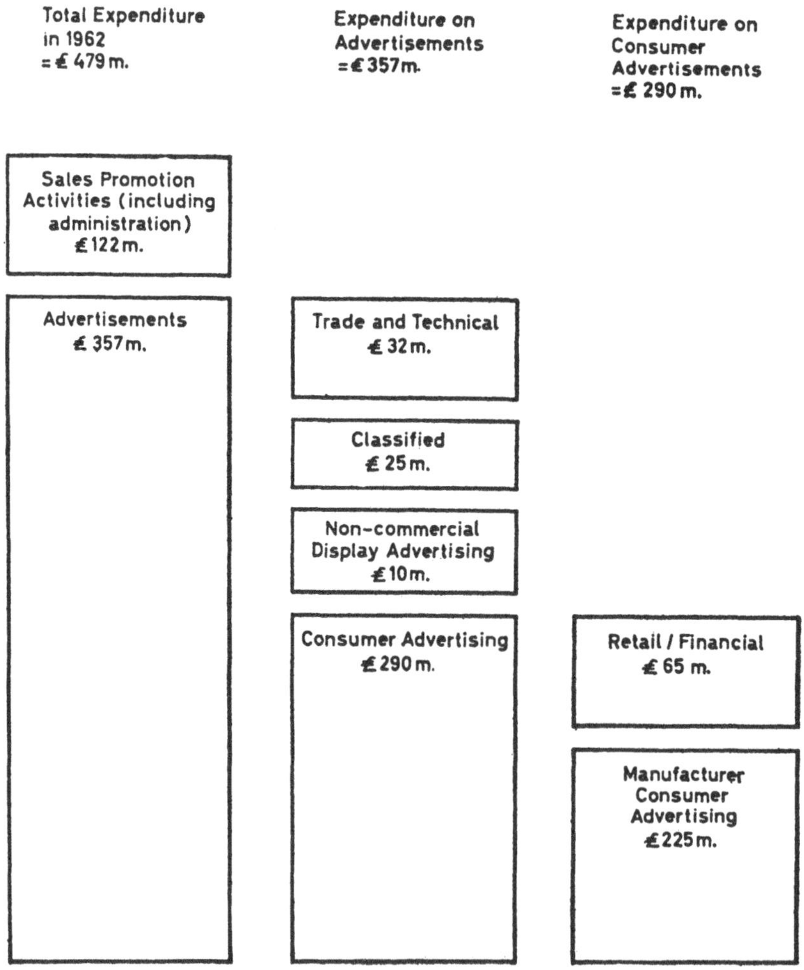

The Element of Subsidy

There is perhaps one further matter which should be touched upon in connection with the foregoing analysis of the cost of advertising. It is an attestable fact that a substantial element of subsidy exists in the final estimates of consumer advertising in respect of newspapers. Between 35% and 60% of the revenue of daily and weekly newspapers and journals in this country is derived from advertising.

Lord Francis-Williams[1] has remarked that 'The daily press would never have come into existence as a force in public and social life if it had not been for the need of the men of commerce to advertise. Only through the growth of advertising did the press achieve independence.' The effect of falling advertising revenue is to be seen all too clearly in the closure of papers and the amalgamation of newspaper interests. The absence of advertising would almost certainly mean the disappearance of a significant proportion of well-known newspapers and journals which currently enrich our lives and the price of the remainder might easily double overnight.

The issue here, however, is not whether advertising is the most effective way of subsidising a free press or the danger of throwing out the baby with the bathwater, but merely that the £290 million spent on consumer advertising does not, in fact, represent the true net social cost of advertising. The

Table 11. Comparison of Advertising Revenues and Net Contributions from these Revenues in 1960

	Advertising Revenue	Subsidy (Net Contribution towards expenses after deduction of costs attributable to advertising)		Surplus as % of advertising revenue
Type of Newspaper	£000 per year	£000 per year	Pence per copy sold	
National mornings:				
Quality	2,700	1,600	5	60
Popular	5,700	2,300	½	40
National Sundays:				
Quality	2,400	1,400	7	55–60
Popular	2,800	900	¾	30–35
London evenings	3,500	1,600	1½	45
Provincial mornings	400	170	2	55–60
Provincial evenings	450	230	1¾	50
Provincial weeklies	70	40	5	60

Note: The basis on which the apportionment of costs between those attributable to advertisement revenue and those attributable to sales revenue has been made was decided upon after consultation with the secretary or chief accountant of three national newspaper companies. All editorial expenditure and all expenditure on publicity was attributed to sales revenue, and all expenses of the advertising department to advertising revenue. 90% of managerial expenditure was attributed to sales and 10% to advertising. The remaining cost items (i.e. production, depreciation, paper and ink, circulation and distribution) were apportioned between sales and advertising according to the average percentage of space which had been used for text and advertisements respectively.

[1] *Dangerous Estate.* Longmans Green. 1957.

report of the Royal Commission on the Press 1961–2 has provided authoritative estimates of the subsidy element, i.e. the contribution towards the expenses of running a newspaper provided by advertising revenue (Table 11).

Applying these percentages of 'surplus from advertising' to the 1962 total advertising expenditure to each type of media the final subsidy element, according to calculations of the Institute of Practitioners in Advertising, can be assessed as follows:

National and London newspapers	£25m
Provincial newspapers	£20m
Magazines and periodicals	£15m
	£60m

The Institute of Practitioners in Advertising also calculates that the subsidy element in television advertising, i.e. the surplus revenue accruing to the television companies after deduction of the costs of advertising placed with them, might be of the order of another £35 million using the cost of providing the BBC television service as a guide to the probable cost of a second commercial channel in the absence of advertising expenditure. The total press and television subsidy element, therefore, in respect of *consumer advertising* in 1962, was probably about £95 million which, together with another £5 million or so in respect of other media (posters, cinema, transport[1] and outdoor signs), brought the total to £100 million. These estimates, it must be pointed out, are based on the assumption that each of these media would continue to operate on the same scale in the absence of advertising as a major source of income. Thus, the net cost of consumer advertising in 1962 was £190 million, i.e. £290 million *less* subsidy of £100 million.

Cost to Manufacturer

Any consideration of the costs of advertising of the individual manufacturer must take account of the use of advertising as a substitute for or complement to other forms of marketing expenditure. The important relationship is not between advertising cost and total marketing cost but between total marketing cost and total sales.

It would not make sense, for example, to reduce the cost of advertising, if to do so meant increasing the cost of some other factor or factors by an amount greater than the amount saved, or, alternatively, to increase the cost of advertising if this resulted in a reduction in other cost factors by an amount smaller than the added amount spent on advertising. For instance, the high proportion of total marketing cost which goes in advertising some durable consumer goods sold direct to the consumer is possible because of the savings achieved on sales force expense and distribution margins.

[1] In 1962 the British Transport Commission advertising revenue from buses, stations and outdoor poster sites was £3·8 million yielding a net income of £2·25 million.

A recent survey by McGraw-Hill[1] of 893 U.S. industrial companies in the machinery, materials, equipment and supplies fields, strongly suggests that when the ratio of advertising to selling expense, i.e. advertising plus direct selling costs (salesmen's salaries, commission, travel and entertainment), is higher, the ratio of selling expense to sales turnover is lower. On average, it was found that 'high' advertisers (where advertising accounted for more than 20% of selling expense) had a 21% lower overall selling cost than 'low' advertisers. The trend was found to be consistent regardless of the volume of sales and of product groups. In the former case, 'high' advertisers in each of four sales-size groups had lower average selling expense, within the range of 16% to 30%, than the 'low' advertisers.

For the machinery group (all special industrial machinery such as machine tools and construction machinery, motors, instruments and controls, transport and communication equipment) the sales expense ratio was 25% lower on average among 'high' advertisers than among 'low' advertisers.

For the materials group (raw materials and ingredients such as steel, industrial chemicals, rubber and plastics, structural products) the difference was 27%. And for the equipment and supplies group (maintenance and operating supplies such as furniture, paper products, lubricants, tyres, valves, machine tool accessories, paint, lighting fixtures, electronic components) the difference was 15%.

In other words, *advertising can contribute to lower sales costs* and, if the net increase in advertising is *less than* the net decrease in selling cost, to more profitable sales. While the results of this survey do not conclusively prove a cause and effect relationship, they at least demonstrate a remarkable coincidence which other manufacturers can test out for themselves. The study suggests that the odds that a company with a high level of advertising will have low selling expense rather than high selling expense are about two to one.

Analyses of this kind applied by the individual company should enable comparisons to be made of the sales costs of different divisions or product lines that have different advertising appropriations and of the effects on selling expense of changes in levels of advertising.

What of the effect of advertising on product sales results and share of market? Data collected by the A. C. Nielsen Company covering sales of twenty-seven categories of packaged grocery products[2] between 1958 and 1962 shed some interesting light on the relationship between advertising and market leadership. The survey revealed that manufacturers of the leading brands in these product groups spent one-third more on press and

[1] *How Advertising Affects the Cost of Selling.* A McGraw-Hill Research Report New York. July 1963.

[2] Baked Beans, Blancmange Powder, Ready-to-Eat Cereals, Processed Cheese, Instant Coffee, Liquid Coffee, Cooking Fats, Corned Beef, Custard Powder, Liquid Glucose Preparations, Honey, Table Jellies, Tomato Ketchup, Luncheon Meats, Margarine, Meat and Fish Pastes, Canned Milk, Sauces, Scourers, Scouring Pads, Soap Flakes Hard Soap, Canned Soup, Packeted Soup, Toilet Papers, Washing Powders.

television advertising in 1962 than they did in 1958 compared with an average increase of 19% for all manufacturers in these groups. Since the leaders were spending at a faster rate than their direct competitors, they increased their share of total advertising from 50·8% in 1958 to 56·0% in 1962 as shown in the chart below. Over the same period their share of sales in their respective product classes moved up from an average of 51·4% to 53·1%.

CHART 34. SALES AND ADVERTISING SHARES OF LEADING GROCERY BRANDS[1]

(27 Grocery Product Classes 1962 v. 1958)

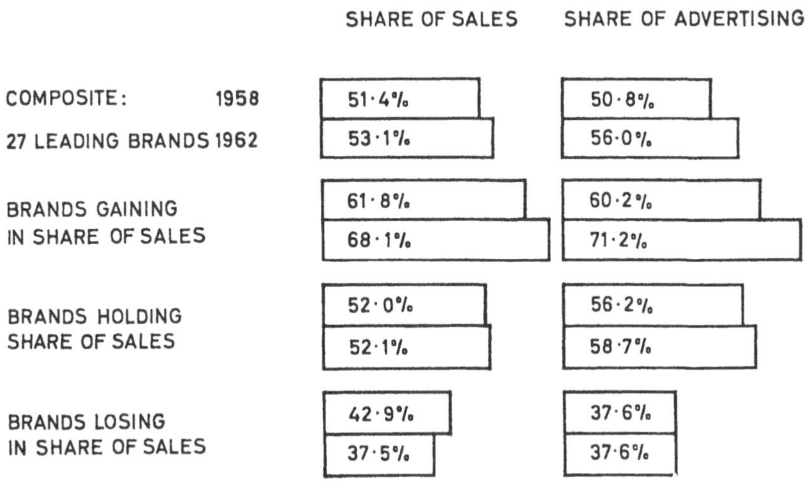

Certain significant comparisons emerge from the above chart according to whether brands gained, held or lost share of market over the five-year period. First, the greatest gains in sales were made by those manufacturers who invested the most in advertising. Second, those brands which held their share of sales marginally increased their advertising investment. Third, those manufacturers who lost some share of sales only held the same share of advertising as in 1958. Again, it is impossible to be certain of the existence of a direct cause and effect relationship.

It is feasible but improbable that the coincidence of higher sales and higher advertising was due to some other factor or factors which gave rise to both. If sales had increased due to these other factors and advertising, allocated on the basis of a fixed percentage of sales achievement, was also increased then such a coincidence would follow automatically. However, it is extremely unlikely that other factors outside of advertising acted in the same direction for all the leading brands across twenty-seven product groups, or that the basis of allocating advertising money was the same for

[1] The Nielsen Researcher. Oxford Edition. January-February 1963.

all the manufacturers concerned. It would seem much more plausible that some relationship does exist between higher advertising on the one hand and higher sales on the other hand; even to the extent of saying that there would appear to be a case for maintaining share of advertising a little ahead of share of sales.

Advertising versus *Price Competition*

It is frequently argued that advertising is a substitute for price competition and that the two are in some way mutually exclusive. Sales, it is said, can be increased either by price reductions so that consumers are persuaded to buy more, or by advertising and promotion so that consumers are persuaded to want more. While this argument may hold in certain very exceptional circumstances, as a general rule, it is based on three fundamental misconceptions.

The first is the belief that any price reduction made possible by using the amount of money being spent on advertising would be a sufficient inducement to the consumer to buy more. For a wide range of products such price reductions spread over the whole of the output of a manufacturer is fractional and, from the consumer standpoint, insignificant.

To begin with, a unit price reduction of less than a halfpenny, which is very often the amount of saving represented by the level of advertising expenditure, is now a physical impossibility. A saving of one halfpenny or a penny per unit is unlikely (except over a narrow range of relatively low-priced goods and services purchased frequently, e.g. matches, bus fares, bread, milk, sugar) to persuade any consumer to buy more of a commodity, whereas an advertising expenditure of the same amount of money might be expected to do so. The higher the unit price of a product the more is this likely to be true.

One way in which a manufacturer seeks to provide effective price reductions is to spread the amount of money available for such a purpose over a portion of his output, e.g. on half his output he could afford to double the reduction in price, and on one-tenth of his output, theoretically, he could afford to give a ten-fold price reduction. This is the reasoning behind the multiplicity of special reduced-price offers, banded packs and the like. All such promotions are, in effect, price reductions whether manufacturer- or retailer-inspired. The retailer himself can often select the product lines and the period of time for making special price offers. On some lines which he can buy in bulk at a favourable discount he can afford to maintain almost continuous price cutting.

As of mid-1963, the A. C. Nielsen Company reported[1] that more than two out of every five grocers (and two out of every three multiple shops) were offering one or more leading brands in any of fifteen food and non-food product classes below the regular price. The chances were the consumer would be able to buy at least one leading brand of coffee at less than regular price in 90% of grocers' shops, a leading brand of scourers in 88%

[1] *The Nielsen Researcher.* Oxford Edition. March–April 1964.

of shops, one or more toilet soaps in 87% of shops and a leading brand of toothpaste in 55% of shops and so on. In December 1963 the average price cuts by retailers, covering twelve food product classes over and above any which might have been available at the same time from manufacturers, was 5·3% for all grocers and 9·1% for multiple outlets.

The second misconception that lies behind the argument that manufacturers advertise in order to avoid direct price competition is that it completely ignores the fact that a great deal of advertising is in fact carried out in support of price reductions and that advertising is indeed a condition of effective price competition. Most retailer advertising is of this nature and a significant share of manufacturers' advertising to consumers is in support of special introductory offers and price promotions. Advertising can thus make price promotion more effective than it might otherwise be by telling consumers of price reductions much faster and more cheaply than other methods.

The third misconception is that price alone is the determining factor in sales. It is not necessary to look very far to see the fallacy of this argument, otherwise everyone would live in the cheapest accommodation, drive the cheapest car, eat the cheapest food and so on. Price is one element, and perhaps the most important one, which enters into our buying decisions, but it is by no means the only one. What the consumer wants from the income he has available to spend on goods and services is a 'standard of living' which represents a particular array of subjective satisfactions. These satisfactions frequently derive from the image he holds of the product or service more than in the reality of the product or service.

Harry Henry in his book on Motivation Research puts the argument with characteristic succinctness when he says: 'So far as concerns food, for example, what a human being *needs* is a certain daily intake of protein, carbohydrate, vitamins and so on: what he *wants*, however, is a selection of familiar and attractive dishes, prepared and served in acceptable forms, and eaten in the ritual situation (with dining-tables, linen tablecloths, china plates, silver cutlery and so on) which for civilised man are as much a part of the meal as the food itself. One might argue that it is a wicked waste of human effort to product linen tablecloths, since food will be quite as nourishing eaten off bare boards . . . but this misses the whole point of the concept of satisfactions.'[1]

Although a brand-image must reflect reality, it comprises much else besides the product's physical characteristics and price. Advertising and promotion are the principal means of building the brand image of a product. This is true for products bought regularly or only bought once in a lifetime. It is also true of many industrial goods and services, e.g. jet aircraft and ocean liners, rail freight services and airlines, banking and insurance services. For some products such as prams, engagement and wedding rings and houses, brand image may be of considerably greater importance than price. Indeed a higher price rather than a lower one may

[1] Op. cit. p. 228.

be a factor in favour of, rather than inimical to, purchase in certain circumstances.

The Advertiser's Problem

Every manufacturer who uses advertising must have asked himself at some stage—is advertising the more economical and/or faster way of communicating my selling message to customers than any other means of marketing communication? He has the choice of a number of alternative courses of action. He can employ a large field sales force, appoint exclusive specialist distributors, give larger margins to distributors, sell by post or door-to-door, or buy up distribution organisations (e.g. public houses, garages, wholesale and retail grocers, etc.) in order to control his own distribution. He can devote himself essentially to the problem of *making* products, leaving it to the broker or dealer to do most of the selling to the customer, the latter often looking to the dealer (rather than the manufacturer) for assurance of value and service. Or, the manufacturer can rely less directly on the distributor to do his active selling for him and add some pressure of his own through direct communication with the consumer, primarily to help his distributor move *his* product faster.

Unfortunately, neither adequate nor independent statistical and cost information exists to enable an attempt to be made to analyse the efficacy of any particular combination of marketing factors. Without such information it is impossible to assess, with any real degree of accuracy, the economic contribution of advertising or other marketing factors in respect of particular industries, product or service groups. It can be assumed, however, that manufacturers use advertising in certain proportions along with other ingredients of the marketing mix because they are convinced that it does contribute effectively and economically to the total marketing effort. It seems unlikely, to say the least, that in today's competitive markets, manufacturers would knowingly and increasingly use a combination of methods which costs more and works less effectively than some alternative combination.

Marketing is not an exact science. Over many years, manufacturers, through the process of trial and error, have improved their techniques, particularly in measuring performance and forecasting future results. When it becomes possible to accurately determine by mathematical means what the best combination of marketing factors should be in any given set of circumstances, there are fair grounds for supposing that manufacturers will be shown to have acted intelligently and to have made some progress in the right direction.

(c) THE ELEMENTS OF ADVERTISING PLANNING

The purpose of each and every advertisement, no matter what medium is used, is to influence *certain* people to think or act in a *certain* way favourable to the advertiser. The basic task of advertising is to reach a target audience, be they members of the general public, trade buyers, specifiers, purchasing officers or other special groups of people, with messages of one sort or another aimed, in the first instance, at changing or reinforcing their attitude of mind and, secondly, at influencing their behaviour. The advertiser seeks to move the people he is trying to influence through the communications spectrum to the point of action as quickly and as economically as possible. It has to be recognised, however, that it may not be possible to achieve this at one fell swoop. It may require several different campaigns to move people from a state of unawareness of a product or service to the point of getting them to take action in the direction of purchasing it.

The planning of advertising involves six basic elements:

1. Identifying the audience to be reached
2. Determining and creating the specific advertising messages to be directed at this audience.
3. Selecting the most effective and most economical media to reach this audience.
4. Scheduling the chosen media to provide the best timing, frequency and impact.
5. Determining the advertising budget.
6. Measuring advertising results.

Clearly, the determination of the audience to be reached and of the advertising messages to be directed at it are very closely related. In other words, what the advertiser has to say and how he says it will depend on to whom it is going to be said. In the first place, what is said must be credible to the recipients, relevant to their problems as potential users of what the advertiser has to offer, contiguous with their past and present experience, and compatible with their existing attitudes and preconceptions.

For example, in planning the advertising for a car the advertiser must first decide to whom his car is most likely to appeal in terms of the potential users' accustomed standards of living, their physical requirements and psychological attitudes towards cars and driving. For some people speed and power are the things they look for in a car. Others look for safety, reliability and trouble-free performance. Some want gadgetry and luxurious comfort, others want simplicity and serviceability. For some, the status that the car confers on its owner is all-important. For others any kind of flamboyance in styling or colour is anathema. The manufacturer, therefore, in deciding what particular sort of people will constitute his most profitable market—and this, in turn, will depend on their pockets as well as their needs and desires—must then determine what he wants to say to them about the car, i.e. what sort of brand image he needs to create and how he can best communicate this image to them.

Market research has an extremely important part to play; first, in identifying the most profitable market for the car; second, in helping to determine the product's basic characteristics and marketing strategy; third, in helping to determine what should be said in the advertising and the best way of saying it; and fourth, in evaluating the results of selected marketing and advertising strategies.

Identification of the Target Audience

Any manufacturer, whatever it is he makes and sells, must attempt to quantify and qualify his potential market. He must try to find out as much as he possibly can about the people who are most likely to be interested in what he has to offer in terms of their number and influence on the final buying decision, their technical requirements, social and economic characteristics, psychological or personality attributes and environmental influences that may in any way affect their freedom or willingness to buy. For example, in many areas of industrial marketing the person who actually does the buying frequently has to purchase within set parameters laid down by the specifier. Thus the advertiser may have to influence a number of targets in relation to any one buying decision.

Social and economic characteristics which must be taken into account by consumer goods manufacturers include sex, age, income level, occupation, size of family, standard of living (as evidenced by ownership of various types of goods, purchase of different kinds of services and income expenditure patterns), geographical location, etc. Much of this information can be culled from official government sources, from surveys and statistics published from time to time by press, television and other media proprietors and by independent research organisations.

For most products, however, the information available is too general for the purpose of marketing and advertising planning, and information directly related to the ability or predisposition to purchase a particular manufacturer's product can only be obtained by means of research undertaken by the manufacturer himself or commissioned by him to an outside research organisation and which is specifically tailored to his particular requirements.

The chief characteristics that industrial goods manufacturers must take account of include the type of customer (e.g. factory, mine, farm, institution or government department), the location of buyers and concentration of the market in terms of geographical, industrial and purchasing criteria.

Psychological and personality attributes are of great importance to advertisers in determining which particular appeals to use in what circumstances. Attitudes, inhibitions, predispositions are rooted in the psychological make-up and personality of the individual. Unfortunately, it has led to the use of a lot of psycho-analytical jargon by market researchers—Oedipus complex, sublimation, introversion, extraversion, etc.—which has frightened or confounded a great many potential users of research. Equally unfortunately, some research has been undertaken in the name of psychological or motivation research which has reflected unfairly on the large amount of very useful scientific and businesslike research carried out. Motivation research has important uses for advertising planning purposes, but is only one technique which can help business men to make better decisions. The best insurance against the misuse of any research technique is to use the services of professionally competent researchers, either within or outside the firm (if outside, then someone who is technically equipped to understand the uses and limitations of research should also be available inside the organisation).

It is usually assumed that whereas psychological factors may play an important part in the customer's choice of car, household goods, food products, toiletries, cosmetics and proprietary remedies, etc., they have very little or no influence whatever on the sale of industrial goods. With most industrial goods, technical performance and service are certainly important considerations. But psychological factors are never completely absent. The attitudes of specifiers, purchasing officers, contractors and architects towards various suppliers of building materials can influence their choice when it comes to awarding contracts, particularly where there is not much to choose between one supplier's material and another's. Moreover, diverse influences may have to be reconciled where there is a diffusion of buying responsibility.

All other things being equal, and in so far as everyone involved in a buying decision is also a human being, there will be occasions when they will prefer to do business with the bigger, though not necessarily more reputable, firms who advertise more extensively and provide them with vast quantities of well-produced literature, not to mention notebooks, scrap pads, cigarette lighters, pens and pencils, and calendars. The man who is not conditioned to some extent by his environment, by the professional, social and other groups to which he belongs and by the persuasive influences that come at him from all directions, has not been born yet.

Environmental factors which are of importance to advertisers are largely concerned with group influences or group behaviour. The groups people belong to—cultural, religious, professional and social—and the status enjoyed by the individual within the group, can be important to manufacturers.

If opinion leaders could be isolated for advertising purposes, the manufacturer and his advertising agency would have an easier task in persuading people to try products or services. Opinion leadership applies to commercial matters just as much as to political, social and other affairs, and in every group of people there are always one or more individuals who emerge as leaders and the group takes on the opinions and attitudes of its leaders. Those outside the group or members of competitive groups will have different leaders with different opinions. New leaders with new attitudes and opinions will break off from established groups and form new or splinter groups of their own and they usually bring their followers or sympathisers with them.

Marketing is very much concerned with group behaviour in the context of the firm and of the market and, therefore, with the interactions between opinion-formers (innovators) and opinion-followers (emulators). If only the manufacturer could break down his market into psychological segments so as to isolate and communicate directly with these innovators and opinion-formers then he would have a most potent selective advertising facility at his disposal. By such means, the attitudes and behaviour of whole groups could be indirectly influenced by precision-aimed advertising. For advertisers this could mean the difference between using guided missiles and lead shot.

Identification of the most likely sales prospects for a manufacturer's product may reveal a number of different market segments each with its own special needs and characteristics. All that this means is that different people buy the same or similar products for widely differing reasons—and, in the case of many industrial products, for widely differing purposes—and that the total potential market for a product will consist of a number of sub-markets or market segments each of which may require a different approach. Over a broad range of consumer and industrial products, a relatively small market segment usually accounts for a large share of the sales.

Just as every product has its intensive and sporadic users, so every market segment has its preferred product. It could be uneconomic to apply the same advertising and selling effort on behalf of a product to a market segment of infrequent or moderate users as to a segment of regular or potentially intensive users. Equally, it could be uneconomic to attempt to sell the same product to each market segment if a new or modified product with a stronger buying appeal to the infrequent or moderate users would sell in much larger quantities and be more profitable. The idea that there is only *one* best all-purpose product for *everyone* is becoming increasingly obsolete. If a manufacturer is to obtain business from as wide a *total* market as possible then he must vary his appeals or offer variations of the same basic product to the different sections or segments of the market.

With toothpaste, for example, preferences vary as between peppermint, spearmint and medicinal-type flavours. One product of a particular flavour is unlikely to appeal to everyone. Other potential toothpaste users may regard the flavour as of very secondary importance and the chemical action or cleaning-power as by far and away the most important consideration. A pure flavour story will have little appeal to these people. With the fluoride toothpastes, for example, masking flavours are used to hide the basic and relatively unpleasant flavour of the stannous or sodium fluoride ingredient. And so the larger toothpaste manufacturers each market a variety of toothpaste with different flavours and active ingredients and use a variety of advertising approaches in order to appeal to all major segments of the market.

Cigarettes provide another example where most manufacturers sell both plain and tipped cigarettes under the same or different brand names and use a selection of different advertising approaches depicting various environmental situations—relaxing or tense, calm or invigorating, alone with one's thoughts or in party mood, indoor or outdoor, etc.

The number of petrols offered by each of the major manufacturers, the availability of optional extras with many consumer durable goods, the introduction of special-purpose soaps and detergents, the development of plastic or aluminium profile sheeting for building and decorative purposes, are further examples of broadening the overall market for the same basic commodity.

In the future, manufacturers' products and advertising policies will undoubtedly reflect a growing awareness of market segmentation based on physical product differences and on customers' psychological differences. Indeed, as products become more alike, the need for psychological segmentation will become greater. But a great deal more research is necessary before marketers are as familiar with the psychological dimensions of markets as they are with their physical characteristics.

Determining and Creating Specific Advertising Messages

Having defined the market or market segments to be reached, the next step must be to decide in what ways it is desired to change or affect the attitudes of the people who make up the market. Before it is possible to change attitudes it is necessary to find out what are the existing attitudes and why people hold the attitudes they do. Motivation research is the only way of finding these things out. Wrong decisions taken at this stage, based on hunch, guesswork or so-called experience, will seriously reduce, if not nullify, the effectiveness of the whole advertising effort.

It is not enough to have a good product. Customers must be made aware that there is such a product. They must be convinced that it is not merely a good product but the best for their own purposes and they must be persuaded to do something about it. In other words, potential customers must be exposed to the product and its advertising, they must perceive the advertising, understand what it is trying to say, retain the key points and finally, in the light of other purchasing influences such as personal selling, shop or stock room display and merchandising, take a decision to buy or not to buy. At any one of these stages—exposure, awareness, comprehension, conviction and action—every manufacturer runs the risk of losing potential customers because what he is saying to them in his advertising is either not meaningful or is irrelevant to their particular circumstances and needs, or is at variance with their own past experience and present attitudes.

Enough research evidence is available to show that the potential customer can be exposed to an advertisement but cannot be made to look at it. People are selective about advertisements and tend only to notice and take in those messages they want to see or hear because the messages fit in with and are relevant to those needs, interests, ideas and beliefs they already have. Failure of advertisements to engage the potential customer psychologically in this way will result in his screening himself off from further contact with the advertiser.

Essentially, the creative advertising task, whether it is performed by someone within the manufacturer's own organisation or by the company's appointed advertising agency, is to turn a purchase proposition—the one most important thing, or perhaps several things, about the product which it is believed will motivate the customer to buy it—into an original advertising idea. This is what 'creativity' or 'the creative process' in advertising is all about. Creative people in advertising—copy writers, script writers, visualisers, typographers, film producers and so on—solve advertising problems and the solutions, expressed in words and pictures, movement and sound, are *ideas*.

The way in which advertising ideas are arrived at is open to a great deal of misunderstanding based on ignorance and unfamiliarity with how the creative process works. The mental picture so often carried of the creative advertising man or woman sitting at the typewriter or the drawing board, pen or brush in hand working to an open-sky brief and waiting for the inspiration to strike, is far removed from the truth. The fundamental starting-point of any advertisement must be the realisation that it is a communication between two people—the manufacturer on the one hand, the customer on the other.

The creative process may be visualised in the following way.[1]

CHART 35. THE CREATIVE PROCESS

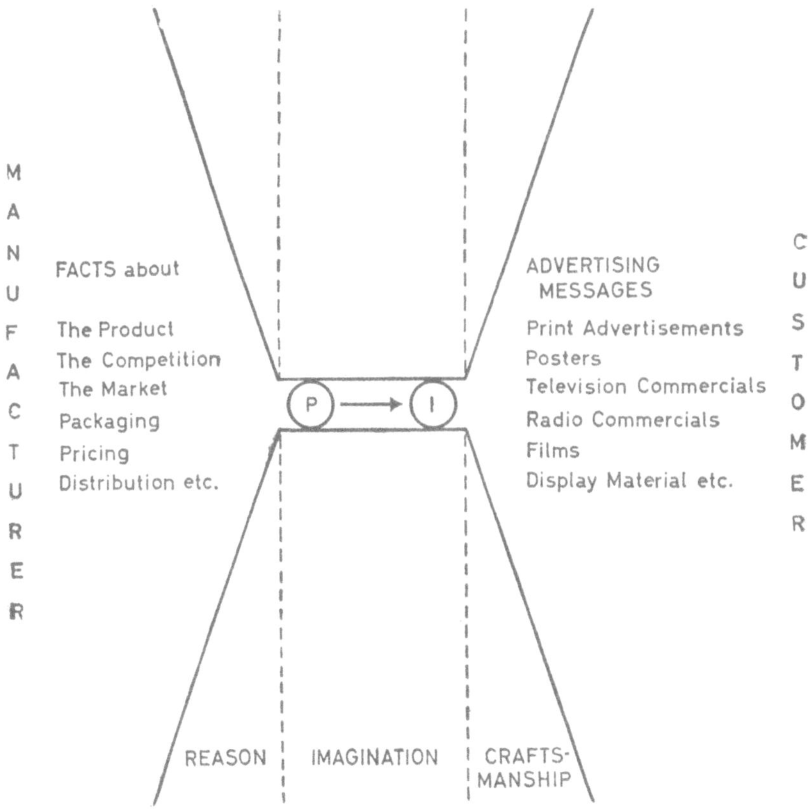

[1] The author is indebted to David Bernstein and to McCann-Erickson Advertising Ltd. for permission to make use of this chart and other material in this section.

The funnel-like object splays out at both ends and has a narrow section in the middle. At one end is the manufacturer, at the other the customer. It is a two-way funnel. Through it, in one direction the manufacturer speaks to the customer through his advertising. Through it, in the reverse direction, the customer speaks to the manufacturer by means of advertising research, customer attitude studies and so on. The customer also speaks to the manufacturer by buying the product.

The importance of communications from the customer, i.e. all forms of marketing intelligence, has already been stressed elsewhere. The major concern here is with communications directed to the customer in the form of advertising although the product itself, its packaging, its pricing, display material and sales promotion are all, in themselves, forms of communication to which creative thinking and planning must be applied.

So far as advertising is concerned what goes into the funnel at the manufacturer's end is facts culled from internal and external sources about the product and the competition, about the market, methods of distribution and so on. The analysis of these facts by trained and experienced marketing men form the basis for marketing and advertising decisions from which a basic purchase proposition or concept is derived; a proposition, moreover, that is related to an identified customer need or desire. Up to this point the accepted rational method of observing, classifying and analysing the facts has been followed and, to a degree, a prediction has been made that the customer will be motivated by a particular proposition.

Creativity starts with the purchase proposition (P) in the diagram and seeks to find an original advertising idea which best expresses and *communicates* the proposition. The purchase proposition becomes an original advertising idea (I) through the application of insight and imagination. It is turned into a physical advertisement by skilled craftsmanship—writing words, drawing pictures, directing photography, seeing, checking and correcting proofs and so on. In the advertising department of a manufacturing organisation or in the creative department of an advertising agency some people are involved in all phases—helping to define the problem, solving it and then actually preparing the advertisements. Others are solely concerned with the craft aspect—actually taking the advertising idea and producing a campaign based on it, i.e. doing adaptations and follow-up advertisements in a series. Relatively so few products are demonstrably and obviously superior to anything else on the market that the problem more often than not is one of communicating significant product *differences* rather than major, perhaps unique, product advantages. Hence, differences between essentially similar products sharing the same basic purchase proposition will often depend upon the unique *creative interpretation* of the proposition.

What the foregoing diagram also illustrates is the restrictive area in which the creative advertising man works—the limitations imposed by the statement of a concise proposition and the request for its imaginative interpretation.

The interpretation of the creative brief is itself subject to the self-discipline that the advertising industry imposes on its own members through an assortment of committees representative of the whole or particular parts of the industry, e.g. The Advertising Standards Authority, The British Code of Advertising Practice Committee, The Joint Copy Committee of The Newspaper Proprietors' Association and Newspaper Society, The Copy Committee of the Periodical Proprietors' Association, The Advertising Advisory Committee of the Independent Television Authority, The Advertisement Copy Committee of the Independent Television Companies Association, The Joint Censorship Committee of the Poster Advertising Industry, British Transport Advertising, The Screen Advertising Association, Proprietary Association of Great Britain, Institute of Practitioners in Advertising, The Advertising Association Advertisement Investigation Department, etc.

In addition, there are a large and growing number of parliamentary statutes restricting, controlling or otherwise affecting what can be said or shown in advertising, when and how. The very large area of advertising not subject to statutory control or regulation is controlled by the voluntary effort of the people who work in advertising, to ensure that no advertising is illegal, dishonest, misleading or fraudulent.[1]

It might be argued that the narrowness of that bit of the funnel in which creative advertising men must work imposes a severe limitation on their creativity, on the basis that a true artist must be free from all constraints. But advertising is not just an art to be judged simply on its aesthetic appeal. The purpose of advertising is to help to sell goods. It is not designed by the advertising man as a means of self-expression nor can it be judged on the basis of whether its creator likes it or not.

Advertising is intended to persuade certain other people to respond in a certain way and therefore involves estimating what other people will do as a result of seeing a particular advertisement. There is little point in any creative exercise unrelated to a specific problem or not directed towards a specific target or the accomplishment of a specific objective. Creative men, unencumbered by fact and given no guidance, may produce a welter of bright ideas. But advertising is a business and cannot escape the commercial disciplines of time and money. It therefore demands not only bright ideas, but right ideas that are based on a rational process of thought, a proper knowledge and understanding of the relevant facts and an informed creativity.

But if advertising is not an art, neither is it wholly a science since at the heart of it is the creative act of getting and developing an idea. At the same time, advertising is coming to depend more and more on the use of scientific methods to gather and analyse the facts on which advertising ideas must ultimately be based, both to ensure a much greater probability of those ideas

[1] For a detailed guide to the voluntary controls set up by the advertising industry see *How Advertising Disciplines Itself.* The Advertising Association. London. May 1964.

being right and, through copy and other forms of communication re-research, to measure their ultimate effectiveness.

(d) MEDIA PLANNING: THE SELECTION OF MEDIA AND MEDIA SCHEDULING

The broad function of media planning is to consider all media—press, television, film, radio, outdoor posters and signs, etc.—in relation to the objective of a specific advertising campaign and to produce a media plan which, on the best evidence and judgment available, is the most effective for the proposed campaign. Having determined the target audience and the specific advertising message to be communicated to that audience, it is the task of the advertising agency's media experts—the media planners and the media buyers—to recommend the most economical medium or combination of media for placing the advertising message before the target group to a given degree over a given period of time. The question of to what specific degree and over what specific period of time will be determined by the advertising task to be accomplished and the size of the advertising budget.

Media planning decisions must be based on the advertising objectives developed for the product which, in turn, will be determined by the basic marketing strategy for the product. The establishment of an advertising strategy, that is, determining whom the manufacturer is trying to reach and what he wants to say to them, is necessary before deciding where and with what frequency he needs to say it.

Factors entering into media planning decisions include the location and accessibility (in terms of media) of the manufacturer's prospective customers, the social, economic and psychological composition of his target audience, the frequency with which the product or service is bought or used, the price of the product or service, the seasonality of the market, area sales strengths or weaknesses *vis-à-vis* competition, the distribution plan with particular reference to major sales drives, and last, but not least, the ideal creative requirements for the campaign in terms of space size or time length, colour versus black and white, product demonstration, minimum acceptable standards of reproduction, etc.

There is still a high element of judgment required in media decision-making although the use of computers is whittling down the area of pure judgment to a degree which could not have been contemplated even five years ago. The ability to apply complex mathematic formulae by such means will reduce much of the routine calculation work and cost comparisons that at present take up so much of the media specialists' time. However, judgment, experience and ingenuity will continue to have an important place in media planning and buying. The biggest computer, like the smallest slide-rule, is only a tool in the hands of its user. What one gets out of it depends on what the user puts into it and it is in this area that judgment, experience and creative use of media (in the sense of finding novel and more effective media solutions to old problems) will remain at a high premium.

Among the major considerations[1] which must weigh heavily in an advertiser's media decisions are the following:

1. Size of the media budget.
2. The nature and scale of competitive media activity.
3. The suitability of the medium.
4. The relative importance of coverage and frequency.
5. The importance of influencing distributors.
6. The degree of flexibility required.
7. The effectiveness of the medium (in terms of the cost of advertising messages delivered to potential customers).

Size of the Media Budget

The size of the media budget is the major determining factor in the choice of media. This will determine whether only one major medium or a combination of several media is affordable. Ideally, the budget should be allocated on the basis of the amount of money considered necessary to achieve the advertising objectives most economically and most effectively in a given set of circumstances. This, however, is only possible when the advertising objectives have been clearly set out in advance. More often than not advertisers and advertising agencies will be able to agree on the choice of the *primary* medium to be used for a particular product within a given budget. This is the medium which, all things considered, will most economically and effectively give a basic minimum coverage of the target customer group. Whatever else happens it is important to do an adequate job in terms of size or length and frequency of participation in this primary medium before adding secondary media.

It is not usually possible to cover all likely customers through the use of one medium. But in any case, within a given advertising budget, a manufacturer has a choice between trying to reach a larger number of customers and reaching a fewer number of customers more frequently. The principle of 'first things first' must always apply. If prospective customers can be graded into sub-groups based on their propensity to buy or use the product and if these prospect-groups can also be identified into specific media groups, then so much the better. Such a happy coincidence, however, is rare except for specialised products used by people who read specialised magazines and periodicals, e.g. do-it-yourself items, yachts, certain photographic goods.

Industrial goods are, in this sense, easier to advertise to actual prospects through a wide range of specialised periodicals and professional and technical journals. As a general rule, the wider the purchase or use of any product the more difficult it becomes to reach prospective customers

[1] This assessment is based on *A Checklist for Sound Media Decisions* by Emerson Foote and Daniel Kinley, presented at the 1959 Spring Meeting of the Association of National Advertisers (U.S.A.) in Chicago, Illinois.

through specialised or a limited list of media. The more ubiquitous the product in use the more ubiquitous the advertising message must be.

Other considerations affecting the choice of primary and secondary media include the necessity or otherwise for colour reproduction (e.g. certain food, fashion and cosmetic products), for product demonstration (e.g. consumer durables, certain food, pharmaceutical and toiletry products as well as the great majority of industrial products) and for special announcements (e.g. new or improved products, special offers, consumer competitions).

The Nature and Scale of Competitive Media Activity

An advertiser is invariably faced with two choices. The first choice is between trying to reach the same audience as his chief competitors or attempting to reach a different audience not being effectively covered, if at all, by his competitors. The second choice is between using the same media as or different media from competitors to reach the target audience.

Many large advertisers consider it desirable to dominate at least one major medium, be it television, newspapers, women's magazines, outdoor posters, professional journals or trade and technical press. Rather than attempt to match his chief competitors in all media, an advertiser may elect to concentrate the greater part, if not the whole, of his media appropriation on one medium in the hope that his product will become identified with that medium and give him a preferred media position, in the same way that another manufacturer may try to obtain special or preferred positions within a particular class of media or a particular publication or television time segment. This tendency to achieve domination in, and identification with, specific classes of media and within specific media is regarded by a large number of advertisers as a very important aim of media planning policy, especially by some of the medium-sized and developing companies, who cannot match the resources and across-the-board media policies of the really big spenders.

The Relative Importance of Coverage and Frequency

'Coverage' means the number of potential customers reached by the advertising message and 'frequency' means the number of times the advertising message is exposed to each of those customers. An advertiser can add more media to his list to get more coverage of his target audience. He can buy more insertions or participations to increase the frequency with which he reaches his audience. However, whereas coverage can be increased only by adding to the *list* of media used, frequency can be increased by adding to the number of participations in each media type, or by adding to the list of media. This must follow because everyone sees a number of different media.

A prospective purchaser of any product may watch independent television, read certain newspapers, popular magazines, periodicals and professional and trade journals, visit the cinema, listen to Radio Luxembourg, or pass outdoor posters in the street or see them in trains, on buses and so on. Every potential customer in his daily life is exposed to a wide variety of media through which the advertiser can reach him or her with his advertising message. He can be exposed to the same message, in different forms, in the newspaper he reads going to work in the morning, the periodicals and journals circulated in his office, the direct mail advertisements he receives through the post, the poster site opposite his place of work, the bus or train he catches home in the evening, the television he watches that night and the magazine he takes to bed with him. All of these opportunities to reach him are open to the advertiser, and the frequency with which the customer is exposed to a given advertising message will be determined by the factors previously mentioned, i.e. size of media budget, choice of primary and secondary media, etc.

The following example shows the use of additional media to provide greater specific coverage and frequency. A producer of a range of special-purpose, unit load bulk materials storing and handling equipment identified three major markets to be developed: heavy chemicals, food processing and pharmaceuticals. One national newspaper and two general magazines were used to establish the overall image of the company and its materials-handling expertise across all markets. Industrial, food and other specialised business publications were added to give greater coverage and frequency in the company's three major specific markets. Direct mail was added to provide even greater frequency on selected key prospects in each of these markets. The object of the direct mail campaign was to acquaint selected customers with a new leasing scheme whereby they could now hire all the necessary equipment rather than buy it outright. The campaign was restricted to those prospects whom the manufacturer knew had bulk-handling problems on a large enough scale to make the new service he was offering of real and immediate interest. Four mailing shots were sent offering a specific service to the selected prospects in each market.

The purchasing and usage patterns for a product are obviously important in determining the relative weight to be given to coverage on the one hand and frequency on the other. Usually, greater coverage is only possible at the expense of greater frequency. Clearly, widely used products with a high repeat purchase pattern require maximum coverage and frequency. Unfortunately, the reverse argument, that for expensive products only bought once or twice in a lifetime coverage is all-important and frequency only secondary, is not always justified. It is certainly not true of a wide range of fairly expensive and infrequently purchased products such as cars, life assurance and fur coats, where buyers are constantly coming into the market as their circumstances and needs change. People need to be constantly reminded of the availability and identity of such things so that when they decide to buy they can make an informed choice on a basis of real preference.

The Importance of Influencing Distributors

The selection of media must take account of the channels of distribution and the attitudes and influence of the distributors upon whom the manufacturer depends for getting his product stocked, displayed and possibly demonstrated before potential buyers. Distributors and stockists often need to be aware and convinced of the effectiveness of the manufacturer's own advertising effort in their local area. This is particularly important (a) where the advertiser gives the name or names of local stockists in his advertisement, (b) where the advertiser and the distributor join together in the same advertisement or different advertisements in the same medium on a co-operative basis, (c) where local advertising of manufacturers' special offers and promotions is needed to ensure the stocking-up and active selling support of distributors in the area. The buying of advertising space in distributors' publications, literature, price lists, etc. by manufacturers is a fairly common practice.

Manufacturers of industrial products who sell to fabricators, converters, installation contractors and secondary suppliers are particularly conscious of the need to plan their advertising and other promotional activities with an eye to the effect they will have on the attitudes and support activity of their key distributors.

The Degree of Flexibility Required

The degree of media flexibility required will depend primarily on the nature of the product and its sources of supply. For products which have a year-in-year-out use and whose sources of supplies are assured, the need for flexibility is not the most important consideration. But for products with marked and, to a degree, unpredictable seasonal peaks and troughs (e.g. cold and flu remedies, sun-tan lotions, de-icers for cars, ice-cream, certain soft drinks), or whose sources of supply are subject to uncertainty and the vagaries of climate (e.g. home-produced and imported canned and fresh fruit, fresh vegetables), then the greater the need for flexibility in media planning. The sudden necessity to switch or cancel media insertions, to change advertising messages or to change expenditure patterns are problems which most advertisers come up against at one time or another.

Within the cancellation limits adhered to by the different media and the physical limitations imposed by the time (and money) taken to produce a press advertisement or television commercial, most advertisers aim to plan ahead as far as possible consistent with the minimum of likely last-minute changes. Clearly, it is easier and involves less risk to cancel media commitments if the necessity arises, than it is to get a valuable media showing at the eleventh hour. For a multi-product company, it is usually easier to transfer the media bookings from one product to another provided it fits in with the manufacturer's marketing plans and meets the media proprietor's requirements.

The Appropriateness of the Medium

It goes without saying that the appropriateness of a particular medium will largely depend on the characteristics of its readers in their role as buyers, specifiers and users of the product or service advertised. The housewife is a buyer of a very wide range of products for the home, her personal use and for the use and enjoyment of her family, friends and guests. Other consumer products are purchased as a result of a combined husband-and-wife decision (which one predominates can be a critical factor in media selection) or on the advice of relatives and friends who may or may not have had personal experience of the product in question. Word of mouth recommendation and personal demonstration are still potent and probably underestimated advertising forces. Some evidence of this is seen in the growth of party-plan selling of cosmetics and household goods, through housewife-agents and buying-club organisations.

Industrial products may be bought by a single chief buyer who has sole purchasing responsibility, or who must buy within the limitations imposed by a specifying authority, or again by a 'buying committee' consisting of both technical and commercial representatives each of whom has some influence on the final buying decision. In a great many cases, a new industrial product has to go through a 'proving period' and be passed by a technical expert or group of experts before a commercial evaluation takes place. The final buying decision will be based on commercial considerations and made by the chief buyer, specifier or commercial director with the advice of other interested parties.

Another measure of the appropriateness of the medium is an intangible thing which goes under the heading of 'editorial content'. There are a number of variables which go to make up the character or personality of any medium and which determine the time and circumstances under which it is read or seen, the degree of authority it carries, the mood in which it is received and observed and the aura of confidence it engenders in its readers. A great deal remains to be found out about these matters, more particularly with regard to the believability and pulling-power that a medium confers on the advertisements which appear in it. There are some media planners who argue that, for advertising purposes, these factors are more important than numbers and that what really matters is the proportion of the potential audience that is influenced by a given advertisement and the degree to which they are influenced in a given direction. In other words, they contend that the quality of the response is more important than quantity of exposure. The judgment and experience of the advertiser and his media planners are still crucial for decisions like these although, with the aid of media research, we are becoming more knowledgeable about the key determining factors which give a particular medium its special character and about the commercial significance of such factors to the advertiser.

In considering the appropriateness of the medium for the advertising message, the media planner has, on occasions, to take account of the appropriateness of the advertising message for the advertising medium. Some media do not accept or may impose conditions on advertising for certain products, e.g. proprietary medicines and treatments, alcoholic beverages, tobacco products. Action has already been taken to ban the advertising of cigarettes on television, and more stringent limitation may yet be imposed on this and other products because of health hazards, the desire to discourage young people from ever starting to use them, and the paternalism of government.

The Effectiveness of the Medium

When all the foregoing factors have been duly weighed in the balance, the final media schedule chosen—the media selected and the frequency of participation—will be determined by cost considerations. Every advertiser would clearly like to be able to select by direct comparison of alternative media combinations that combination which provides the maximum number of effective advertising messages delivered to potential customers at the lowest possible cost. Unfortunately, it is not quite as simple as this because three important variables enter into any inter-media comparison: (1) the effective cost of the different media, (2) the effectiveness of the advertising message as between different media, (3) the ability of the different media to reach potential customers.

By *effective cost* is meant the cost per thousand readers, viewers, or listeners who actually see or hear the advertisement as opposed to the number of opportunities which the audience has to see or hear it. While the 'number of opportunities to see the advertisement' or 'the number of advertising impressions' which a given media schedule provides can sound impressive enough when talking to distributors about the scale of the advertising effort being put behind a particular manufacturer's product, so far as the manufacturer is concerned the real cost is the cost of getting *x*-thousand readers or *y*-thousand viewers to see his advertisement. Special discounts made available by the media proprietors—on 'package deals' of one sort or another, the purchase of space in special issues, the purchase of time at special periods or times of the year—further complicate the issue.

The effectiveness of the advertising message is as much a matter of the relative effectiveness of each medium to deliver the message as it is a matter of creating the advertising message itself. The latter is the result of sound reasoning, imagination and craftsmanship. The former comprises a number of elements which will vary in effectiveness with each advertising medium—the 'image' and authority of the medium, visualisation facilities (colour, sound, motion, reproduction), editorial content, immediacy of action required (reminder advertising or quick response), etc.

Having established who his potential customers are and where they are located the manufacturer is finally forced to ask himself which particular media combination will result in the most economic delivery of his advertising message to these prospects.

Inter-media comparisons based on the earlier criteria, i.e. budget, competitive activity, frequency versus coverage, etc., can be made. But a comparison of the cost per thousand between television and women's magazines, or between national press and outdoor posters, is considered by many media experts to be virtually impossible. Unfortunately, media planners have to make such comparisons and they do have to choose from among a number of possible alternatives on some sort of cost basis. The fact that absolutely accurate statistical comparisons are not within their grasp at the present time does not mean that media selection can be left solely to the toss of a coin or to the mystical incantations of the media buyer.

Over the years, media experts have been adding to their scientific knowledge and methods of media selection and buying. Based on the marketing strategy for the product, a number of specific advertising objectives are developed. Then for each medium under consideration, the best way of using each media type, e.g. television, national or provincial newspapers, magazines, profession and trade journals, outdoor, etc., in order to accomplish the advertising objectives, is determined. For each type of media, the costs per thousand readers (or viewers), using two or three alternative combinations of size (or length) and frequency of participation, are calculated and compared. The particular medium which emerges as the most economic is then reviewed in the light of all the other relevant criteria discussed previously to determine the extent to which secondary media may need to be added to secure greater coverage or some other important requirement, or to what degree these other criteria off-set the difference in cost per thousand between the first choice and other media.

The calculation of the *effective* cost per thousand, that is to say, the number of people who actually see a manufacturer's advertisement, is not such an easy matter. Media and audience research surveys already provide a limited amount of information in respect of the readers who note and read particular advertisements in certain publications and of the number of television viewers tuned into particular programmes or time segments.[1] But such data do not at present provide the necessary detailed guidance on the proportions of the various media audiences who may be expected on average to 'take-in' a particular advertisement. It may eventually be possible for the manufacturer to assess accurately the real cost per thousand effective advertising messages delivered to potential customers. For the time being, he must make do with comparisons on the basis of the cost per thousand readers (of a particular issue of a publication) or viewers (of a particular television programme or time segment) exposed to or having the opportunity to see his advertisement regardless of the proportions of readers or viewers who in actual fact do not see it or take it in.

[1] Social Surveys (Gallup Poll) Ltd. carries out regular noting and reading checks of print advertisements in a selected list of publications. Television Audience Measurement (TAM) Ltd. supplies programme audience figures for all commercial television stations for each day of the week broken down by individual programmes and time segments.

Because of the difficulty in measuring, let alone forecasting, the results of advertising, manufacturers have tended in the past to use certain rule-of-thumb criteria in working out what to spend on advertising.

Thus, some companies use the *ratio method* by which a fixed percentage of sales revenue is allocated to advertising based on average sales performance over a period of years, on actual sales revenue earned in the previous year or an expected sales revenue in the forthcoming year.

Other companies use the *unit method*, i.e. a fixed advertising rate per unit of sale, say, 2*s*. per case or per gross of product, or £1 per installation. Using either method, the size of the advertising budget tends to increase as sales increase and to be cut back when sales decline. But the need for increased or reduced advertising is not necessarily related to current sales experience. Budgeting for advertising cannot follow the same unchanging arithmetic rule from one year to the next any more than can the budgeting for the total business.

Some companies use the *competitive comparison method* in arriving at their advertising budgets. This relates their expenditures to what the major competitors are estimated to be spending or to the average rate of expenditure by the industry as a whole based on either the ratio or unit methods. Whilst it does not have the direct simplicity of either of these two methods, the competitive comparison method does have the advantage that a company maintains its relative position *vis-à-vis* the industry and its competitors. Apart from the difficulty of accurately assessing what competitors are spending or what the industry average is, the main disadvantages are that neither competitive budgets nor an average budget for the industry need bear any relationship to an individual company's market objectives or requirements. At best, the company may maintain its competitive position; at worst, its budget may be either inadequate in relation to the company's sales needs or uneconomic (especially when added to other marketing expenses which in the case of competitors are not usually discoverable).

A comparatively few companies use the *task method* whereby advertising budgets are based on the jobs to be done. These change from year to year as market conditions and prospects change, as advertising, selling and other costs continue to rise, as greater competition develops and as new product and profit opportunities present themselves. The task method requires that advertising money should be allocated on the basis of the advertising task to be accomplished. It assumes that the company is capable of realistic sales forecasting, of setting realistic advertising goals and of correctly gauging the funds necessary to achieve them.

For a company's established products, the trend of the market and the volume of competitive advertising must be taken into account in setting advertising budgets. Increased advertising expenditure in certain areas may be necessary to counter special competitive activity or to capitalise on competitive weakness. Or lower advertising expenditure may be indicated in a rapidly declining market. On new products, relatively heavy spending may be necessary to establish and maintain an early foothold in the market or to ensure that a new product gets up a good head of steam for the next phase of the marketing operation.

Advertising expenditure, especially on new products, needs to be looked upon as an investment. Any form of investment is undertaken to ensure the maintenance of a desirable rate of return or to secure an improved rate of return on the money spent. Just as investment in new plant is undertaken to build up future levels of output so investment in advertising is undertaken to help build up future levels of sales. The cost of advertising, like the cost of plant extension, cannot always be completely recouped in the first, second or even third year. The costs incurred, and the returns obtained, may need to be spread over a period of years.

For fiscal reasons companies make out their accounts on an annual basis, but this does not mean that everything stops at the end of the accounting period. There is no logic, from a purely marketing point of view, in trying to balance the books on an arbitrary chosen day of the year. Whatever the accounting necessities that lie behind the balance sheet—and there are many good reasons why an annual reckoning is necessary—company operations continue, money continues to be paid out and returns continue to flow in.

Thus, more and more companies are planning their marketing expenditures, including advertising, for three years, four years or longer periods ahead. Such plans enable the company to work out revenue and expenditure projections based on different sets of assumptions as to expected sales volumes at varying levels of marketing expenditure. By comparing such alternative projections it is possible for management to select that projection of revenue, expenditure and profit which, in terms of the period of time that must elapse before a break-even point is reached and in terms of the rate of profit earned thereafter, proves to be the most acceptable. A typical pay-out plan has already been shown earlier.[1]

The scale of advertising investment and the length of the pay-out period acceptable to a particular company will depend most importantly upon the following factors:

(a) Its overall objectives—the degree to which the company needs to protect and, if possible, increase the return on an already substantial investment in a particular product field especially where under-utilised capacity exists; or the need to reduce business risk by insuring against product obsolescence through diversifying into other fields related to its existing product-line; or its reluctance to settle for anything less than product leadership in its major markets; or, finally, its desire to enter a rapidly growing market with long-term profit potential.

[1] See p. 148.

(b) Its attitude to marketing investment—some companies view marketing investment differently from other forms of investment, e.g. plant and equipment, and expect all products to break even in their first year.

(c) Its profit goals—management profit goals may be long- or short-term and the sales volume and profit potentials for any product will be related to the product itself, the size and long-term trend of the market, the strength of the product's appeal, the degree of differential advantage it enjoys compared with the major competition, and the anticipated length of the product's life cycle.

(f) MEASURING ADVERTISING RESULTS

The advertising budget probably represents the largest amount of money disbursed by manufacturers with no precise measure of what it can be expected to achieve. The spending of large sums of money on advertising without some system of accountability can be compared to conducting a business without a book-keeping or accounting department. Advertising accountability has lagged far behind general management accountability in that the latter is held responsible for accomplishing certain specific and, usually, measurable results in relation to money spent. Sound business operation demands that expenditure and results be related. The idea of holding advertising accountable for accomplishing certain *sales* results is certainly not new. But there is now a growing body of expert opinion that the sales criterion, as applied to advertising in isolation, is based on a fundamental misconception.

A pioneering study of the problem of measuring advertising results has been carried out by two American organisations—The Association of National Advertisers and The National Industrial Conference Board—and their reports[1] suggest certain methods of arriving at a practical solution.

The crux of the problem is that the causal relationship between advertising and sales is, generally speaking, limited, and, as yet, unmeasurable. Advertising is only one component within the marketing mix that leads to a sale. Others include product or service features, pricing, packaging, distribution, personal selling, sales promotion, merchandising and point of sale display.

Additionally, no single marketing operation exists in a vacuum—competing operations, changes in tastes, attitudes and preferences, seasonal factors, and changes in the general economic climate or in the conditions affecting a particular industry, ensure that things are always in a state of flux. It is always dangerous, therefore, to assume that if sales go up, or sales go down, advertising alone is responsible. Sometimes this may be true as when advertising is far and away the predominant variable, or

[1] *Defining Advertising Goals for Measured Advertising Results.* Association of National Advertisers Inc. *Measuring Advertising Results.* National Industrial Conference Board.

when it calls for immediate buyer response, e.g. mail order, coupon response, request for demonstration or product sample. Even here, the number of mail order enquiries [other than on a cash sale basis], coupon responses, product sample enquiries and requests for demonstrations does not directly measure the effectiveness of the advertising in terms of actual sales results. The conversion rate, i.e. the ratio of actual sales made to enquiries received or demonstrations given, is the critical factor and this can depend on many factors other than advertising, e.g. the effectiveness of the sales follow-up, the customer's assessment of product or service features and value for money.

Advertising is a means of communication. Its results can only be measured in terms of communication goals, in terms of the cost per advertising message delivered per customer for a given result. In other words, according to Colley,[1] 'an advertising goal is a specific communication task, to be accomplished among a defined audience to a given degree in a given period of time'.

An advertising goal, as distinct from a total marketing goal, cannot be measured by sales figures or share of market. A legitimate marketing goal might be to increase sales of a product during a specific period by 25% over the same period of the previous year. The advertising goal could be to increase awareness among potential customers, from a level of, say, 25% to a level of 40% over a six-month period, that the company makes the product in question *or* to establish a preference for the product among 15% of these customers over the same period.

Advertising accountability consists of setting and measuring agreed advertising goals. It does not, in itself, consist of measuring the size of an audience exposed to advertising nor of counting the number of people who have noted an advertisement, nor whether people like or dislike the advertising—important as these measures are. It is concerned solely with the overall changes that occur in mental attitude and behaviour as a direct result of advertising.

At a later stage it may be possible to relate these attitude changes directly to buying action but, for the present, too little is known about the relationship between the establishment of certain favourable attitudes and actual purchasing or intention to purchase. In particular, not enough is known about the effect of repetition or about the time lags involved in the response to advertising or the way it dies away in time. These relationships and time lags would appear to depend on the nature of the particular product and its rate of purchase, the particular choice of media, the pattern of size and frequency of advertisements and the creative content of specific advertisements.

The most important and difficult part of the accountability procedure is the setting of advertising goals. The following principles were suggested by Colley:[2]

[1] Ibid.
[2] Ibid.

(i) An advertising goal should be a succinct statement of the communication aspects of the marketing job. It should *not* encompass results (such as sales) that require a combination of several different marketing forces.
(ii) The goal should be expressed in writing—in finite, measurable terms.
(iii) Goals should be agreed upon by those concerned at both creative and management levels.
(iv) Goals should express realistic expectancy in the light of calculated market opportunities. They should not express vague hopes and desires arrived at without factual foundation.
(v) Benchmarks should be set up against which accomplishments can be measured—customer knowledge, attitude, buying propensity, etc.
(vi) Methods to be used at a later date in evaluating accomplishment should be set up at the time the goals are established.

However, making goals specific does not necessarily make them right. Careful analysis must precede the setting of goals. Market and motivation research can help the manufacturer to determine such basic things as the most important product or service benefits (real or imagined), the people who are most likely to buy the product or service, the reasons why some buy and others fail to buy, the attitudes and predispositions that need to be changed, the media through which prospects may best be reached and so on. It will be appreciated that there is little point in setting goals where there is no known method of measuring the progress made. Media research, audience research and copy research are all useful tools of measurement but they do not carry the advertiser far enough in measuring the actual results of his advertising—the extent to which people's knowledge and attitudes may have been affected by the advertising.

A system of measuring advertising goals will involve a great deal more *communications research* in the following areas:

(a) Product/Service Awareness—the measurement of the degree to which advertising has succeeded in making the target customer group more aware of the existence of the product or service.
(b) Product/Service Knowledge—the measurement of the degree to which advertising has succeeded in increasing the target customer group's knowledge and comprehension of important product or service features and customer benefits.
(c) Product/Service Image—the measurement of the degree to which advertising has succeeded in reinforcing or modifying the product or service image in the intended direction.
(d) Product/Service Acceptability—the measurement of the degree to which advertising has succeeded in convincing the target group of the desirability and acceptability of the product or service.

Advertising communications research, in other words, is designed to measure the extent to which members of the target group are moved through one or more of the levels of awareness, comprehension, conviction and action. Allied to other market measurements such as the pre- and post-testing of individual advertisements and studies of media coverage and effectiveness, communications research is the means of bringing the manufacturer and his advertising agency nearer to achieving a workable system of advertising accountability than at any time in the past. In the early stages, the setting and measurement of advertising goals will not be an easy task and wide errors of judgment are to be expected. Better judgment and greater accuracy will come from experience of using the technique.

(g) THE ROLE OF PUBLIC RELATIONS

Public Relations, as defined by the Institute of Public Relations, is 'the deliberate, planned and sustained effort to establish and maintain mutual understanding between an organisation and its public'. It is not, therefore, the casual or haphazard act of public spiritedness undertaken with due regard to maximum publicity, or the occasional press handout or trade reception. It is an organised attempt to promote all company activities and interests in every way possible, short of paid-for advertising, to the various groups of people whom the company seeks to influence.

Public relations covers many diverse activities and many 'publics' including a firm's own employees and shareholders, potential employees and investors, customers, suppliers, financial institutions and government departments. As companies grow and diversify they find their relationships with various groups of 'publics' become more and more complex and that these relationships can exert an important influence on many facets of company activity. The job of public relations is to advise company management of any changes in the opinions of its various 'publics' and of the implications of its actions and policies (or lack of them) for the opinions of these groups.

Public relations can influence various groups to regard the organisation in a certain way—as leaders in research and technological innovation; as people with civic responsibility and public spiritedness; as a vigorous, resourceful 'get-things done' organisation; as a big organisation that values the custom of the small man; as a good organisation to work for (applicable to both existing employees and potential recruits); as a good investment opportunity (of particular importance in relation to the financing of new projects or acquisitions through new capital issues); or, at long range, as an organisation whose products or services can be bought with confidence and reliability.

In the final analysis, whatever people's attitudes are towards the organisation, these will be reflected in their attitudes towards its products or services, towards doing business with it or towards working for it. With regard to this latter point, the result is not without importance in personnel relations. Company or group morale is as much a function of external image as of internal administration and communications. Well-conceived public relations can do much to enhance employees' sense of pride in the organisation's ideals, achievements, growth record and concepts of service to the industrial community or to the general public. While this is never the sole purpose of public relations, it can be a valuable by-product, especially where sales representatives in daily contact with customers are concerned.

The sales representative should never be placed in the position of having to make excuses for, apologise for or defend the company's activities, products, service, etc. Well-planned public relations has a most important backing-up role to play in support of the field selling effort. It can never be a substitute for hard-selling product advertising. It can and should be used to create a favourable long-term climate in which the company product advertising and sales representatives' personal efforts can be made to work more effectively.

Harry Henry's observations about product or brand images[1] apply equally to company images. What the outside world thinks about a business operation is not simply the end-result of a production line manufactured to a given specification. It is the total personality of the company which consists not only of its products and service but also all the ideas that customers or other special groups of people have about it—the picture that they have in their mind of the sort of organisation it is, what sort of people work for it, what sort of people they will demonstrate themselves to be if they do business with it and so on. At the same time, the image of an organisation is never completely independent of reality. Bad products or indifferent service will not help an organisation to build a favourable image for itself, but all other things being equal, e.g. product quality, product range, service, etc., it is better to be liked and highly thought of than not.

Public relations must look inward at the company's own employees and outward at customers, suppliers, financial institutions, trade unions, local business or trade associations, central and local government authorities, semi-official bodies concerned with developments in the firm's locality, and other influential groups.

The task of internal public relations is to ensure that every key employee has all the facts he needs to appreciate what the organisation is setting out to do, what his role is to be and how he can best contribute to the achievement of company plans and objectives. Policy briefing meetings of company managers, seminars and indoctrination courses, educational and instructional films, company magazines or news bulletins are just a few of the activities that should feature in a planned internal public relations programme aimed at increasing company-mindedness, active participation in company affairs and greater understanding of and enthusiasm for what the organisation stands for.

[1] Op. cit. pp. 88–91.

The way in which the company regards itself internally will be reflected in the image it projects to the outside world—through executives talking to managers of other businesses, through management and sales representatives talking to customers, through employees talking to friends, relatives and neighbours, as well as through what is said or not said in advertising, sales literature and other forms of product publicity—in fact, through the sum total of its individual and collective abilities to communicate a sense of pride in the organisation and enthusiasm for its ideas and achievements.

Public relations media are much the same as those used for advertising purposes, i.e. press, television, films, radio, exhibitions and word-of-mouth. The organisation of special events such as trade shows, formal 'openings' by important or big-name personages, conferences, receptions, symposia, routine factory visits for customers and other influential guests, are all important aspects of public relations activity. By these methods public relations can communicate news of the company and its activities to outside groups. New products or services, research developments, new factories, plant and facilities, personnel appointments, manufacturing or trading agreements with other companies at home and abroad make news and it is the job of the public relations expert to exploit these newsworthy elements in corporate activity and communicate them in the most useable and acceptable form to the appropriate news media.

Product promotion is also an important area of public relations activity. Its purpose is to back up product advertising, and to favourably predispose customers towards the company's products which are subsequently advertised. Press or magazine articles, television or radio features which mention companies or products or achievements can do much to boost the interest in and sales of a product, particularly if the public relations man can obtain a specific name mention. For, in effect, a favourable write-up or mention implies an endorsement which is often more potent than the manufacturer's own claims. In other words, the source of information or recommendation can be as important as the information itself, and the chief value of product publicity lies in the trust and confidence people have in the editorial authority and integrity of the medium carrying it.

Public relations, unlike advertising, does not usually try to develop a single theme or proposition. Every sales point is considered with a view to appealing to many different interests and publics. Successful product publicity depends on the widest possible contacts with hundreds of different media and editorial interests and on the ability of the public relations adviser to meet their specific requirements and provide the type of news or feature article that will interest each particular editor. Thus, public relations is a highly personalised business requiring a constant flow of news releases about a company's activities or its products adapted to the needs of the particular medium. For example, each medium will usually want an 'exclusive' or at least a different approach from its competitors, which partly explains why a single universal theme does not work as well for product publicity purposes.

Public relations, then, is a technique of communication aimed at promoting a company and its products to a much wider range of publics than either advertising or sales promotion. While it is true that a considerable amount of paid-for advertising is undertaken for institutional or corporate reasons, the scope of public relations is far broader. Public relations includes corporate relations and product publicity campaigns but it covers much else as well. Hence, it is not unusual for the Public Relations Officer in a company to report, not to the Advertising Manager, but to a more senior management executive or directly to the chief executive himself.

How the professional public relations executive is positioned in a company, where the function exists at all, will reflect the importance and emphasis that the company attaches to its public relation activities. If the Public Relations Officer is regarded as a sort of corporate antenna whose job it is to transmit signals to the Board room covering any and every aspect of the company image, internally and externally, and to transmit messages from the Board room to company employees and outside groups, then he will probably report directly to the Board or its appointed representative. If, however, he is regarded as a product publicity specialist, pure and simple, then he is more likely to be responsible to the chief advertising executive.

The role of the public relations executive is open to much mis-directed criticism if only because the purpose of public relations is not so easily defined or understood and its end-results are not always self-evident or capable of measurement. Company goodwill and a good reputation, which may be said to be the general long-range aims of public relations, are not easily or quickly acquired. A well-conceived public relations programme can help build up a company's reputation and create an aura of confidence around its trade-marks, products and service concepts among key groups of importance to the company.

(h) THE SALES PROMOTION LINK

Sales promotion is the vital link between personal selling by a manufacturer's sales representatives and his advertising direct to consumers and trade customers. It comprises a variety of techniques aimed at providing special incentives to buy. These techniques are employed by both manufacturers and distributors. From the manufacturer's standpoint, the targets for his sales promotional effort are both the distributor and the final customer. In most cases he does not sell his product direct to the final user and must therefore stimulate buying action on the part of the wholesalers and retailers who are *his* direct customers. The wholesaler, in turn, must persuade his retail customers to buy from him. Finally, the retailer must provide buying inducements to the shoppers who patronise his store.

Sales promotion comprises three distinct groups of activities. First, it covers those specific incentives of the manufacturer aimed at persuading distributors to order and actively sell his products, at getting wholesalers and retailers to put that little extra sales effort behind his products, e.g. a special cash discount or bonus on all orders over a certain size or placed before a certain specified date, an offer of one or two bottles or cans of the product free with every dozen ordered over a specified period, a chance to enter a sales or display competition in which the successful distributor stands to win a new car, a free holiday or valuable cash prize. These activities are generally known as *Trade Promotions*.

Second, there are those specific incentives provided by producers of fast-moving consumer goods, aimed at persuading the consumer to buy particular products at particular times. These activities are known collectively as *Consumer Promotions* and include such things as free samples, reduced price offers, '2-for-the-price-of-1' banded pack offers, in-pack or send-away premiums, couponing, competitions and the like.

The third group of activities comes under the general heading of *Display* which takes in product display and demonstrations and related point-of-sale material, e.g. showcards, price-markers, banners, mobiles, floor bins, wire baskets, counter dispensing units, posters, window stickers, shelf-strips, and moving displays.

Most trade and consumer promotions are usually of a temporary nature and used to achieve specific short-term sales objectives such as stocking up the retailer in anticipation of a major advertising scheme or ahead of a competitor's promotion; introducing a new product or a new size, colour, or flavour of an established product for the first time and getting the widest possible consumer sampling; restoring a loss in brand share of sales due to strong competitive activity; or selling off old or excessive stocks.

In these competitive times, sales promotion activity must be a continuing feature of the manufacturer's marketing effort. For the average retailer, in-store display and product promotion are the lifeblood of his business. No manufacturer can afford to assume that his product has, for the time being, had enough sales promotion and display support—and the two invariably go together—for this is inviting the consumer to try some other manufacturer's brand.

It is the manufacturer's responsibility to demonstrate to each of his distributors the advantage that his product offers to the latter's customers and why stocking and promoting the product is a good business proposition in terms of turnover and profit. The distributor must be persuaded that the manufacturer's advertising and promotional effort is going to create a demand for the product among his local customers, and therefore merits a preferred position or special display in his shop. The manufacturer should make specific suggestions on stock and display requirements, on the size, type and location of special displays inside the shop, on what display material is likely to be most effective and on how the distributor himself might merchandise the product through special pricing and promotion features. Finally, the manufacturer should offer technical and physical assistance in the planning and preparation of displays and special promotional events in all possible worthwhile outlets.

It will be appreciated that these observations apply particularly to the consumer goods field, where the opportunities for making impulse sales by means of special display features, special pricing and promotions are very much greater. The industrial goods manufacturer is no less interested in demonstrating to his distributors the advantages of handling and recommending the company's products at every conceivable opportunity. The industrial goods distributor is just as much concerned with rates of turnover and profit as his counterpart in consumer goods. The industrial goods manufacturer may employ different tools and use different degrees of emphasis to get distributors' support. Advertising support may be less important and the supply of outstanding sales and technical literature more important. Planned visits to the plant by distributors and prospective customers and the organisation of or participation in exhibitions are also of greater importance to the industrial goods manufacturer.

The location of responsibility for sales promotion and merchandising planning varies from company to company. Its actual physical location—whether it is under the sales manager, the advertising manager, the brand or product manager—is of less importance than the provision of the proper organisation for co-ordinating and integrating it with the other key marketing functions. The fact that sales promotion is frequently 'housed' in the advertising department merely reflects a growing recognition that the presentation of products or services is a single unified *communications* activity, calling for the application of imagination and creative skill by the manufacturer and his professional advisers. Viewed in this way, there would appear to be a case for grouping together the various creative communications activities within a company—sales communications, advertising, public relations, sales promotion and merchandising—to constitute a 'creative communications function' alongside the marketing information and research, product planning, selling and distribution functions.

(i) ADVERTISING ORGANISATION

There are two major types of advertising organisation, the manufacturer's own advertising department and the advertising agency. Few manufacturers prepare their own advertisements or deal directly with media proprietors. It would not pay any but the very largest commercial organisations to maintain full-time creative staffs comprising copy-writers, artists, photographers, typographers, producers and media specialists. The approval of advertising and media plans, the determination of advertising budgets and the approval of physical advertisements are the final responsibility of the manufacturer's own advertising executives but the actual creation of advertisements and the preparation of media plans are, in most cases, the responsibility of the agency. The degree of control exercised over the advertising agency's work and output will depend on the degree of advertising sophistication among company executives, the number of executives concerned with advertising and the importance the company attaches to the contribution that advertising can make to the profitable development of the business.

The Manufacturer

Three typical examples of how the advertising function is organised within the manufacturing organisation are shown below.

CHART 36. ADVERTISING ORGANISATION—*Large Food Products Manufacturer*

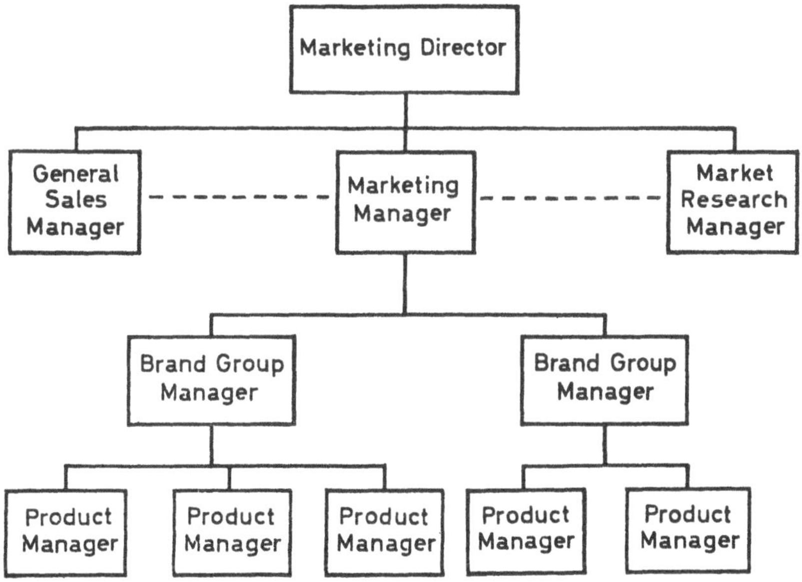

This company operates a Product Manager system. Each Product Manager reports to one of two Brand Group Managers, who in turn report directly to marketing management. The Product Manager is responsible for the determination, implementation and control of advertising policy in respect of his product, for the briefing of and continuing liaison with the company's appointed advertising agency, and for the review and evaluation of agency performance. The company retains two agencies, one handling the advertising for three different products under one brand name, the other handling the advertising for two entirely different products catering for a different market under a second brand name.

The responsible Brand Group Manager co-ordinates the individual product advertising and sales promotion budgets and approves all advertising and media plans on his assigned products. The company does not employ an Advertising Manager, the overall direction and control of the company advertising effort being one of the main functions of the Marketing Manager. Public relations are handled by outside professional advisers who work directly for the Marketing Director.

CHART 37. ADVERTISING ORGANISATION—*Large Electrical Appliance Manufacturer*

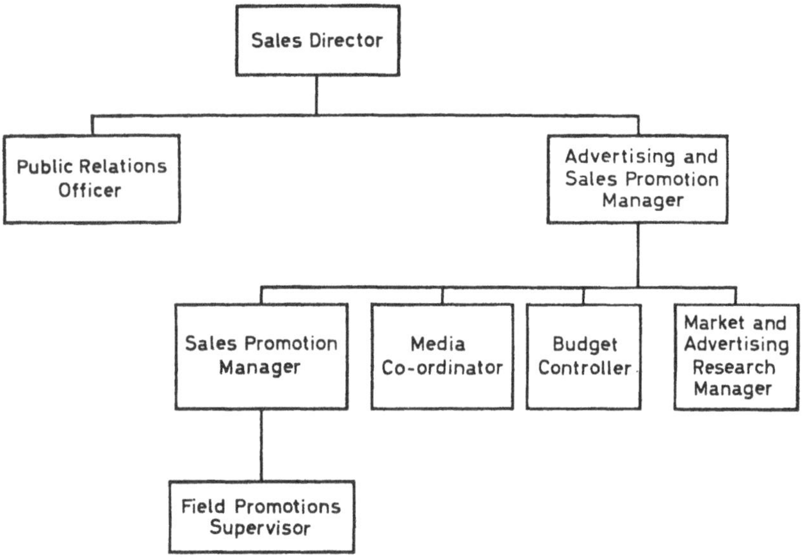

In this company there is a well-developed advertising department under an Advertising and Sales Promotion Manager. The latter reports to the Sales Director who has effective control of overall marketing policy. The firm engages in both domestic household appliances and industrial installations each of which is handled by a different advertising agency.

The Advertising and Sales Promotion Manager carries special responsibility for both domestic appliance and industrial advertising and promotional activity in which the company features importantly. Within the department, there is: a Sales Promotion Manager who organises, with the assistance of a team of promotion representatives, in-store activity for the company's products; a Media Co-ordinator whose main job it is to integrate the company's media buying activities through its two appointed advertising agencies (a large amount of direct mail, trade advertising and co-operative advertising with important local stockists and customers is carried on); a Budget Controller who ensures that all agreed budgets are adhered to and moneys spent according to plan; a Market and Advertising

Research Manager (the company spends several thousand pounds a year on advertising and media research). A Public Relations Officer reports directly to the Sales Director of the company.

CHART 38. ADVERTISING ORGANISATION—*Medium-sized Household Cleaning Products Manufacturer*

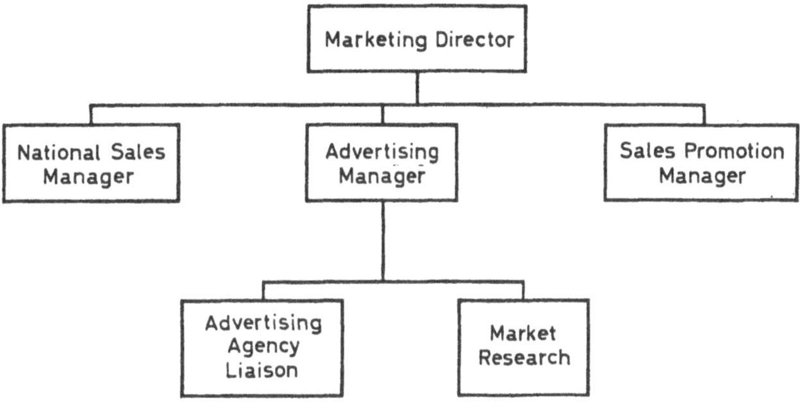

This company employs an Advertising Manager who reports to the Marketing Director. He has complete and sole responsibility for the advertising and is the sole contact between the company and its advertising agency. He is also responsible for commissioning any market or advertising research through the agency or other external research organisation. He has no line authority over any other company executive. Sales Promotion is the responsibility of another executive who also reports to the Marketing Director. The company retains a firm of public relations consultants who advise the Chairman and Managing Director of the company.

None of these ways of organising the advertising function within a company is foolproof. Its smooth working will be the result of careful planning, unambiguous briefing and guidance of the agency and innumerable internal and client-agency meetings. The most common danger to be avoided in large-scale firms is the failure to delegate full authority down the line with the result that advertising has to be cleared and approved at several different levels. Since advertising is still very much a matter of personal judgment, the existence of too many people with authority to make changes but not enough authority to give final approval can have a stultifying effect on campaign planning. At the other extreme, a too rigid control by the company of its advertising agency can inhibit the agency's creative output and kill off many a good advertising idea at birth.

The Advertising Agency

The advertising agency's prime responsibilities are the creation of advertising and the placement of that advertising before the proper audience. First and foremost, its organisation structure must facilitate both of these. Other specialist services in non-advertising areas have been developed to help clients in their overall marketing planning. In some agencies these additional activities are an integral part of the total service whereas in others they are regarded as 'optional extras' which the client pays for. In Chart 39 the basic services common to most agencies and the main optional services are shown. The latter are indicated by the broken-line entries.

(j) THE FUNCTIONS OF THE MODERN ADVERTISING AGENCY

The development of the 'marketing perspective' in business management has changed the traditional role of the advertising agency in a number of important aspects. The day is long gone since the advertising agency was regarded as being concerned purely with space-buying and space-filling. These functions are still of fundamental importance in the modern advertising agency but a great deal has happened in the meantime in determining what space is bought and how it is filled. The modern advertising agency's contribution to its client's business operations begins long before the space is filled (the physical preparation of advertisements) and continues far beyond their appearance (the buying of advertising space).

As more and more manufacturers have ceased to be essentially involved with the problems of *making* products and have become more involved with the problems of *presenting* products, so the functions of the advertising agency have developed to meet the changing needs of the manufacturer and in ways for which it is peculiarly suited.

In the first place, the transference of the customer from the periphery to the centre of the manufacturer's business thinking and planning involves greater knowledge of the customer and his problems and the recognition of the importance of communicating the right things back to the customer (the right products and service, packaging, pricing, advertising and promotion).

In the second place, just as the *making* of products involves the integrated use of a variety of technical skills and facilities, so the *presentation* of products must be a single integrated activity which makes use of a variety of communication skills, materials and facilities.

Communications to and from customers is the advertising agency's essential business. There are few skills so basic to the implementation of the 'marketing perspective' than the ability to think and plan from the viewpoint of the customer or user and to look at marketing as largely a problem in creative communication of one sort or another.

The Customer's Viewpoint

The advertising agency has a continuing primary interest in understanding the customer and in making the maximum use of research to study customer motivation and behaviour across many different product fields.

CHART 39. ADVERTISING AGENCY ORGANISATION

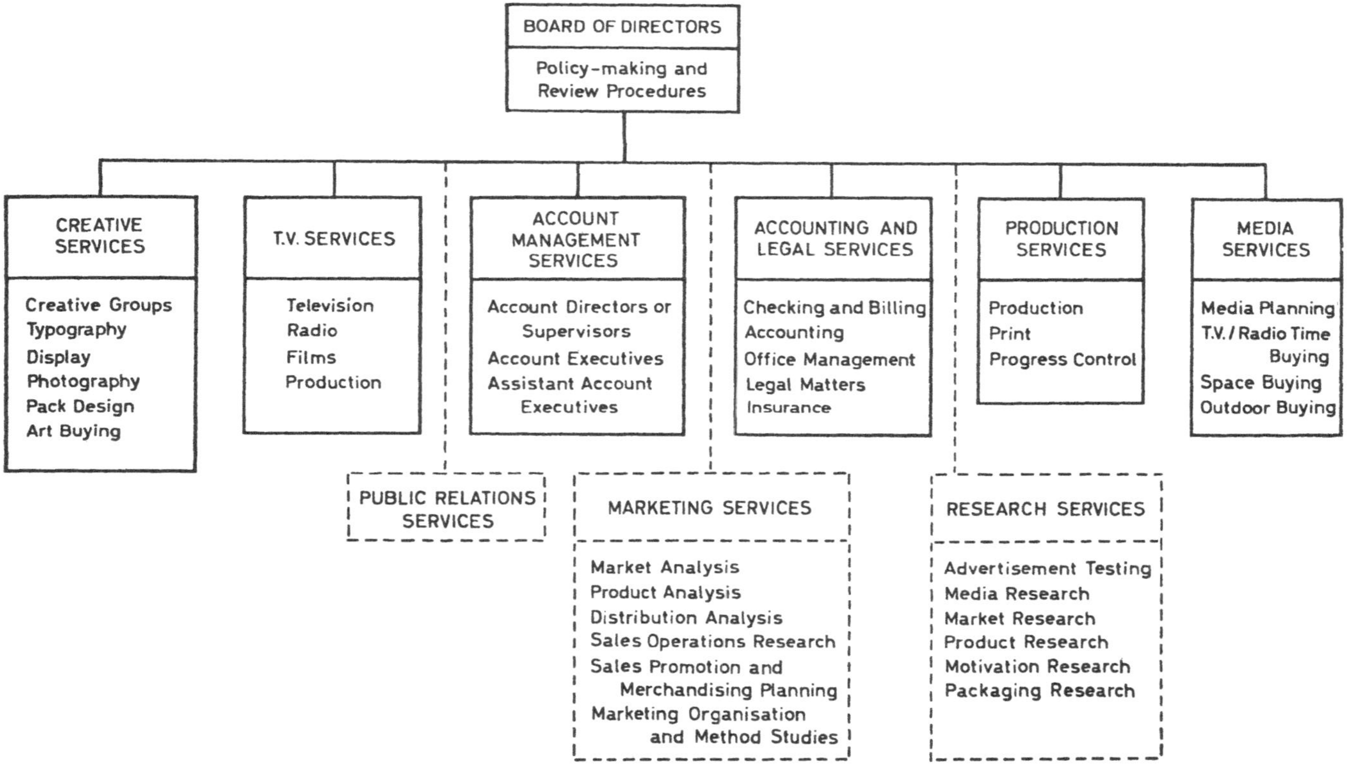

Such knowledge, to a greater or lesser degree, has always been fundamental to the performance of its basic advertising function.

Knowing the consumer, however, is not just applicable to advertising. It has important implications for product development, packaging, pricing, distribution methods, sales promotion and merchandising. These are all methods of communicating with the customer or user. They all have the same aim—the differentiation of the product in the consumer's mind. If it is accepted that advertising aims at differentiating products in the consumer's mind *after* the products have been made then it can be a relatively short step to 'factor-in' this differentiation into the product itself (or its packaging, pricing, distribution) at the outset.

Thus an agency, by virtue of its knowledge of the consumer and its creative (idea-producing) ability, is well placed to make a significant contribution to new product development and product planning in all its phases.

Particularly is this likely to be the case as more and more products are developed to meet the specific requirements of different segments of a market. Such products and their supporting advertising must reach out for specific types of people and select them out of the total population. The trend towards greater market segmentation will continue because more people with more money to spend will add to the total size of markets and make them worth splitting up and because, as consumers develop more sophisticated tastes and become more selective, manufacturers will see greater profit opportunities in catering for these differences.

The Marketing Responsibilities of the Advertising Agency

Since an advertising agency is a consumer-oriented organisation specialising in the field of creative communication, and hence already engaged in one very important aspect of selling, it can, with further specialisation, provide practical help and advice over a wide range of marketing problems.

From the agency's own standpoint such a development represents both a logical extension of its traditional creative role and the need to be familiar with and understand its clients' marketing processes and problems. The agency should be able to assess the effect of decisions made in the non-advertising areas of the clients' business on the effectiveness of the advertising itself and on the total marketing effort, and should be equipped to advise in these decisions. Since advertising is only one of the factors influencing the presentation and sale of a product, a bad decision, lack of co-ordination or bad timing in any part of the marketing process can nullify or at any rate reduce the total effectiveness of the component parts.

Involvement in the clients' basic marketing thinking and planning on a continuing basis offers greater stability and integration in the client-agency relationship and increases the agency's chances of producing more effective advertising. The benefits accruing to the manufacturer from such a relationship can include better advertising, expert advice in other non-advertising matters and an outside objective viewpoint on the relative strengths and weaknesses of the company's marketing operations. The objective review and evaluation of policy is one of the hardest tasks confronting any business organisation because of its deep involvement in and commitment to present performance and the necessity of justifying past performance. The built-in conservatism of many company managements, personality problems, policy constraints, and the 'it-hasn't-worked-in-the-past-so-why-should-it-work-now' frame of mind can seriously impede any objective assessment of company policies and practices.

The profitable use of the advertising agency as a sounding board and as one important source of objective evaluation of company marketing policy is only possible in an atmosphere of mutual confidence and respect for each other's professional competence and integrity. Because the agency is likely to have on its staff professional people with a broad knowledge and experience across many markets and product fields outside a particular client's immediate area of interest or know-how, it can bring an objective frame of mind to bear in assessing (a) the company's marketing strengths and weaknesses, (b) the effects of specific promotions at the trade and consumer levels, of product introductions and test market operations, (c) the level and quality of product distribution and display, (d) the effectiveness of the company's sales communications activities—and so on. The carrying out of independent field checks by advertising agency personnel is, in fact, fairly common practice nowadays and it seems likely that more clients will use their agencies in this and other ways as an important source of marketing intelligence and performance evaluation.

A manufacturer may choose one or all of an agency's specialised services according to his own real or imagined requirements. At one end of the spectrum there are agencies which spend a considerable amount of executive time and effort on developing package designs, sales communications, point-of-purchase display materials, consumer promotions (premiums, coupon schemes, competitions, etc.) and merchandising ideas (related-item and other special offers and selling 'events') for their client's products. Several of these agencies have separate departments or associated companies staffed by experts in each of these fields.

One or two of the very large agencies, while not offering personal selling facilities to their clients, even provide special sales and merchandising training courses for manufacturers' representatives. Agencies providing specialised marketing services do so in order to assist client managements with the planning of overall strategy. They make comprehensive proposals covering not only advertising but also product development, packaging, pricing policy, sales promotion, distribution, display, merchandising, public relations and consumer research—in fact, a completely integrated marketing communications programme for presenting a consistent and distinctive image of the company and its products to everyone concerned in any way with their sale or purchase. This means *planned* verbal and visual communications through all media at the company's disposal. Clearly, for the advertising agency to play such an integral part in the client's day-to-day business, it must have continuing access to top management thinking and a thorough appreciation of management's objectives and policies.

A marketing department in the larger advertising agencies generally serves two functions. First, it exists to advise and assist agency personnel in preparing effective advertising and promotional plans and materials. Second, it works directly on problems of concern to client management such as sales organisation and field selling methods.

Typically, the work of an agency marketing department may involve some or all of the following spheres of activity.

1. Market Analysis—economic trends and forecasts; industry and company position and trends; assessment of market size, segments, trends and potentials; analysis of competition; planning and evaluation of test markets.
2. Product Analysis—product line and range analysis (*vis-à-vis* competition); packaging; pricing; new product development.
3. Distribution Analysis—appraisal of distribution channels; analysis of distribution methods; analysis of distributors' margins and trading policies; retail audit analysis; distribution developments and potentials; trade opinion and attitude research.
4. Sales Operations Research—headquarters staff structure and operations; sales records and statistics; sales reporting and control procedures; field sales supervision; manpower performance, training and development; personnel selection and recruitment; compensation and incentives; sales communications research; selling and distribution cost analysis.
5. Sales Promotion Planning—merchandising plans and materials; consumer promotion plans and materials; trade promotion plans and materials, display plans and materials; competitors' sales promotion activities.
6. Marketing Organisation and Methods—determining functions to be performed; establishing the structure; defining executive responsibilities and relationships; defining marketing and advertising objectives; preparing marketing plans and budgets.

The provision of such services involves more than a change of outlook by the advertising agency. It requires certain structural changes to allow the results of marketing research to be fed into agency planning procedures. It requires the co-ordination of a greatly enlarged team of specialists and a planning system which enables them to be brought in at the right moment and to the required degree. It calls for a major investment in staff, services and facilities over and above those normally required to buy and fill advertising space.

At the other end of the spectrum there are agencies which, from lack of opportunity or inclination, do not enter into their clients' business in this way. A great many manufacturers deliberately avoid involving their agencies to anything like this degree. The best that the agency can hope for in such circumstances is that some top management executive in the client organisation is responsible for central planning, co-ordination and control of the marketing effort and that the agency's advertising contribution is properly integrated with the other marketing forces.

7

Co-ordinating and Controlling the Marketing Functions

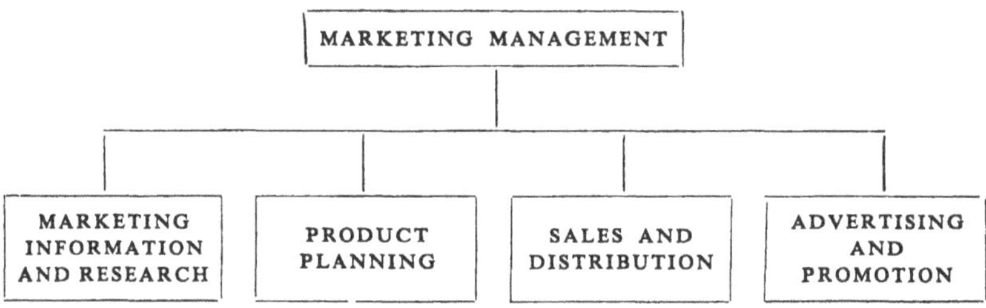

(a) CO-ORDINATING THE SPECIFIC MARKETING FUNCTIONS

The effective co-ordination and control of marketing operations depends on (1) organisation, (2) technique, (3) programming and (4) the evaluation and review of results.

Marketing Organisation involves the grouping of related activities into responsible management units and the definition of the working relationships between such units. The larger the firm and the wider the range of products to be marketed the more likely it is that the most effective form of organisation will be that which groups activities into functional management units—market information and research, product planning, sales and distribution, advertising and promotion—under a marketing 'supremo'. There is a limit to the number of functions which any one executive can exercise in relation to the products under his control. The more products he is responsible for the fewer the functions he can be expected to carry out. Conversely, the greater the number of functions for which he is responsible the fewer products he will be capable of handling efficiently.

Marketing organisation also involves the selection, review, promotion, pay and status of key management executives. It means finding and placing the right men in the right management jobs and making sure that there are good men coming up under them. For this reason it is essential to carry out an annual review of key management jobs and personnel. Once the position of each of these key executives has been reviewed and their status, pay and

CHART 40. CO-ORDINATION AND CONTROL OF THE SPECIFIC MARKETING FUNCTIONS

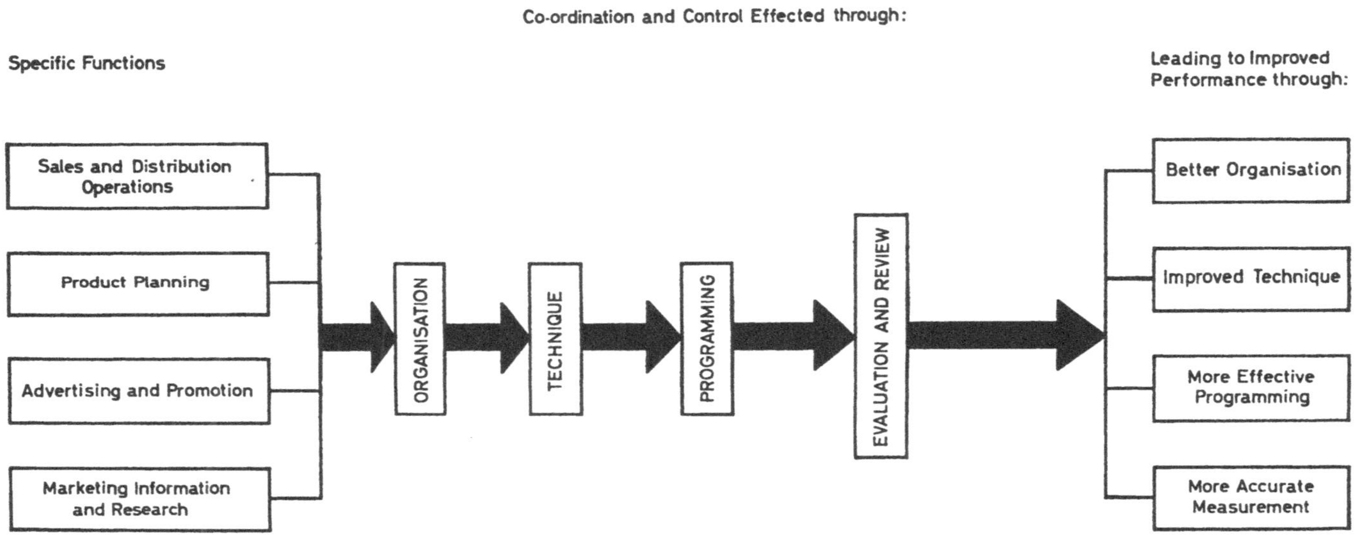

promotion settled then the review and remuneration of executives down the line can be dealt with without reference to top management.

Under a functional organisation structure each senior management executive is responsible for the selection, performance, review and remuneration of the staff under him. No functional management executive has any line authority over any but his own staff. Each functional manager is responsible directly to the Marketing Director or his senior management equivalent. Lateral communication between functional departments is absolutely essential to ensure the planned integration of effort and so that the contribution made by each separate specialised activity is related to the requirements of the whole.

Marketing Technique is concerned with the methods used to control and carry out a programme of work and the individual work tasks which together make up the programme. It is concerned with the development of new and better methods of controlling and accomplishing work and with the motivation and training of staff in the use of these methods. Two methods in particular are proving to be of great value for marketing control purposes. These are 'Budgeting-by-Product' and the concept of the 'Overall Marketing Budget'.

'Budgeting-by-Product' focuses attention on profit-planning for each of the company's products so as to ensure that resources are allocated to each product on its own merits and potential and in relation to the contribution it makes to total company profit. A multi-product company will usually require a different balance of marketing activities and allocation of resources for each of its products and these, in turn, must be aggregated and integrated into a total company marketing budget. The advantages to the company of the budgeting-by-product method are the improved quality of profit-planning, greater profit-consciousness of personnel, more effective comparison of budgeted goals with actual performance for each product, and more reliable indications of areas requiring management investigation and action.

The concept of the 'Overall Marketing Budget' is a logical consequence of the recognition of the fact that the allocation of company resources as between different products and their different marketing requirements must be centrally controlled and administered in accordance with an overall company marketing plan or programme. The marketing budget, which is built up from individual product budgets, *relates total marketing or sales goals to total marketing expenditures.* At a later stage the Overall Marketing Budget must be incorporated into an Annual Operating Budget along with other individual budgets relating to capital expenditure, maintenance and repair, etc. Beyond this, some company managements develop long-range corporate budgets covering the next three, five or even ten years.

Marketing Programming sets out the specific work tasks to be performed, the timing and sequence in which they are to be carried out and the specific degree to which they are to be accomplished. It is also concerned with the assembly and allocation of resources necessary to accomplish the set programme of work. The physical basis of marketing programming is the 'Annual Marketing Plan', in respect of each product or service supplied by the company.

A *written* appreciation of the company's markets, incorporating a clear statement of the marketing objectives for the forthcoming year and the action to be taken to achieve the objectives, is still the exception rather than the rule with the great majority of business firms. By 'Marketing Plan' is meant something a good deal more comprehensive than a mere 'Advertising Plan' or 'Sales Plan'. Some sort of plan probably exists in every organisation but very often it exists only in the mind of the chief marketing executive and, if committed to paper, exists only in a series of unco-ordinated memoranda to the various departments concerned with different parts of the marketing operation. In such circumstances there is a greater likelihood that the executives responsible for implementing the plan never see the whole picture but only that part which relates to their particular piece of 'doing'. The main reasons why formal written marketing plans are not prepared are the belief that such overall plans are not necessary, the shortage of time, the lack of qualified personnel or the feeling that a written plan reduces flexibility of operation.

A written marketing plan is the means of knitting together a host of sub-plans—selling and distribution plans, advertising and promotional plans, etc.—which together make up the overall plan; it is also the means of communicating these plans to everyone concerned with their implementation. The latter, if they are to act intelligently, need to know what their particular roles are in relation to the whole. The other principal advantages of committing such plans to paper are that: (a) the facts upon which the marketing programme is based are kept up-to-date; (b) the facts and thinking upon which the product marketing programme is based are brought together in one document; (c) the information necessary to fill in new personnel on the background to the marketing programme is available in one place; (d) the evaluation and review of current and past programmes is made obligatory—each year the basic marketing strategy is reviewed in the light of actual performance and of the degree to which the company achieved or fell short of its goals.

The actual format of a marketing plan is a matter for the individual company depending on circumstances and its own special requirements. The following suggested outline is intended to be no more than a typical check-list of the major points that a number of marketing companies find desirable or useful to include when writing up their annual plans.

Suggested Outline for Annual Marketing Plan

Part I—Historical Review and Current Situation Report covering:
- (a) The Product(s) or Service(s)
- (b) The Market(s)
- (c) The Competition.

Part II—Statement of Marketing Goals and Strategy.

Part III—Plan of Action in respect of:

(a) Product or Service Features and Development
(b) Packaging
(c) Pricing
(d) Field Selling and Distribution
(e) Sales Promotion
(f) Advertising
(g) Public Relations
(h) Market Research
(i) Timing.

Part IV—Marketing Budget.

The most important part of the Plan and the one from which all else flows is the *Historical Review and Current Situation Report*. The Product or Service section should include a description of the product or service and its main features past and present, improvements, price history, a sales history, a review of advertising and promotional activity and any market research findings. The Market section should cover size of market, overall trends and trends within the market, location of market (classes or types of consumer, geographical variations, etc.), seasonality, customer or user attitudes, motives for buying and using, purchasing and using habits, etc. The section on Competition should compare the company's product or service with competition as regards quality, price, distribution, trade attitudes, consumer acceptance; the amount, type and effectiveness of advertising and promotional activity; and share of market trends both long- and short-term.

This part of the Marketing Plan should be completely factual and objective. This is not to say that it should be just a recitation of the facts without explanation. It is not always easy to face the real facts in a given situation or to interpret them without apportioning responsibility for previous shortcomings. But, in practice, the major causes of deviations from the previous annual plan must be isolated, measured (if possible) and explained so as to provide a basis for corrective action in the future.

From this analysis of the past and present situations a forward plan and strategy can be developed. Marketing goals may be expressed in several different ways—in terms of the return on capital invested, case or unit sales volume, percentage share-of-market, net sales revenue, or gross profit on sales, etc. Specific advertising goals might be expressed in terms of the percentage of a particular target market made aware of important product or service features, recognising a particular package design, recalling key elements of the advertising message, entering a competition, sending away for a premium item, etc. over a fixed period of time.

The Plan of Action brings together the different sub-plans dealing with each separate marketing activity and designating responsibility for action.

A time-table will show how the various components are to be integrated —who does what, when and to whom.

The final part of the Plan is the Overall Marketing Budget which sets out planned marketing expenditures against expected marketing results.

The Evaluation and Review of Marketing Results requires the measured comparison of operating results against planned performance and the continuing review of marketing organisation and personnel, marketing procedures and techniques, and marketing programmes. It also includes the evaluation and review of the methods of measurement and assessment themselves. Control depends on being able to measure activity in terms of inputs (resources) and outputs (results) and measurement involves quantification. Many marketing parameters are not easily quantified, e.g. changes in attitudes of mind, measures of propensity or tendency to buy, demand elasticities in relation to advertising and promotional stimuli. A number of relatively new techniques of measurement, largely developed in the field of operations research, have been touched upon elsewhere. Meanwhile, marketing men cannot avoid the necessity for measurement. They must simply do the best job they can with the instruments they have. But they must also be constantly on the look out for and ever ready to experiment with new techniques from other fields of activity. Only in this way will they learn more about their subject and find ways of improving performance through better organisation, better technique and more effective programming of work.

(b) CO-ORDINATING MARKETING WITH OTHER MAJOR MANAGEMENT FUNCTIONS

Co-ordinate with the marketing function are the other management functions of production, finance and personnel. Marketing personnel must also maintain close liaison with the Purchasing and Technical Research Departments (whether these be located under production or somewhere else) and with the Legal Department, which is often linked with Finance.

Co-ordination with Production and Technical Research.

Marketing management must liaise with production management to ensure that output of the right products is available at the right times, in the right places and in the right quantities to meet sales requirements. At the same time the marketing man, in attempting to match production resources to his sales requirements, must at all times be aware of the production department's strengths and limitations. He will capitalise on these strengths and avoid making demands that would impose too great a strain on or result in reduced profitability of plant operations.

It makes no sense to make a product which is unsaleable because the price is too high, because the quality is below what the customer requires, or because the company cannot deliver on time. Many small firms and some large ones have found themselves in serious difficulty because marketing or sales management accepted more orders from customers than the factory could meet profitably or deliver on time. It is equally bad business to sell a product at a price which can only be met by lowering quality and/or service.

Among the chief factors which the marketing man will need to take into account in preparing his marketing plans are the following:

(i) *Plant Capacity:* It will be advantageous if the marketing programme utilises existing under-employed equipment and plant facilities. If it makes excessive demands on an already over-stretched factory and calls for the employment of additional machines, manpower, supplies and services, then production and shipping delays, rising costs and reduced profit margins are likely to ensue, at least in the short-run.

(ii) *Production Know-how and Engineering Skills:* There is a much greater marketing risk involved in moving outside the company's acknowledged production know-how and engineering skills, particularly where new products and processes are concerned. The marketing man, desirous of having something different to sell against competitors, should temper his requirements to what is feasible in the factory and make the maximum use of accumulated production experience and know-how.

(iii) *Plant Flexibility:* The ability of the factory to respond to changes of plan and to meet marketing opportunities as they arise will depend on the adaptability of men and machines, flexibility of plant layout, and the degree of plant utilisation at any given period of time. Marketing men should avoid sudden changes in plan calling for revised production schedules to meet emergency situations wherever possible, since these will usually raise costs, reduce profit margins, and may lower quality standards and cause production breakdowns.

(iv) *Standardisation:* Product modifications and new products which make maximum use of standardised components, materials and processes are preferable to products that require special parts, ingredients or processing. The marketing man will usually find it necessary to arrive at a workable compromise between what is desirable and what is feasible within the limits of affordability.

(v) *Quality Standards:* the customer is the final judge of quality—a term which is open to differing interpretations. Customers demand a certain quality at a certain price. This 'quality' may be different from the marketing man's idea of quality and will usually be different from the production man's idea of quality. The latter's insistence on technical perfection—which will normally be very expensive to achieve—must be tempered by what customers want and find acceptable at the price they are prepared to pay. It is the marketing man's job to provide the company's customers with products which meet their requirements in terms of design, performance, quality *and* price. The products may not be the cheapest but neither need they be the most expensive.

(vi) *Technical Research:* Developing the right new products, improvements to existing products and new uses for existing products are more likely to ensue as a result of collaboration between marketing and technical research into products, materials and processes. The whole product planning process depends on such collaboration. The introduction of new cost-reducing methods of manufacture and the standardisation of materials and components can be of great marketing significance if it means a widening of the company's competitive differential advantages.

Strong technical orientation is particularly necessary for the industrial goods marketing man dealing with complex products, installations, applications and adaptations to specific customer requirements. The marketing man's detailed knowledge of market characteristics and requirements can aid the technologist in developing and adapting new materials and new processes—many of which have their original applications in the military and strategic fields—to commercial uses, e.g. heat-resistant ovenware developed from materials used in space research, cigarette filters and industrial protective clothing developed from materials first used in atomic energy establishments, special aluminium alloys developed for use in high speed military and civil jet aircraft, commercial computers developed from military prototypes and so on. Many new product ideas will undoubtedly come from advances in miniaturisation, dehydration, quick-freezing, ultrasonics, etc.

The marketing man has a lot to learn from production and research staff about manufacturing processes and research possibilities. If he is wise, he will use this knowledge when framing his marketing plans. However, the benefits are not all on one side. The marketing man can contribute to greater production efficiency and profitability in a number of ways. In a sense, the marketing man is the spokesman for the company's customers. In this role, he can advise the production department on matters of practical concern to the customer such as product performance in use, the adaption or modification of the product for improved performance, or for different applications. He can guide the research programme along more profitable lines in relation to the development of new uses for existing products, of modifications to existing products which may expand the market for the company's output, and of completely new products for existing or new applications. A major problem in most companies is to decide on the order of priorities for research projects within a limited research budget. The marketing man, because of his intimate knowledge of markets and customers, is, therefore, particularly well qualified to advise on the 'marketing' priority of various projects, since it is the aim of everyone to bring the most promising products to the marketable stage in the shortest possible time. The marketing man should be the catalyst in this process. The marketing man is also able to assist production and research people in testing out product ideas and prototypes among customers.

Finally, marketing management can contribute significantly to manufacturing efficiency through the provision of accurate forecasts of forward production requirements. The efficient programming of production depends, to a very great extent, on knowing in advance what quantities of output will be required at specified times and on being able to rely on an even flow of production orders throughout the year. If the orders placed on the factory help to eliminate seasonal peaks and troughs, so much the better.

Co-ordination with Purchasing.

Close contact with the Purchasing Officer or Buying Department is also necessary to ensure that sales requirements are not handicapped by sudden or unanticipated shortages in important manufacturing materials and components due to the marketing executive's failure to keep them informed of forward-plans and commitments. Conversely, the holding of excess stocks of materials and components due to faulty forecasting or the marketing executive's failure to inform the Buying Department of reduced requirements, ties up capital which could be usefully employed in other directions. Two examples serve to show what can happen through lack of co-ordination between the marketing and buying departments.

First, a manufacturer of a consumer durable found himself unable to deliver a large consignment of a new model which had sold in much larger quantities than expected. Whereas the production people were told of the forward-order position in good time and were therefore able to put on an extra shift, the paint shop could not because the Buying Department had not been given adequate warning of additional paint requirements. Nearly £350,000 was tied up for ten weeks in stocks of unsaleable goods.

Second, a packaged food manufacturer ordered a large quantity of a particular item for a self-liquidating premium, i.e. for which the consumer had to send one packet top plus a postal order for 3*s*. 6*d*. The Buying Department ordered an initial quantity with a further and even larger reserve order for delivery six weeks later. Bad forecasting of the rate of off-take of the premium and the failure of the Sales Promotion Manager to advise the department not to re-order, resulted in the equivalent of two years' supply of premiums being purchased. The undistributed stock was sold back to the original supplier at a net loss to the company.

Co-ordination with Finance.

Business is concerned with the calculus of gain and loss measured in financial terms. The marketing man, whose job it is to make a profit from the sale of the company's output, is intimately concerned with costs and budgetary methods. While the intricacies of high finance are best left to the professional accountant, the marketing man must be thoroughly familiar with the firm's costing methods and budgetary control procedures. He must understand the way in which costs are built up and allocated to individual products and how budgets are arrived at. For he is responsible for implementing the budget and for controlling the costs of marketing operations, and he will be ultimately judged on the basis of his financial performance. The intelligent application of the concepts of 'budgeting-by-product' and the 'marketing budget' require a strongly developed cost- and profit-consciousness on the part of marketing executives.

The marketing man must also be in contact with the firm's legal advisers whether they are employed by the company or retained by it. There are Acts of Parliament and official regulations covering most aspects of doing business—product formulation, manufacture, description, pricing, packaging, advertising and promotion, conditions of sale, conditions of employment, etc. There are laws and regulations affecting patents, trade marks registration, licensing agreements, customers' claims and complaints. There are legislative enactments dealing with restrictive trading practices, monopoly arrangements, hire purchase, price agreements and so on. Moreover, there seems to be every indication that the number and scope of such regulations, both official and those collectively imposed by industry itself, will increase rather than diminish and that quick and easy access to sound legal advice is therefore of considerable importance to the marketing man.

Co-ordination with Personnel.

The Personnel Department, if such exists, is usually responsible for the recruitment, selection, placement, training and indoctrination of company staff. While selection procedures are by no means perfect, it would be foolish to dismiss them out of hand and rely solely on personal judgment and intuition. There can be no cast-iron guarantee that the person selected for a particular position will be the best of the candidates who present themselves for interview or that the selectors will place him in the right job. The best that one can hope to do is to reduce the risk of error to more tolerable limits. In this respect, marketing management have a particular interest in locating and retaining good marketing men. Highly trained and experienced marketing men are still a relatively scarce and, therefore, expensive commodity. Anything that can be done to help marketing management to find and place such men is to be welcomed. But this means that those responsible for recruiting, screening and short-listing potential candidates must have a clear understanding of the nature of the work to be done by the person appointed, his status, and relationship within the department to which he is assigned, his development prospects in terms of responsibility and remuneration, and the necessary educational background, personality, aptitudes and experience needed for the job. The closest consultation is therefore necessary between Marketing and Personnel in order to arrive at clear job descriptions and executive specifications—a more difficult task in the case of marketing personnel than for many other types of specialist personnel such as engineers, chemists, physicists, metallurgists, etc. The sources of potential candidates for a particular position, the media used to reach them and the manner of advertising to them, i.e. whether to use a box number, the company name or operate behind the anonymity of a selection agency—are all matters on which Personnel and Marketing should consult one another.

The indoctrination and, where necessary, the training of new employees must also be worked out together by Marketing and Personnel so that the person gets the best training in relation to his eventual assignment and responsibilities. Whereas general indoctrination is ordinarily the responsibility of Personnel, specific marketing training is the proper responsibility of the Marketing Department.

Finally, assessment of marketing personnel must be left to marketing management. It is sound practice to allow a man to be judged by his peers rather than 'outsiders' who may not know all the circumstances or be in possession of all the facts. Assessment must be fair and impartial and must be seen to be so by the individual being assessed. In other than the most exceptional circumstances where prejudice or personal reasons might prevent an unbiased judgment, management has a clear responsibility to assess the performance of the executives under it. Management's prime duty, above all others, is to prepare for its own eventual replacement and to develop and promote good men to positions of higher responsibility. For the future of any enterprise, even if the factory should be burned to the ground and everything else is lost depends, in the last resort, on people.

Index

C

D

E